Software Architecture 1

Software Architecture 1

Edited by
Mourad Chabane Oussalah

Series Editor
Jean-Charles Pomerol

ISTE

WILEY

First published 2014 in Great Britain and the United States by ISTE Ltd and John Wiley & Sons, Inc.

ISTE Ltd
27-37 St George's Road
London SW19 4EU
UK

www.iste.co.uk

John Wiley & Sons, Inc.
111 River Street
Hoboken, NJ 07030
USA

www.wiley.com

Library of Congress Control Number: 2014934511

British Library Cataloguing-in-Publication Data
A CIP record for this book is available from the British Library
ISBN 978-1-84821-600-6

Table of Contents

Preface

Over the past two decades, several languages have been proposed to describe software architectures to promote the development of architecture-focused applications. In general, these languages provide formal or semi-formal notations for describing and analyzing software systems. They are usually accompanied by tools designed to analyze, simulate and, sometimes, generate the code for modeled systems. Software architectures have made a real contribution in the development of complex distributed systems. Their main characteristics lie, on the one hand, in their power to manage levels of abstractions and levels of expression in a system and, on the other hand, in their ability to take into account the modeling of the structure and behavior of a system. It is widely accepted today that one of the critical issues in the design and development of any complex software system is its architecture, i.e. the organization of architectural elements that constitute it. Good architecture can facilitate the production of a system's critical properties (reliability, portability, interoperability, etc.). Conversely, bad architectures can have disastrous consequences on the system. Moreover, good architectures can serve as the system's "conscience" during its development. In fact, a good architecture guides the evolution process of a system, for instance by indicating which aspects of the system can be modified without compromising its integrity.

Nowadays, new engineering applications, particularly those dedicated to the design and development of object-oriented, component-based, service-oriented, agent-oriented and model-based distributed information systems, have highlighted the evolving nature of manipulated architectural elements and structures associated with them. The sustainability, adaptability and scalability of such systems has become a very important economic issue. In fact, as these systems often require several years (human resources / months) of development and updating, it becomes imperative for these systems to allow for a consequent life and especially to respond to the changing requirements of software architecture manufacturers, builders of applications and end users. In this context, the academic and industrial communities proposed the design and development of new open software architectures (i.e. those that are able to communicate and interface with other architectures), which can be adaptable (i.e. they can be designed according to the operating conditions and different application domains) and scalable (i.e. they will be capable of being completed/modified to take account of services not anticipated in their initial design).

In fact, the software architecture provides a good response to the inherent requirements of complex systems such as:

– the requirement to use and reuse these systems in different environments and contexts. It is thus necessary to be able to remodel (adapting, evolving and re-engineering) so that they can meet, on the one hand, the requirements of their specific usage (e.g. distributed infrastructure, limited resources and different points of view on the composition of different functions) and, on the other hand, new technological requirements (component, service, architectural views, etc.);

– the requirement to reduce development and maintenance costs of these systems by designing them for reuse and composition of reusable architectural elements (objects, components, services and agents). These architectural elements can be identified and extracted from existing systems to be reused in future developments;

– the requirement to update these systems quickly and with minimal cost. In this case, it is necessary to automate the transformation process (structural and behavioral) and promote the reuse of these activities (reuse the evolution process);

– the requirement to control their complexity (understanding and developing these systems, etc.) while handling them with a high level of abstraction.

Nowadays, in light of this, a number of proposals have emerged on component-based and service-based architectures (SOA), agent-oriented architectures and model-based architectures. In any case, the challenges include the improvement of quality and productivity, and the industrialization of software production.

Also, with such a large number of proposals and solutions, it was necessary to review the research and applications concerning architectures in software engineering.

Therefore, we propose a book entitled *Software Architectures*, which deals with object-oriented, component-based, service-oriented, agent-oriented and model-based software architecture paradigms, with different techniques and architectural methods for analyzing architectural features, models of representation of patterns and styles, their formalization, validation and, finally, the engineering approach in which these coherent and autonomous elements can be managed.

This book is primarily intended for project managers, project owners, architects, designers, developers and users of software architectures, engineering university and school teachers, engineers, Master's degree and doctoral students and, finally, engineering students.

Mourad Chabane OUSSALAH
March 2014

Chapter 1

Object-Oriented, Component-Based, Agent-Oriented and Service-Oriented Paradigms in Software Architectures

Recent years have seen object-oriented, component-based, agent-oriented and service-oriented paradigms coexist and develop in parallel. This has led to the emergence of similar or specialist concepts that are often juxtaposed with misinterpretations of vocabulary. These misinterpretations are exacerbated by the existence of hybrid approaches that borrow elements from the four paradigms. Moreover, modern applications that combine these paradigms emphasize this ambient intertwining and the overall understanding becomes more difficult.

The purpose of this chapter is to clarify the boundaries between the paradigms by proposing a conceptual comparative framework based on two quantitative and qualitative approaches. The principle is to concentrate on differentiation of the conceptual aspects that are directly related to the paradigms, as opposed to an approach that compares the different technologies for implementing these paradigms. The aim is to offer

---

Chapter written by Abdelkrim AMIRAT, Anthony HOCK-KOON and Mourad Chabane OUSSALAH.

architects a better understanding of the implications and consequences of choosing one or the other of these paradigms.

1.1. Introduction

According to Wikipedia, "A programming paradigm is a fundamental style of computer programming that deals with how solutions to problems must be formulated in a programming language". This chapter focuses on four key paradigms in the field of software development, namely *object-oriented software engineering* (OOSE), *component-based software engineering* (CBSE), *agent-oriented software engineering* (AOSE) and *service-oriented software engineering* (SOSE). These paradigms will be studied and analyzed in light of real-world construction approaches of distributed applications.

A software development paradigm specifies how an information technology (IT) solution to a problem must be formulated in accordance with clearly defined concepts and mechanisms. It determines the order in which to deal with the problem and provides the means to develop this order, to follow its principles and to implement it in practical terms. Thus, a software development paradigm has its own particular style of developing IT solutions, in terms of analysis, design and development.

By nature, a paradigm is independent of function-specific issues; however, it can encourage certain types of application in order to support specific qualities. However, these qualities are usually associated with specific repercussions. When a paradigm is well suited to an implementation issue, it reduces the need for a costly integration process and isolated solution tests by using a common conceptual framework.

In this chapter, we propose a conceptual framework based on a *top-down* approach. The principle of a *top-down* approach is to concentrate on the differentiation of conceptual aspects directly related to the paradigms, as opposed to a *bottom-up* approach that examines their technological differences. Our comparison-based conceptual framework relies on two approaches: a quantitative approach based on the concepts of product and process, and a qualitative approach based on quality criteria that organize the characteristics of each paradigm. These approaches will assist in clarifying the conceptual and technical misinterpretations of these different paradigms.

1.2. History

Figure 1.1, drawn from [SOM 04], shows the evolution of software engineering. We can see the progression from the lines of code in structured programming to current trends or approaches such as service-oriented and model-based paradigms[1].

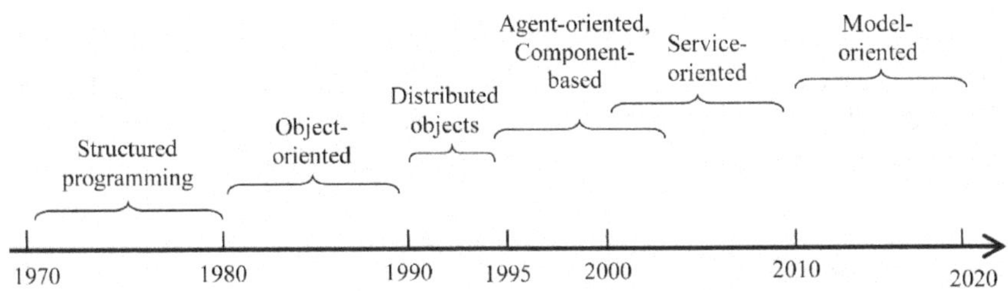

Figure 1.1. *Evolution of development paradigms*

1.2.1. *Object-oriented paradigm*

Object-oriented paradigm (OOP) is a design- and programming-oriented paradigm that emerged in the early 1960s and was developed by Alan Kay's work in the 1970s [KAY 93]. It consists of the definition and interaction of software modules called objects: an object represents a concept, an idea or any entity in the physical world [OUS 99]. It has an internal structure and behavior, and it is able to communicate with other objects. The aim of OOP, therefore, is to represent these objects and their relationships; communication between objects via their inter-relations facilitates the implementation of the intended functionalities.

The Simula-67 language laid the first foundations, i.e. those of object-oriented languages: class, polymorphism, inheritance, etc. [COX 91]. However, it was actually with Smalltalk 71, followed by Smalltalk 80 (Dan Ingalls) [GOL 83], inspired largely by Simula-67 and Lisp, that the principles of object-oriented programming, based on the work of Alan Kay, would be established: object encapsulation, messages, typing and polymorphism (via subclassification); other principles, such as inheritance, are either derived from these or fall within the implementation.

1 In this chapter, we will deliberately ignore the model paradigm as proposed by the OMG and focus on the object-oriented, component-based, agent-oriented and service-oriented paradigms, which makes space for a sufficiently extensive chapter.

The 1980s witnessed the proliferation of object-oriented languages: Objective C (early 1980s), C++ (C with class structure) in 1983, Eiffel in 1984, Common Lisp Object System in 1987, etc. The 1990s saw the golden age of enhancement of object-oriented programming in different sectors of software development. Currently, the object-oriented approach is considered as the reference model for other approaches.

The object-oriented has been completed with the *remote method invocation* (RMI) mechanism, with the aim of introducing the concept of distribution in the programming model. RMI is mainly based on the principle of *object request broker* (ORB) [GAS 92, VIN 97].

1.2.2. *Component-based paradigm*

The component-based paradigm was proposed by McIlroy [MCI 68] in which he implemented an infrastructure on Unix using *pipeline* components and filters. Component-based development appeared in the early 1990s in response to the failure of the object-oriented approach to meet the requirements of reuse and composition. The component-based approach extends the object-oriented paradigm by stressing the importance of reuse, the separation of problems and the promotion of composition [PAP 07].

Reading and understanding an existing code is always a tedious task for developers; however, it is highly advantageous to be able to reuse an existing code in the form of a component. In fact, a developer only needs to know what a component includes, and not how it was implemented. In addition, in the component-based approach, a clear distinction is made between the development of a component and that of a system. In the first case, we focus on the arrangement of the component and in the second case, we focus on the assembly and composition of compatible components.

1.2.3. *Agent-oriented paradigm*

The agent-oriented paradigm appeared in the 1970s under the leadership of distributed artificial intelligence (DAI) where Hewitt [HEW 73, HEW 11] proposed the concept of actors, i.e. competing interactive autonomous entities. In the mid-1990s, collective models called multi-agent systems (MASs) came into existence. In these models, an agent is treated as a self-contained entity with certain capabilities that enable it to carry out its services or use the services of another agent through interaction. Organization-based multi-agent systems (OMASs) are among the new models [FER 03].

Agents are distinguished by their social ability to cooperate, coordinate and negotiate with each other [HYA 96]. Autonomy and high-level interactions are the main points of difference between agent-based and object-oriented, component-based and services-based approaches. Agents can be classified into the following two categories:

– Reactive agents, which wait for an event to happen before responding to changes in their environment.

– Proactive agents, which take decisions on their own initiative in their environment.

Software agents have their own control *thread*, encapsulating not only their code and state, but their invocation too. These agents may also have rules and individual goals, appearing as active objects with invocation initiative. In other words, when and how an agent can act is determined by the agent itself.

In the agent model, communication is usually asynchronous. This means that there is no predefined flow of control from one agent to another. An agent can initiate an internal or external autonomous behavior at any time, and not only when it receives a message [HEW 77].

Agents can respond not only to invocations of specific methods, but also to observable events in the environment. Proactive agents can actually question the environment for events and other messages to determine what measures to take.

1.2.4. *Service-oriented paradigm*

The service-oriented paradigm is a relatively new software development, dating from the early 2000s, and well established in the field. SOSE is directly inspired by real-world organization methods in trade between multinationals, and is based on the classic notion of service.

The origin of SOSE comes from requests related to systems that need to be able to withstand increasingly volatile and heterogeneous environments such as the Internet and Web services [CAS 03], ambient intelligence environments [WEI 91] or business applications run on corporate networks such as *enterprise resource planning* (ERP) systems [PAP 07]. The productivity of a supplier and their responsiveness to changing needs are major issues that SOSE attempts to provide solutions to in software development.

The service is a software entity that represents a specific function. It is also an autonomous building block that does not depend on any context or external service. It is divided into operations that contain specific actions that the service can provide. A parallel can be drawn between operations and services, on the one hand, and methods and classes in the OOSE, on the other hand. SOSE also has a concept of composite service built by combining service descriptions. The implementation of service composition takes place during the *runtime* phase.

A key element of SOSE is the pattern of service interaction, also known as service-oriented architecture (SOA) that enables a range of services to communicate with each other. SOA is a means for design and an understanding of a software system to provide services to applications or other services via the publication of tracked interfaces.

A service is an action performed (a function rendered) by a provider for a customer; however, the interaction between the supplier and customer is established via a mediator (which may be a bus) responsible for bringing various participants together. Services are usually implemented as coarse-grained software entities. They encompass and propose system entities. These systems can also be defined as the application layers. The concept of a service represents a processing entity that respects the following characteristics:

– Coarse-grained: operations offered by a service encapsulate several functions and operate on a wide range of data, unlike with the component-based concept.

– Interface: a service can implement several interfaces and several services can implement a common interface.

– Architecture: each service is described by an architecture that enables us to understand what it does, in which conditions, at what price and with which non-functional properties.

– Discoverable: before a service can be called (*bind, invoke*), it has to be found (*look-up*).

– Single instance: unlike components that are instantiated on demand and can have multiple instances at the same time, it is a single service. It corresponds to the *singleton design pattern.*

– Loosely coupled: services are connected to customers and other services via standards. These standards ensure decoupling, i.e. the reduction of dependencies. These standards are eXtensible markup language (XML) documents, as in the case of Web services. However, several communication techniques manage the heterogeneity of services implementations so that they can still communicate. In the context of SOSE, coupling encompasses all concepts of the dynamic discovery of services and automatic changing/replacement of these services.

SOSE considers an application as a set of services interacting in a accordance with their roles and regardless of their location in order to withstand heterogeneous and loosely coupled software systems. The Web service is an example of a service where we use three basic elements: web services description language (WSDL) (an XML meta-language) as a description language, universal description discovery and integration (UDDI) registry to enable localization and a transfer protocol, such as hypertext transfer protocol (HTTP) or simple object access protocol (SOAP).

SOA is essentially a collection of services that interact and communicate with each other. This communication merely consists of a data return or an activity (coordination of several services). SOA is an interaction model application that implements services. This term originated between 2000 and 2001.

There is a hierarchy of services corresponding to the different layers of the technical architecture of a solution. SOA is a very effective solution to the problems faced by companies in terms of reusability, interoperability and reduction of coupling between systems that implement their information systems.

SOA became mainstream with the emergence of standards such as Web services in e-commerce, business to business (B2B) or business to consumer (B2C) based on platforms such as J2EE or NET.

1.3. Software architecture

For many years, software architecture was described in terms of boxes and lines. It was not until the early 1990s that software developers became aware of the crucial role that software architecture plays in the successful development, maintenance and evolution of their software system. A good software architecture design can lead to a product that meets customer needs and can easily be updated, whereas an improper architecture can have disastrous consequences that can lead to the withdrawal of a project [TAY 09].

1.3.1. *Object-oriented software architecture*

Object-oriented modeling creates diagrams, text specifications and a programming source code based on object-oriented concepts to describe a software system. Object-oriented modeling languages are methods and techniques to graphically analyze and represent software systems. There are several methods of modeling objects such as designing object-oriented software (DOSS) by Wirfs-Brock, object-modeling technique (MOT) by Rumbaugh, OOSE by Jacobson or object-oriented analysis and design (OOD) by Booch. However, nowadays, most of these methods have been integrated into Unified Modeling Language (UML) by Booch *et al.* and, therefore, are no longer practiced by analysts. Object-oriented software architecture is used to describe a system as a collection of classes (entities to be abstracted and the encapsulation of functionalities) that can have objects (instances) and communicate between themselves by sending messages [OUS 99, OUS 05].

1.3.1.1. *Advantages and disadvantages of object-oriented software architectures*

Object-oriented software architectures offer several advantages as follows:

– They are based on well-defined methodologies to develop systems on the basis of a set of requirements.

– They often provide direct mapping from specification to implementation.

– They are familiar with a large community of engineers and software developers.

– They are supported by commercial tools.

However, they suffer from a number of shortcomings. The most significant are as follows:

– Significant limitations in terms of granularity and scale-up.

– Low level of object reuse, partly due to the tight coupling of objects. In fact, they can communicate without using their interface.

– The structure of object-oriented applications has poor legibility (a set of files).

– Most object-oriented mechanisms are manually managed (instance creation, management of dependencies between classes, explicit method calls, etc.).

– There are few or no tools to deploy executables on different sites.

– They only specify the services provided by object implementation but do not, in any way, define the requirements of these objects.

– They provide little or no direct support to characterize and analyze non-functional properties.

– They provide a limited number of primitive interconnection mechanisms (method invocation), making it difficult to account for complex interconnections.

– They offer few solutions to facilitate the adaptation and assembly of objects.

– They find it difficult to take account of object-oriented developments (adding, deleting, modifying, changing communication methods, etc.).

– They are not suitable for building coordination patterns and complex communication.

– They have limited support for hierarchical descriptions.

– They make it difficult to define the overall systems architecture prior to the complete construction of the components.

1.3.2. *Component-based software architecture*

Component-based software architectures describe systems as a set of components (processing or storage units) that communicate with each other via connectors (interaction units). Their goals are to reduce development costs, improve the reuse of models, share common concepts between system users and finally build reusable off-the-shelf component-based heterogeneous systems. To support the development of such architectures, it is necessary to have formal notations and tools for analyzing architectural specifications. *Architecture description languages* (ADLs) stand as a good solution for this purpose [OUS 05, TAY 09].

1.3.2.1. *Advantages and disadvantages of component-based software architectures*

In component-based software architectures:

– interfaces are generally first-class entities explicitly described by ports and roles;

– interactions are separate from the calculations and are explicitly defined in most ADLs;

– non-functional properties are taken into account;

– hierarchical representations are semantically richer than simple inheritance relationships;

– ADLs are enhanced by architectural styles defining a design vocabulary framed by a set of constraints on this vocabulary;

– the overall description of system architecture can be specified before completing the construction of its components;

– the level of granularity of a component or connector is higher than that of an object or an association.

However, component-based software architectures:

– provide only high-level models, without explaining how these models can be connected to the source code. Such connections are important to preserve the integrity of the design;

– remain an *ad hoc* concept known by the academic community. Currently, the industrial world is becoming increasingly interested in this discipline of software engineering;

– despite the ISO/IEC/IEEE 42010:2011 standard[2], there is no real consensus because different notations and approaches for describing software architectures have been proposed.

1.3.3. *Agent-oriented software architecture*

OMASs are effective systems, which meet the challenges of designing large and complex MASs. MASs are a paradigm for understanding and building distributed systems, where it is assumed that the processing elements – i.e. agents, which are autonomous entities able to communicate – have a partial knowledge of what surrounds them and have their own particular behavior, as well as a capacity to execute themselves independently (see Figure 1.2). An agent acting on behalf of a third party (another agent, a user) that it represents without necessarily being connected to it, reacts and interacts with other agents. The social capacity for cooperation, coordination and negotiation between agents is one of their main characteristics [WOO 09].

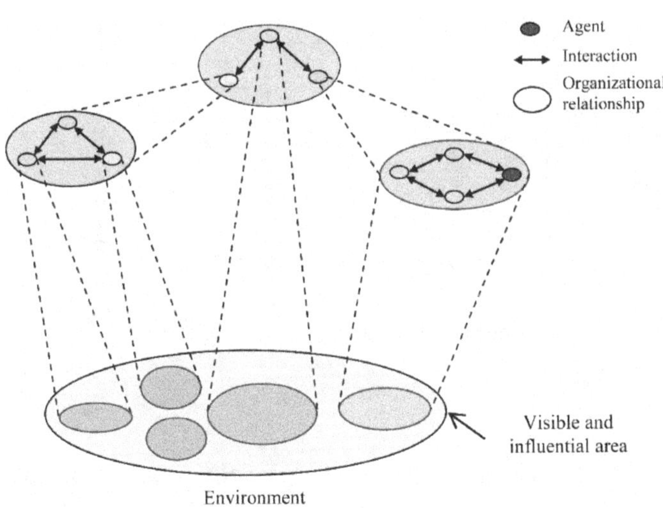

Figure 1.2. *Canonical view of organizational multi-agent system [JEN 01]*

2 www.iso-architecture.org/ieee-1471/.

To summarize, a framework for specifying agents must be able to capture at least the following aspects of a MAS:

– beliefs that the agents have;

– interactions that agents have with their environment;

– the objectives that officials are trying to achieve;

– actions that agents perform and the impact of these actions.

1.3.3.1. *Advantages and disadvantages of agent-oriented software architecture*

In agent-oriented programming, the concept of software architecture is replaced by a further knowledge-driven concept called organization. An organization is made up of a set of roles and relationships between these roles. Figure 1.3 shows that a role can be played by one or more agents and an agent could also potentially play more than one role simultaneously. A role is an abstraction of an agent; it allows for a more generic description of the architecture as well as the interaction between agents [WOO 09].

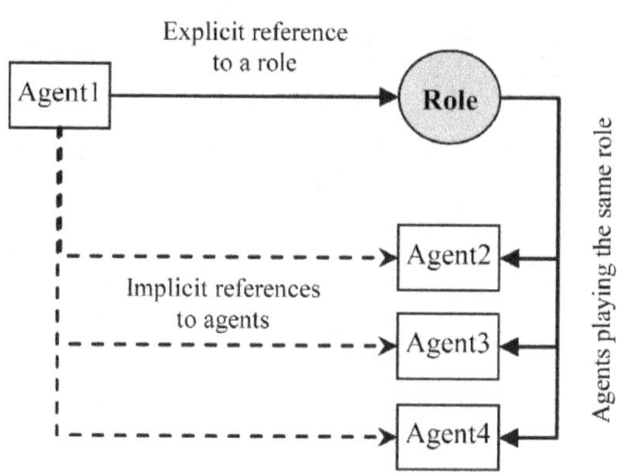

Figure 1.3. *Coupling between agents*

Generally:

– agent-oriented architectures support competition and distribution;

– agent-oriented architectures integrate business and technical perspectives;

– relationships between agents are therefore very dynamic and partly managed independently or via organizations;

– MASs take the coupling and collaboration concept between entities further (coordination, decomposition, negotiation, etc.);

– MASs use coupling mechanisms dynamically and indirectly (intermediary agent, directory agent, etc.);

– MASs propose semantic coupling guided by knowledge and by a social organization of work.

By contrast, in agent-oriented software architecture:

– the agent-oriented paradigm does not support non-functional properties;

– they usually have only one input, thus they are not compositional;

– agent-oriented architectures are generally difficult to verify.

1.3.4. *Service-oriented architecture*

SOSE is based on the concept of SOA [OAS 08, PAP 07], which defines a conceptual framework to organize the construction of application based on services. SOA introduces the concepts of service providers and consumers.

– A service provider is the actor responsible for the development, deployment, execution and maintenance of the service when it is required. In addition, when the service expires the provider takes care of the termination of the service activities.

– A service consumer is the actor who uses services according to their needs.

In the beginning, suppliers and consumers are independent – i.e. the supplier during the implementation of its services has no prior knowledge about the future consumers, nor how they might reuse that service. Thus, the SOA is based on a third actor called the *service broker* [OAS 08].

The *service broker* is the actor associated with a service registry that enables the relationship between consumers and suppliers who are unaware of each other. Suppliers publish their services in these registries, which are then used by consumers to identify those that match their needs.

Suppliers and consumers commit to a contract of use, in terms of respect for the service interface for the consumer and compliance with functional and non-functional properties promised to the supplier. Figure 1.4 summarizes the organization of a SOA.

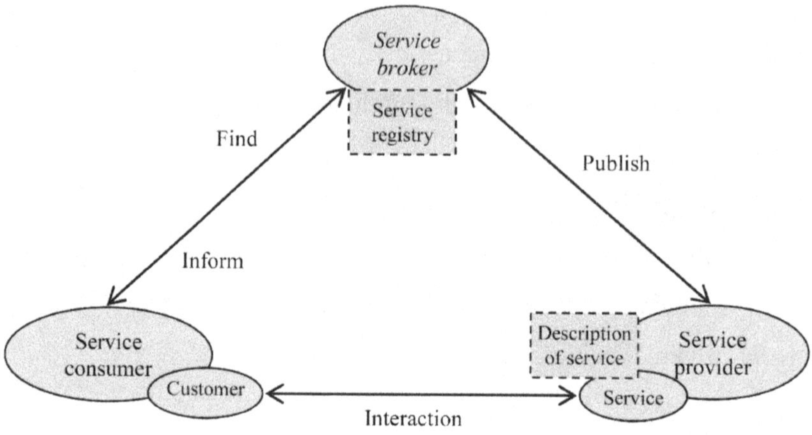

Figure 1.4. *Service-oriented architecture organization*

1.3.4.1. *Advantages and disadvantages of service-oriented software architecture*

– SOA provides dynamicity via the mechanism of discovery and dynamic service selection.

– The service-oriented paradigm supports distribution as well as the management of non-functional properties.

– The service-oriented paradigm does not support the aspect of competition (in the sense of having parallel processing capabilities).

– SOA offers high internal consistency (using a pivot exchange format, usually XML).

– SOA provides loose external coupling (using an interoperable interface layer, usually a Web service, and through the discovery and dynamic selection of services).

– SOA can develop a complex product by integrating different products from different suppliers, regardless of the platform and technology used. Thus, it helps us to manage the complexity involved.

However, service-oriented software architectures:

– are not suitable for applications with graphical user interface (GUI) functionalities. These applications could become more complex if they use SOA architectures that require a large volume of data exchange;

– also, in the case of stand-alone application or for short-term usage, the SOA will become a burden;

– are a performance problem for the SOA, a complex mechanism with too many messages exchanged and unnecessary complexity for a number of software packages; not suitable for systems with very strong time constraints.

1.4. The two dimensions of the conceptual framework for comparison: quantitative and qualitative

The aim of our conceptual framework for comparison is to fill the gaps around the clear identification of differences between OOSE, CBSE, AOSE and SOSE. The goal is to give users a better understanding through the use of a comparative summary of the four paradigms in order to assist them in deciding on the use of one of these paradigms. This aspiration involves a grasp of their respective concepts, in their definition and then in the analysis of impacts on quality.

This comparison between object, component, agent and services serves the same purpose as the comparison between objects and components [OUS 05, SZY 02]. The common goal is the analysis and understanding of the differences in a unique, comprehensible framework.

Thus, the approach we develop follows a *top-down* pattern, which, as opposed to previous *bottom-up* works, focuses initially on the conceptual levels, directly on the paradigms before seeking to derive the qualitative implications. This high-level focus allows the definition of an overall framework capable of handling four paradigms. In this definition of the comparative framework, we seek both:

– generality in identifying categories and subcategories of the comparison framework that should not be dependent on a particular paradigm, but rather provide an outside perspective on which elements of the four paradigms may be projected. This generally prevents us from favoring one paradigm over another, and also ensures the reusability of the framework, which can be used to compare various other development paradigms;

– minimalism in the selected categories and classified elements, which must only extract the essence of the paradigms required to identify their differences;

– completeness in identifying differences that allows us to fully understand the impact on the quality of the choice of one paradigm over another. Completeness of this framework provides the opportunity for users to customize the qualitative analysis.

1.4.1. *Conceptual differences*

The four paradigms studied have a very similar approach based on the construction of systems from existing or future software entities. They have a common goal of maximizing reusability that is directly derived from the object. They share the same overall development process that consists of identifying software entities (object, agent, component or services) that meet the needs, and then combining these entities to make the final application. They are based on the same concepts of composition, for the construction of new entities from existing ones to ensure a consistent approach where any entity can be seen as an object, agent, component or service. Thus, this approach facilitates incremental development and exploitation of knowledge.

However, although these four paradigms have the same overall goal, the concepts behind the notions of objects, components, agents, and services are different.

Thus, we confront the following four aspects:

– difference in utilization and owner's responsibility;

– difference in coupling;

– difference in granularity;

– difference in cooperation and problem-solving.

1.4.1.1. *Difference in use and owner's responsibility*

A component is called "off the shelf" [CRN 06, HEI 01] by adopting a piece of technology, the component, which is available for developers. The latter recover a block of software component and ensure its incorporation based on their requirements.

A service focuses on the use of a function provided by a third party [DUS 05, NIT 08, OAS 08, THE 08]. A service consumer only uses the result from the invocation of the target service.

These two views seem close at first; however, they have a significant impact on the allocation of responsibilities between supplier and consumer. To illustrate this distinction, we take an example of the video game industry on personal computer (PC). This industry is mainly based on two models of content distribution:

– The classic model: purchasing a game in a specialist shop or downloading on the Internet.

– The cloud gaming model: purchasing a subscription to play available games directly on an Internet platform.

The classic model illustrates the object-oriented, component-based and agent-oriented approach. The cloud gaming model illustrates the service-oriented approach.

1.4.1.1.1. Responsibility of an object, component or agent

The first classic model corresponds to a player who buys a copy of a game. This copy is collected either on a physical medium, usually a DVD, or in a dematerialized form (cloud) via download platforms such as STEAM[3]. The player is then responsible for installing the game on his/her own machine, i.e. its deployment. It is only after this installation that he/she can launch the application and start playing.

This distribution model corresponds to a component-based approach. Typically, the game (the component) comes with an instruction manual (the documentation) that defines a number of consumer-end constraints. These constraints are of two kinds:

– Deployment constraints: the provider of a PC video game sets the minimum system requirements in terms of computing power (CPU, graphics card, RAM, etc.), storage capacity (hard drive), audio resources, etc. The

3 http://store.streampowered.com.

customer's system must meet these requirements to be able to install and run the game. The installation process itself presents constraints whether it is the exact location on the hard disk or the connection requirements to the Internet, key authentication, etc. In OOSE, CBSE and AOSE these installation constraints are typically defined by the chosen component model [CRN 11]. Each model is associated with a particular system environment before it can be used. Moreover, this model provides deployment rules associated with these components.

– Usage constraints: each game provides a list of specific commands that determines how to interact with it and the resulting actions that are necessary to progress through the levels (game play, level design, etc.).

These elements provide the rules to be complied with if the user wants to take full advantage of the proposed component. In OOSE, CBSE and AOSE these user constraints are typically defined by the contractual interface of the entity (object, component and agent). Compliance with this interface is crucial to ensure the correct use of resources according to the possibilities previously determined by the supplier of the entity.

1.4.1.1.2. Responsibility of a service

The second distribution model, called *Cloud gaming*, illustrates the concept of service. In this model, the player pays the right to play a game that is running on a remote platform under the responsibility of the supplier. He/she only needs the interface and the appropriate connection to access the platform. In fact, the player is no longer responsible for operating the game on his/her own machine. The only information he/she requires is how to access this platform and how to play the game. Hence, deployment constraints no longer exist in relation to the installation of the game; only usage constraints remain. This lack of operation has several advantages. On the one hand, it simplifies the exploitation of resources by removing efforts that accompany the understanding of the installation phases. On the other hand, it ensures the optimal use of these resources. In fact, the application runs directly on the provider's environment. The latter therefore has full control of its execution. Thus, it is more likely to ensure the quality promised to its customers.

In our example, the quality of a video game (fluidity, graphics, etc.) varies depending on the system on which it is installed. Being run on a remote platform, this game has the same quality for each player connected.

In addition, users who originally did not have the required system configurations will benefit from this service. Thus, constraints on the customer only decrease to their communication capacity.

Finally, another significant advantage of this service-oriented model relationship between customers and suppliers is the transparency of service developments as long as the latter do not change the initial usage constraints (connection interface, protocols, etc.). As it is, the new versions are directly accessible without the need to adapt on the consumer-end. On the contrary, in a component-based approach, if the customer wants to take advantage of these developments, he/she must collect and deploy the game himself/herself. Problems associated with this deployment may occur if the customer's system no longer supports the updated component. Cloud gaming illustrates this advantage where different versions of the same game follow one after the other in a transparent manner to users. As for the classic distribution, it requires players to collect a particular patch and then its deployment on their machine in order to develop the version of the game. These new versions can potentially require a hardware upgrade at the consumer-end (for example, to support an improved graphics engine) whereas it is not required in cloud gaming. Thus, collecting the patch, its installation and the ability to use the new version of the game may incur additional costs. These additional costs are generally not present in the service-oriented approach where the customer pays for this function, whereas in the component-based approach the customer pays for one component at a time and within a given release version.

However, the main drawback of this service-oriented relationship between the customer and the service provider is the total reliance of the first system on the second system as well as the reliance on different media of communication between them. As it is, a failure of these elements, which are outside the sphere of the customer's actions, sees its inability to act on the issue. In turn, it is the contract previously established with the supplier that characterizes the consequences of these failures in terms of compensation for the customer.

Within the framework of *cloud gaming*, these failures, which are out of the customer's control, are, for example, an error in the game's platform or even loss of Internet connectivity linked to the Internet service provider (ISP). Thus, the service-oriented paradigm pushes the owner's responsibility to the maximum, compared to the component-based paradigm, and therefore decreases the customer's responsibility. Indeed, the CBSE, the *off-the-shelf* approach, implies that the supplier is solely responsible for the development of its component, the associated Quality of Service required and its maintenance.

In the SOSE approach, the supplier is also responsible for the deployment, execution and management of their service. The service consumer is solely responsible for the communication and for the compliance of usage constraints.

1.4.1.1.3. Multitenant nature

An application is called "multitenant" [JAC 05] if it offers functionalities to many users simultaneously. It therefore manages numerous instances at the same time and allows multiple isolated instances to be hosted in order to guarantee accurate results to its various customers.

Similarly, an instance being run is dedicated to manage multiple parallel connections. In our example of video games, *cloud gaming* platforms support a large number of players in parallel. For each of these players, they must maintain a particular context in order to retain their respective information. This information is of two kinds:

– *Contract* groups: the set of data related to the contract between the customer and the supplier that govern the use of the service (in our example: monthly subscription account number, quality, etc.).

– *Runtime* groups: the set of data required to run the application throughout the use of the service (in our example: experience gained, games played, persistent universes, etc., in order to reproduce exactly the status where the player stopped in his/her game).

This multitenant principle is not necessary for an object/ component/agent. In fact, although it may belong to multiple compositions, at runtime, different instances of the component are created and each are created under the responsibility of a customer in the context of a particular composition.

To conclude, from a usage and owner responsibility perspective, object-oriented, component-based and agent-oriented paradigms are close.

1.4.1.2. *Difference relating to coupling*

Coupling is a concept that we identify as one of the key breaking points between OOSE/CBSE and AOSE/SOSE. This concept expresses all the possible dependencies between conceptual and software entities. Reducing coupling guarantees a number of intuitive benefits in terms of isolating errors, easing additions and removal of entities reused, reconfiguration, etc.

In fact, OOSE and CBSE have a broad mandate in the type of applications they wish to implement, whereas the SOSE and AOSE mechanisms are built to support the development of applications that run on highly volatile, cooperative and heterogeneous environments.

This difference is consecutively illustrated by their respective connection for, on the one hand, the management of heterogeneities, and, on the other hand, the automation of other mechanisms.

1.4.1.2.1. Management of heterogeneities

The aim of the service-oriented paradigm is the independence it has with implementation technologies. A service must be accessible and usable without any assumption on its implementation, on the potential users or on how to use this service. This problem is well known in CBSE but is not as critical as in the SOSE issue. As it is, there are a large number of component models [CRN 11]. To develop a new system, the designer must choose a particular model and use only the components complying with this model as the collaboration between different models is very difficult [CRN 06]. Thus, although the CBSE has proven its effectiveness in software reuse and maintainability, it does not specifically target certain difficulties encountered by developers in relation to changes in platforms, protocols, devices, Internet, etc. [BRE 07].

For its part, the SOSE advocates a single homogeneous service-oriented model [ERI 08], to be standardized and used by all, to encapsulate all types of resources and hide their heterogeneous nature during development.

1.4.1.2.2. Comparison to automation mechanisms

Automation contributes to the definition of the SOSE itself, and therefore the vast majority of research seeks to automate mechanisms such as service publication, discovery, selection and composition. As it is, the decoupling between requirements and services used, discovery at runtime, the definition of collaboration and, finally, the dynamic establishment of communications were the main goals set from the start in the development of the service paradigm. This principle of automation is pushed to its maximum by the concept of self-adaptation [NIT 08], which seeks to coordinate all mechanisms related to the service-oriented paradigm to allow for reactive or proactive contextual adaptations.

Although the process automation is a key element of research in CBSE and represents many of its current challenges, it is not an integral part of the conceptual origin of the CBSE or the definition of a component model [CRN 11].

Thus, with respect to the heterogeneity and automation, SOSE aims to produce loose coupling at all levels, from development to execution.

1.4.1.3. *Difference in granularity*

In the field of software engineering, granularity corresponds to a relative measurement of the size of architectural elements that make up the applications. The software engineering community speak then of coarse-grained systems or fine-grained systems [BEI 07], which are, respectively, associated with their composition by the assembly of high and low granularity blocks. These notions of high and low granularity are determined by the importance of the encapsulated resources by architectural elements. This importance is relative to the underlying complexity of the implementation and usage of these resources.

Understanding granularity became prominent with the development of CBSE [BEI 07, MOH 08]. In fact, this granularity represents one of the first points of distinction between an object and a component. The object responds to the lack of clarity, understanding, and thus the handling of systems, which are decomposed into too many objects or objects that are too large. Thus, different component models offer different granularities [BEI 07], and these proposed variabilities for the size of the building blocks reinforce the importance of choice in the decoupling of the application in order to maximize the quality of the resulting architecture.

The concept of granularity is intuitively understandable, which counteracts with the vagueness of its formalization where the clear delineation between high granularity and low granularity remains to be defined. However, the current understanding is sufficient to establish a hierarchy between SOSE, CBSE, AOSE and OOSE, where service-oriented paradigms are usually described as more coarse-grained than component-based, in the same way that the component-based paradigms are typically seen as coarse-grained in relation to agent-oriented paradigms and fine-grained in relation to object-oriented paradigms.

We justify this comparison of granularity between the service-oriented/ component-based/agent-oriented/object-oriented with two commonly encountered realities:

– Technical reality: where component-based models are often used to build new SOSE services from scratch or from legacy systems. CBSE related technologies can intervene at all phases for SOSE system realization, from the services implementation, to their adaptations in order to integrate them taking care of the heterogeneities (as different runtime environments, languages, protocols, interfaces, etc.), or even in order to provide the level of abstraction necessary for the composition of pre-existing services. This relationship between service-oriented paradigms and component-based paradigms is the same between component-based/agent-oriented and object-oriented paradigms, where the object-oriented paradigms are commonly used to implement components or agents.

– Conceptual reality: linked to the very nature of the service and processes associated with it. The previous sections have highlighted a set of inherent properties of the SOSE such as loose coupling, heterogeneity management, automation degree, the distribution of responsibilities or even the multitenant. Although these concepts are already present in the CBSE, the thrust of SOSE is to push them to their maximum. To ensure these developments, complex processes must be executed. Thus, the singularly coarse-grained nature of the service-oriented paradigm comes from a need for balance or dilemma between the cost of support of the service processes, the size of the encapsulated resources and the relevance of their placement on the network.

The technical reality is offset against the component-based approaches such as [AND 08, OAS 09] which, during the implementation of the SOSE applications consider the service of the interface of a component as a service within SOSE term. In this respect, the SOSE service is seen as a subset of the interface. However, the ratio of the implementation of one by the other remains the same.

1.4.1.4. *Difference of cooperation and problem-solving*

The concept of cooperation and problem-solving is a concept stemming from the field of DAI, in coordination with the multi-agent approach. The main problem in the study of cooperation in distributed problem-solving is to understand how agents wishing to accommodate each other, may interact with each other to form an effective team. Two forms of cooperation are defined, the sharing of tasks and the sharing of results, which correspond generally to discerned phases in the study of problem-solving. In both of these types of cooperation, R. Davis and R. Smith are particularly interested in its control and communication. In the division of tasks, the control is directed by the goals and the agents are represented by the tasks they are committed to perform; the problem lies in the distribution of the tasks. In sharing results, the control is data-driven, the agents are represented by knowledge resources, and the problem lies in the communication of the results [BOU 92, SMI 81].

A cooperative strategy is necessary in order to perform tasks effectively when problem-solving involves several agents. The purpose of a strategy is to ensure overall consistency from local decisions and enable the effective use of communication. Two classes of cooperative strategies are defined: organizational strategies and the distribution of information strategies. The first class deals with the decomposition of a global task into subtasks and assigning these subtasks to the agents. They aim to identify the most appropriate agent to decide which plan to follow. For instance, an organizational strategy chooses an agent, which has the largest selection of possible actions. Strategies on the distribution of information indicate how and when agents must communicate. For example, one of these strategies specifies that we should not repeatedly send the same information to an agent [BOU 92, CAM 83].

Cooperation refers to a judgment value on the overall activity of a set of agents. The judgment of cooperation is influenced by several indicators such as the number and the persistence of conflicts as well as the synchronization of different agents' actions. The mechanisms that allow us to weigh these indicators are called cooperation processes.

Durfee has identified the cooperation indicators. These indicators were empirically determined from the observation of cooperative situations. The following list of indicators is not exhaustive [DUR 89]:

– Coordination of actions: this indicator relates to the adjustment of the direction of the agents' actions over time (synchronization) and in space.

– Parallelization: this indicator is based on the distribution of tasks and their concurrent execution.

– The sharing of resources: this indicator relates to the use of resources and skills such as information, results and equipment.

– Robustness: this indicator relates to the system' ability to compensate for the failure of an agent.

– Non-redundancy: this indicator reflects the lack of redundant activities, for instance, selective communication.

– The non-persistence of conflict: this indicator reflects the lack of blocking situations; it is based on the agents' ability to prevent conflicts or to solve them by default.

The cooperation and problem-solving concept is absent in the OOSE, the CBSE and the SOSE because their basic entities are reactive and not proactive in nature as it is in the case of the agents.

1.4.1.5. *Summary of conceptual differences*

We have shown our conceptual framework for comparison between the four paradigms. The first purpose is to complete the continuing lack of coverage in the literature about the clear specification of the conceptual differences between object-oriented, component-based, agent-oriented and service-oriented paradigms.

We therefore chose a top-down approach, which focuses first, on the conceptual aspects of the different paradigms before developing qualities, which are derived from them.

1.4.2. *Quantitative dimension*

Structural elements and mechanisms, which characterize the four paradigms, can be classified into two categories: products and processes.

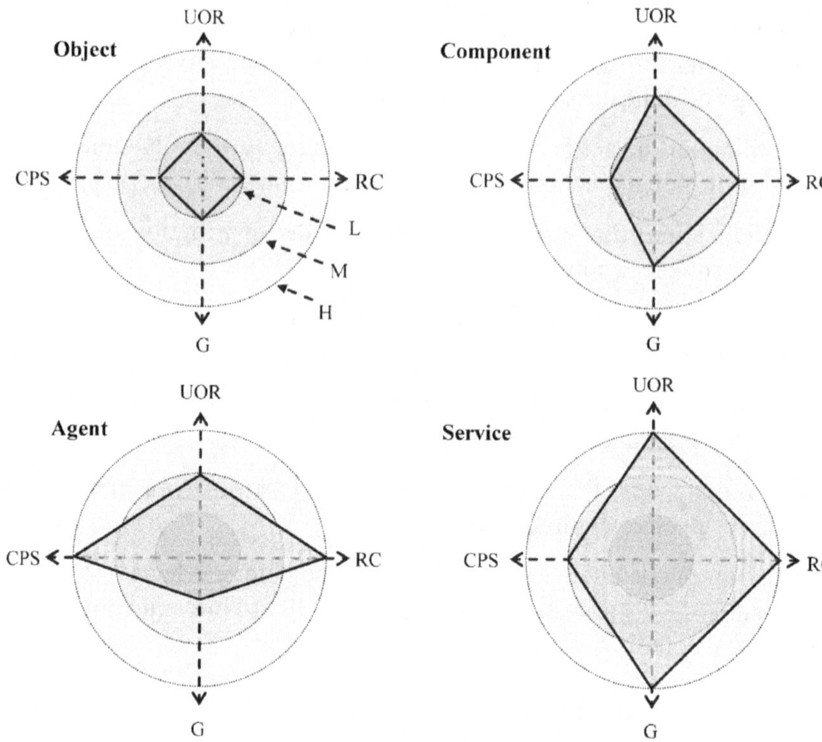

Figure 1.5. *Summary of conceptual differences between the four paradigms (UOR: usage and owner's responsibility; RC: relation to coupling; G: granularity; CRP: cooperation and problem-solving; L: low; M: medium; H: high)*

1.4.2.1. *Product and process*

A product is a software or conceptual entity that is the result of an action or process. A process is an action or series of actions that is used to create or modify a product and thus *obtain* a product as a result. Products are divided into two subcategories:

– simple architectural elements: the basic building blocks of a paradigm;

– composite architectural elements: complex products built from existing architectural elements. Their structure clearly identifies the reused architectural elements and their relationships.

Each subcategory is further divided into two groups according to two levels of abstraction: the *design-time* and *runtime*.

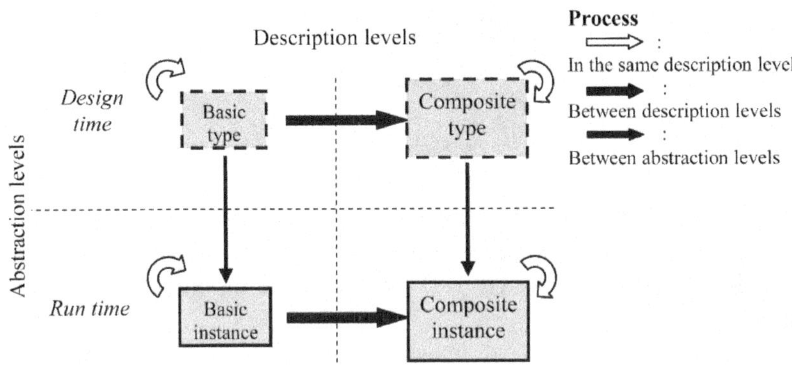

Figure 1.6. *Abstraction and description levels: distribution of products and processes*

The process category focuses on the principle of reuse, i.e. how to reuse software entities in order to build new composite ones. Conventionally, a component can be a single or composite architectural element. These notions of component and composite define two levels of description. Thus, processes are grouped according to the levels of abstraction and description:

– In the same level of description: this category groups processes that target and generate products of the same level of description (Figure 1.6: white arrows). This category is divided into both design-time and runtime.

– Between levels of description: this category groups processes that target products of two different levels of description (Figure 1.6: dashed arrows).

– Between levels of abstraction: this category represents the processes that ensure the transformation of products from the design-time to runtime (see Figure 1.6: black arrows).

Figure 1.6 shows the distribution of products and processes on a single representation. A composite "A" is made up of a set of components such as "B" which is defined as a simple architectural element. Both products have their performances at design-time and runtime. The various arrows represent processes that are being studied. The white arrows are the processes related to the same level of description and abstraction. The dashed arrows are the processes that make the link between the levels of description and have their representation at the design-time and the runtime. The black arrows are the processes that make the link between the levels of abstraction and thus ensure the transformation from the design-time to runtime.

1.4.2.2. *Comparison between paradigms*

1.4.2.2.1. Product

Single architectural elements

The single architectural elements of the object-oriented paradigms are the *class* at design-time and the *instance* (object) at runtime. The same distinction is made for the CBSE between component type and connector type products [AMI 09, GAR 97] and their component and connector instances.

Connectors [CRN 11] are mediators in connections between components, i.e. they are used as intermediaries between these constituent components. They have a twofold function: (1) enabling indirect compositions between components and (2) the introduction of additional functions through the glue code, which they encapsulate.

In AOSE, we describe an entity that is capable of acting in an environment that can communicate directly with other agents as a "single agent"; it has its own resources and skills and provides services to its environment. The concept of the single agent is used interchangeably in the design-time and runtime phases.

In SOSE, the boundary between levels of abstraction is much less clear and most existing work refers to a service as a runtime entity [STO 05, THE 08]. However, a notion of abstract service exists in some approaches [CAV 09]. This concept is used to distinguish between the requirements sought by the architect to define its application and services actually available in the system to meet these requirements. However, an exact clarification between abstract service and concrete service remains to be defined. We also mention the concept of service description, which is a major product of the SOSE [OAS 08]. As it is, each runtime representation of a service is associated with its service description, which is the target of many processes involved in the exploitation of resources.

Composite architectural elements

The four paradigms share the composite notion. The object-oriented paradigm is based on the concepts of composite class and composite object. The CBSE relies on concepts of configuration and composite component types at the point of design. For their runtime, it relies on their configuration and composite component instances.

In the context of this study, we consider a composite agent as a MAS, which is composed of a set of single agents representing active entities of the system with a set of relations that unite the agents with each other. Neither the agents nor the MAS, however, are explicitly composable in contrast to the organization-based agent systems that are compositional.

The notion of service composition and, ultimately, of the SOSE's composite service is mainly at the runtime. Indeed, most of the existing works consider the composite service as the execution of a collaborative scheme between services by a composition engine. However, some approaches [GEE 08, ZEN 03] introduce the instantiation concepts of a collaborative scheme from abstract templates that describe them. We choose to consider this similar representation with OO types of collaborative schemes, such as design-time entities, and instances of collaborative schemes such as runtime entities. In addition, a collaborative scheme is classically associated with two patterns of services coordination, such as choreography and orchestration [RSA 08], which have technologies that support their representation at the point of design-time and runtime. We define a composite service encapsulating the composition of services in a similar manner in the composite service type and composite service instance.

1.4.2.2.2. Process

To elaborate the main differences between paradigms, we describe a selection of the most relevant and widely accepted processes by the community.

At the same level of description:

– *Design-time*: the object-oriented paradigm is primarily based on the process of association and inheritance. The CBSE is based on the horizontal composition [BAR 06, CRN 11] between architectural elements of the same level of description. This horizontal composition corresponds to the process of establishing connections between components. We can also mention versioning, selective inheritance and refinement processes. In the same level of description, the SOSE processes focus mainly on handling collaborative schemes between services. We mention the process of choreography, which is one of the principle supports for reuse and does express direct communications between services.

– *Runtime*: communication processes between architectural elements are the major concern in this category. OO and CBSE are based mainly on call function processes, while the SOSE inevitably includes additional processes. Typically, services have to be discovered and selected dynamically (process discovery and selection of services). Then these services coordinate their actions through a process of choreography that defines the succession of invocations of service. In addition, a front-end process of service publication is required to make the service available to potential customers (see Figure 1.4).

Between levels of description:

– *Design-time*: the OO is based on the composition process to produce composite components. The CBSE is based on vertical composition that links components and composites. Vertical composition (or hierarchical) [BAR 06, CRN 11] consists of a sub-component encapsulated in a composite component. This composition is anti-reflexive to avoid cycles, i.e. that the same component cannot be found at several levels of the hierarchy. It assumes the consistent combinations of behavior for the composite with the behavior of its constituents. Moreover, the constituents are hidden for the requests of the composite customers. The SOSE is based on the orchestration process that models vertical communications between the composite service and its constituent services.

– *Runtime*: the communication processes between constituents and composites are the essence of this category. OO and CBSE are based on different call processes. In CBSE, these calls are sometimes referred to as the process of delegation. In SOSE, the coordination of the process of services invocations from the composite toward its constituents is called orchestration. Similarly, the process of discovery and dynamic selection of services are required to identify the constituents of the composite service.

Between levels of abstraction:

– The OO and the CBSE are based on the instantiation process to link types to their instances. The AOSE is based on the concepts of generic role (part of the *design-time*) and specific role to a domain (part of the *runtime*). The SOSE is based on the concepts of abstract service and concrete service respectively as elements of *design-time* and *runtime* [HOC 11]. However, the transition from one to the other is based on the discovery process and selection of services process. The transition from one type of collaborative scheme to an instance of collaborative scheme is based on instantiation. The transition from one type of composite service to an instance of composite service corresponds to the combination of discovery and selection of its constituent services and the instantiation of collaborative schemes, which guide their behavior.

Table 1.1 presents a summary of the comparative study between paradigms from the product and process point of view.

Product		Object	Component	Agent	Service
Single element	Design-time	Class	Component type, connector type	Agent	Abstract service
	Runtime	Object	Component, connector	Specific role to a domain	Concrete service, description of service
Composite element	Design-time	Composite class	Type of configuration, type of composite component	SMA/organization	Type of collaborative scheme, type of composite service
	Runtime	Composite object	Configuration, composite component	Composite role	Instance of collaborative scheme, instance of composite service
In the same level of abstraction	*Design-time*	Association, inheritance	Horizontal composition, selective inheritance, versioning, refinement	Multiple roles	Choreography
	Runtime	Call method	Call function	Call transmission	Choreography, discovery and selection, invocation, publication
Between levels of description	*Design-time*	Composition	Vertical composition	Composition of roles	Orchestration
	Runtime	Call method	Call function, delegation	Call transmission	Orchestration, invocation, discovery and selection
Between levels of abstraction		Instantiation	Instantiation	Specific role to a domain + individual knowledge	Discovery and selection, instantiation of scheme

Table 1.1. *Product and process: comparison between paradigms*

1.4.3. *Qualitative dimension*

Existing research studies related to software quality define a number of criteria such as performance, safety, robustness, flexibility and development. [BIA 07, KIT 96]. Each of these studies has outlined their own organization of these criteria. The definition of these quality criteria and the way to apprehend them are being shaped based on the perspective of the target user via these measurement frameworks. Indeed, understanding a quality can vary between the stakeholders involved; whether they are architects, designers, developers or others. In addition, the scope of the system directly influences the importance of these criteria. We therefore try to cover all of these variations by offering the possibility for users to define their own vision of the qualities that interest them most. In the first instance, we identify the set of paradigm factors that influence software quality. Then we compare OOSE, CBSE, SOSE and AOSE approaches following these factors. Second, the user defines the quality criteria that they want to measure by combining the previous results.

Using the various previous analyses and by placing the four object-oriented, component-based, agent-oriented and service-oriented paradigms within the conceptual framework, it emerges that they share the following quality factors:

– *Reusability*: the support and ease of a product or a process related to a software development paradigm to be reused in the same way or through a number of changes.

– *Composability:* the support and ease of a software development paradigm to safely combine architectural elements to construct new systems or composite architectural elements.

– *Dynamicity:* the support and ease of a paradigm to develop applications that can adapt their behavior dynamically, automatically and autonomously to meet changing requirements and changing contexts as well as the possibility of errors.

These three factors represent the qualitative nature that led to the definition of the object-oriented, component-based, service-oriented and agent-oriented development paradigms. Figure 1.7 illustrates this analysis and provides a high-level view of their primary points of interest and traces the chronological evolution of the concerns for the software engineering community.

Reusability is the oldest of the three concerns. The earlier developers quickly became aware of code repetition in an application and have therefore sought to define mechanisms to limit repetition. The object-oriented paradigm focuses on this concern and its development is one of the outcomes of this research. The object-oriented concept facilitates the conservation and the transfer of experience gained across different systems. It further deepens reuse, which, at the outset was intended to reuse the code as it is through the inheritance process that we are able to evolve saved data and behavior in order to meet special requirements. Thus, the object-oriented paradigm provides high reusability which has paved the way for more complex applications and thus for the identification of new limits in terms of granularity, software architecture, communication abstraction, etc. These limits have therefore led us to a shift in concern towards composability.

Thus, the software engineering community has developed and introduced the CBSE to overcome this new challenge. Szyperski's famous phrase "components are for composition" [SZY 02] illustrates this case perfectly. By definition, a component must have a design specifically established to support the potential composition to allow interoperability. Component models and associated technologies (CORBA *component model* CCM [OMG 12], COM + [MIC 13], Fractal [BRU 06], etc.) exist to provide specific development and deployment frameworks needed to support composition patterns. Such models impose component formats in terms of the construction of codes and deployment rules [CRN 11]. Thus, the CBSE strengthens the control of composability and clearly formalizes the associated processes. Ultimately, this formalization raises the solid foundation needed for automation opportunities. Part of the software community has therefore redirected itself towards the dynamicity concern as the predominant aspect. Thus, SOSE has been developed from the experience gained from objects and components; however, at the outset, it focused on how to improve dynamicity. The SOSE seeks to provide an appropriate response to highly volatile environments and thus overcome the constraints imposed by the general purpose of the CBSE.

Figure 1.7 summarizes these displacement-related concerns. Research from the OOSE focuses mainly on reuse and discusses some composability and dynamicity. The CBSE focuses on composability, which strengthens reusability and also seeks to automate its processes. The SOSE focuses mainly on the dynamicity of existing processes to ensure reuse and composition. As for the AOSE, it gives more importance to the dynamicity without significant improvement of composability factors and reusability factors; however, it focuses on the cooperation and coordination of agents to solve a problem.

The comparison between object-oriented, component-based, agent-oriented and service-oriented paradigms (which one is more reusable, more modular and more dynamic) taking into account the three quality factors, is very difficult because it depends on the perspectives of the individual who compares. The results vary depending on the contexts in which he/she is positioned and in which he/she positions each of the four paradigms, namely object-oriented, component-based, agent-oriented and service-oriented software entities. For example, from the point of view of a low-level developer, an object will be easier to reuse than a service, whereas conversely, from a business perspective, a very high-level service will be more easily reusable.

Thus, our conceptual comparison framework attempts to take this reality into account by providing these users with all the information required to express their own analyses and qualitative comparison. These qualitative factors are based on a classification of the material provided by the paradigms, which we grouped by their qualitative criteria.

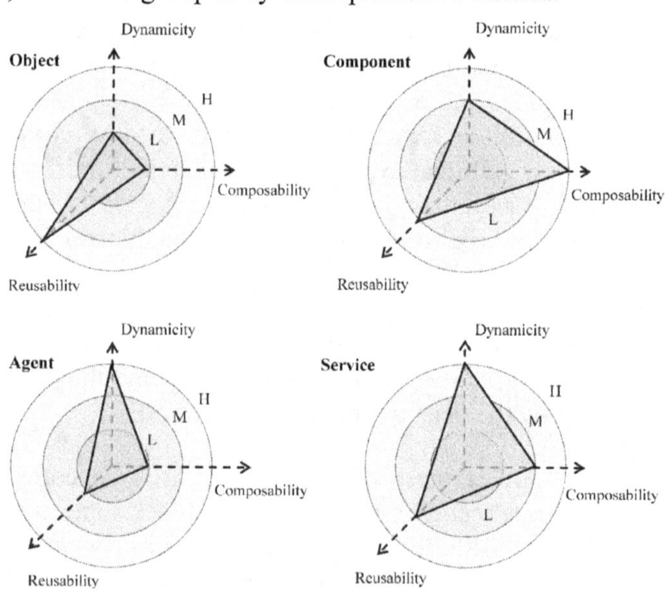

Figure 1.7. *Evolution of overall concerns between paradigms (L: low, M: medium, H: high)*

1.4.3.1. *Qualitative criteria for comparing development paradigms*

We have identified eight main qualitative criteria that are common to all software development paradigms. These criteria have a significant impact on the overall quality of the system development process produced as a result:

– *Explicit architecture:* capacity of a paradigm to define the clear architectural views of an application, i.e. to provide the means to identify and explain the functions associated with the products that make up the application as well as the processes between these products.

– *Communication abstraction:* capacity of a paradigm to abstract the communication between an application's functions and to learn and understand these communications from one tenant so that they can be easily handled.

– *Expressive power:* is the expressive potency of a paradigm in terms of capacity and optionality of creation. It is based on the number of concepts and processes provided to specify, develop, handle, implement and execute applications.

– *Loosely coupling:* is the potential reduction between product-process dependencies.

– *Evolution capacity:* this is the potential of a paradigm to evolve its products and processes. It is based on analysis and judgment value considered on the different processes that support these evolutions and their targets.

– *Owner's responsibility:* this corresponds to the assignment of responsibilities between suppliers and consumers. These responsibilities focus on the reused software entities in terms of development, Quality of Service, maintenance, deployment, execution and management. This distribution reflects the degree of freedom granted to consumers by the supplier.

– *Concurrency:* in resource-intensive applications that have a demanding need for computational power, concurrency is the most promising solution. Further, concurrency is also highlighted by the recent progress on the hardware side, such as the introduction of *multi-core* processors and *graphic cards* with parallel processing capabilities. The main challenges of the competition are to preserve consistency and to prevent against deadlock and dependent behaviour.

– *Distribution:* different classes of distributed applications exist according to where the data, the users or computation are distributed. As an example of these classes, we have the *client/server* applications (CS) as well as *peer-to-peer* (P2P) computing applications. The challenges of distribution are manifold. Among the major concerns of distribution we have future extensions and interoperability, which are often hampered by a heterogeneous infrastructure component. In addition, the different scenarios of most applications are, nowadays, increasingly dynamic with a flexible set of interacting components.

1.4.3.2. Comparison between paradigms

Table 1.2 presents the values assigned to the eight criteria used to assess the differences between the OOSE, the CBSE, the SOSE and the AOSE. The results are given following three levels of importance (high, medium, low), which are awarded for each criterion and express our analysis of the four paradigms. This comparison establishes a relative assessment between the paradigms (relative to each other).

		Paradigms			
	Quality criteria	Object	Component	Service	Agent
1	Explicit architecture	L	M	M	L
2	Communication abstraction	L	M	H	M
3	Expressive power	H	M	L	M
4	Loose coupling	L	M	M	H
5	Evolution capacity	L	H	M	M
6	Owner's responsibility	L	M	H	M
7	Concurrency	L	M	H	H
8	Distribution	L	M	H	H

Table 1.2. *Comparison of development paradigms (L: low, M: medium, H: high)*

Software architecture is the cornerstone criterion for the CBSE and the SOSE, unlike the OOSE and the AOSE, which have not taken this concept in their initial definition. To fill this gap, in UML 2.0, OMG introduced the concept of component and connector to describe a software architecture based on the object-oriented mechanisms.

In communication abstractions, the SOSE provides the best communication abstraction, based on the encapsulation provided by the services in addition to the isolation of communications in a collaborative scheme. In CBSE, communications are located within different connectors that share the overall behavior. The fine granularity of the object-oriented paradigms accentuates this disadvantage due to the explosive number of collaborations between objects, which is mainly due to the multiple method calls between objects.

Loose coupling is a key issue for the different paradigms. Object-oriented systems involve a set of strongly coupled classes, while the CBSE, the SOSE and the AOSE target a reduction of this coupling to make it looser.

Regarding the expressive power, the OOSE handles a large number of concepts such as inheritance, levels of abstraction, levels of description, granularity and reflection. These concepts are expressed through different programming languages such as Java and C++. The CBSE is largely inspired by the object-oriented paradigm, but it has not yet reached the same level of maturity. Finally, the SOSE has the lowest expressive power, because it combines the same shortcomings, plus inaccuracies on levels of abstraction, as the component-based paradigm.

The evolution capacity is directly related to the notion of explicit architecture. Software architecture can be depicted on a graph of nodes and edges. Evolution processes can be grouped according to their target: nodes, edges, or the graph. Typically, the OOSE does not have this notion of explicit architecture. The OOSE evolution process focuses only on nodes and edges. Instead, the CBSE and the SOSE handle the concept of explicit architecture and therefore offer an evolutionary process on three targets. However, the most important maturity of the CBSE and the explicit management of the levels of abstraction have enabled the community to go further and to propose evolution processes at the meta-architecture and meta-meta-architecture levels.

Owner's responsibility: the SOSE pushes the owner's responsibility to the maximum where the service provider is responsible for the development, Quality of Service, maintenance, deployment, execution and management. In contrast, the CBSE shares responsibilities at the deployment level where the customer becomes responsible for instantiating the component in its implementation, execution and management. In OOSE, the class is typically in white box implementation, where the customer is free to manipulate it at will but he/she has full responsibility of the class.

Concurrency and distribution: AOSE is built around the aspects of concurrency and distribution. These two criteria have appeared in a number of important research studies and have led to the emergence of DAI. With this new approach, the work is done by a group of agents, which act in the same environment and must sometimes resolve conflicts caused by this distribution of expertise.

The analytical method used can only establish a relative order between the paradigms compared, where one paradigm is more effective than the other on a particular criterion. However, in the current framework, the results obtained are limited to relative hierarchies. We believe that this comparison framework between the four paradigms is a step in their qualitative assessment process.

Figure 1.8 shows the use of the eight criteria to assess differences between OOSE, CBSE, SOSE and AOSE. The results are given in three levels of importance (low, medium, high), which are awarded for each criterion and express our analysis of the current status of the three paradigms. Also note that Figure 1.8 shows a graphic interpretation of data presented in Table 1.2.

1.4.3.3. *Perspective of qualitative analysis*

The conceptual framework that we propose is built to make way for the definition of the user's own assessment of qualitative perspectives. The chosen approach is that the user expresses their knowledge by specifying the perspective through which they want to study the four paradigms being compared. A particular perspective corresponds to the user's focus on a specific factor. It defines a formula for evaluating this factor by combining the results received from the previous comparison, i.e. following the steps of our eight quality criteria.

A qualitative perspective is the combination of:

– the chosen factor to compare the paradigms;

– the expression of the user's expertise in relation to this factor.

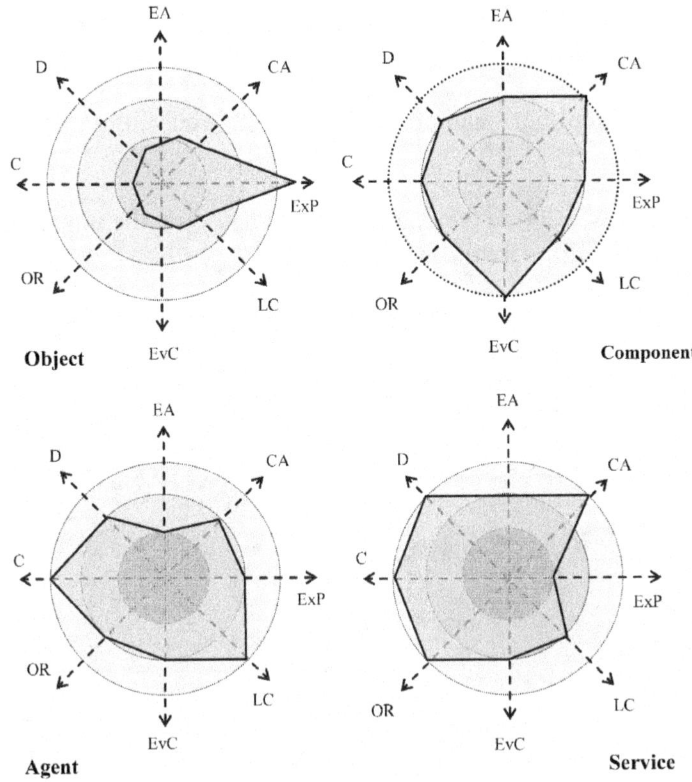

Figure 1.8. *Comparison of criteria with respect to the four paradigms (EA: explicit architecture; CA: communication abstraction; ExP: expressive power; LC: loose coupling; EvC: evolution capacity; OR: owner's responsibility; C: concurrency; D: distribution)*

Thus, we define a standard formula, which models this ability to customize:

Quality = Q (α_1, α_2, α_3, α_4, α_5, α_6, α_7, α_8)

The α_i coefficients express the importance of the eight quality criteria, which is given by the user with the target factor. The Q function defines how the coefficients are combined along with the measurements of properties.

A perspective is therefore a qualitative window based on the eight criteria and their results. As an illustration, we assess the four paradigms following our personal viewpoint on the three selected quality factors: reusability, composability and dynamicity that represent the core concerns of OOSE, CBSE, SOSE and AOSE paradigms.

1.4.3.3.1. Example of qualitative perspectives: reusability, composability and dynamicity

In Figure 1.9, we divide the quality criteria based on the impact they have on the different quality factors.

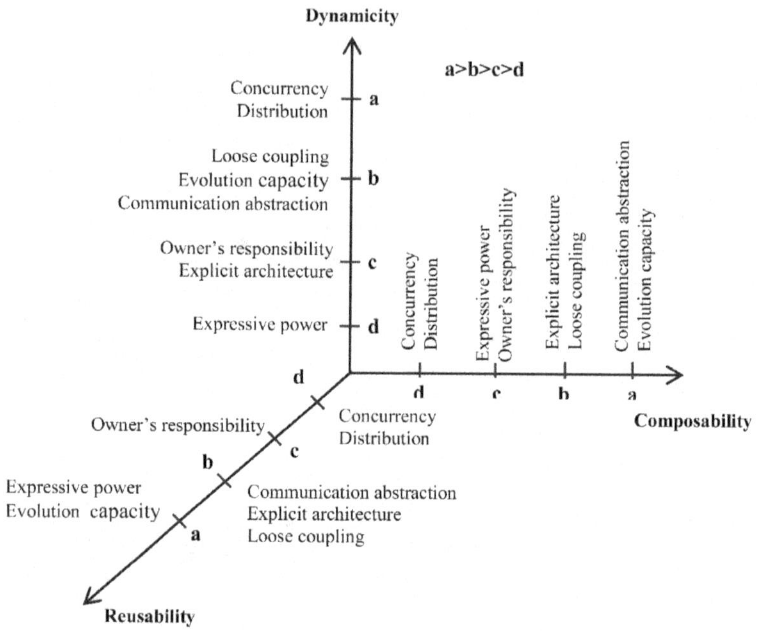

Figure 1.9. *Perspectives expressions of reusability, composability and dynamicity*

Reusability is mainly influenced by the expressive power and evolution capacity with an "a" coefficient, followed by the communication abstraction, the explicit architecture and low coupling with a "b" coefficient, the owner's responsibility with a "c" coefficient and finally the concurrency and the distribution with a "d" coefficient, where (a, b, c, d) represent coefficients of importance of each criterion with respect to a quality factor, with (a> b> c> d). From there, we define a set of formulas that combines this distribution and the results of the previous classification of the four paradigms. To calculate a numerical measure, we associate a weight to each level of Figure 1.8 of 1, 2 and 3 for low, medium and high levels, respectively. For example, for the reusability of the factor (r) of each paradigm, we obtain the assessment of the quality function Q_r:

$$Q_{r,\,object} = b\alpha_1 + b\alpha_2 + 3a\alpha_3 + b\alpha_4 + a\alpha_5 + c\alpha_6 + d\alpha_7 + d\alpha_8$$

$$Q_{r,\,component} = 2b\alpha_1 + 3b\alpha_2 + 2a\alpha_3 + 2b\alpha_4 + 3a\alpha_5 + 2c\alpha_6 + 2d\alpha_7 + 2d\alpha_8$$

$$Q_{r,\,agent} = b\alpha_1 + 2b\alpha_2 + 2a\alpha_3 + 3b\alpha_4 + 2a\alpha_5 + 2c\alpha_6 + 3d\alpha_7 + 2d\alpha_8$$

$$Q_{r,\,service} = 2b\alpha_1 + 3b\alpha_2 + a\alpha_3 + 2b\alpha_4 + 2a\alpha_5 + 3c\alpha_6 + 3d\alpha_7 + 3d\alpha_8$$

Composability is generally influenced by the communication abstraction and evolution capacity with an "a" coefficient, then, by the explicit architecture and loose coupling with a "b" coefficient, the owner's responsibility and expressive power with a "c" coefficient and finally the concurrency and distribution with a "d" coefficient where (a> b> c> d). From there, we define a set of formulas that combines this distribution and the results of the previous classification of the four paradigms. To calculate a numerical measure, we associate a weight to each level of Figure 1.8 of 1, 2 and 3 for low, medium and high levels, respectively. For example, for the composability factor (cp) of each paradigm, we obtain the assessment of the quality function Q_{cp}:

$$Q_{cp,\,object} = b\alpha_1 + a\alpha_2 + 3c\alpha_3 + b\alpha_4 + a\alpha_5 + c\alpha_6 + d\alpha_7 + d\alpha_8$$

$$Q_{cp,\,component} = 2b\alpha_1 + 3a\alpha_2 + 2c\alpha_3 + 2b\alpha_4 + 3a\alpha_5 + 2c\alpha_6 + 2d\alpha_7 + 2d\alpha_8$$

$$Q_{cp,\,agent} = b\alpha_1 + 2a\alpha_2 + 2c\alpha_3 + 3b\alpha_4 + 2a\alpha_5 + 2c\alpha_6 + 3d\alpha_7 + 2d\alpha_8$$

$$Q_{cp,\,service} = 2b\alpha_1 + 3a\alpha_2 + c\alpha_3 + 2b\alpha_4 + 2a\alpha_5 + 3c\alpha_6 + 3d\alpha_7 + 3d\alpha_8$$

Dynamicity is mainly influenced by concurrency and distribution with an "a" coefficient, then the communication abstraction and evolution capacity and loose coupling with a "b" coefficient, the explicit architecture and owner's responsibility with a "c" coefficient, and finally the expressive power with a "d" coefficient where (a> b> c> d). From there, we define a set of formulas that combines this distribution and the results of the previous classification of the four paradigms. To calculate a numerical measure, we associate a point at each level of Figure 1.8 with 1, 2 and 3 for low, medium and high levels, respectively. For example, for the dynamicity factor (d) of each paradigm, we obtain the assessment of the quality function Q_d:

$$Q_{d,\,object} = b\alpha_1 + a\alpha_2 + 3c\alpha_3 + a\alpha_4 + a\alpha_5 + b\alpha_6 + a\alpha_7 + a\alpha_8$$

$$Q_{d,\,component} = 2b\alpha_1 + 3a\alpha_2 + 2c\alpha_3 + 2a\alpha_4 + 3a\alpha_5 + 2b\alpha_6 + 2a\alpha_7 + 2a\alpha_8$$

$$Q_{d,\,agent} = b\alpha_1 + 2a\alpha_2 + 2c\alpha_3 + 3a\alpha_4 + 2a\alpha_5 + 2b\alpha_6 + 3a\alpha_7 + 2a\alpha_8$$

$$Q_{d,\,service} = 2b\alpha_1 + 3a\alpha_2 + c\alpha_3 + 2a\alpha_4 + 2a\alpha_5 + 3b\alpha_6 + 3a\alpha_7 + 3a\alpha_8$$

In summary, the conceptual framework provides a comparative picture between object-oriented, component-based, agent-oriented and service-oriented paradigms. These categories identify the important software development paradigm characteristics and provide a common applicable framework to assess the OOSE, the CBSE, the AOSE and the SOSE in a fair manner. This assessment is quantitative and qualitative in nature and offers an overall understanding of their similarities and differences. However, the quantitative assessment described is only relative, i.e. it establishes a relationship of superiority between the paradigms but measures neither their values nor their differences. The example of perspectives shown above resulting from this relative assessment therefore provides relative results.

Figure 1.10 summarizes the functioning of our conceptual framework for comparison. The quantitative aspect represents the processes and products of the corresponding paradigms that are the pillars of the eight properties. These properties characterize the quality criteria and serve as vocabulary for users to express their own perspectives on the qualities that concern them.

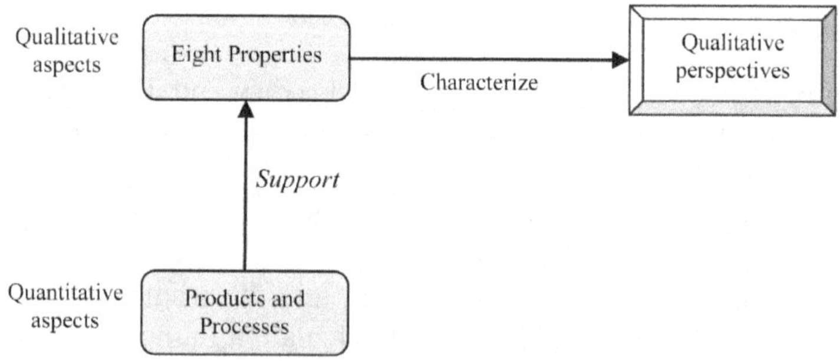

Figure 1.10. *Overall functioning of the conceptual framework*

1.5. Approaches for integrating development paradigms

Several alternative approaches for integrating paradigms were categorized by the entities they aim to combine (object, agent, component and service). These approaches are based either on conceptual proposals or combinations of technical and conceptual proposals (e.g. *middleware*, see Table 1.3).

The active object-oriented model is an example of an object-oriented and agent-oriented combination, which represents an object that conceptually runs on its own thread and provides an asynchronous execution of method invocations. It can thus be considered as a higher level concept for concurrency of the object-oriented systems [SUT 05]. Further, language extensions to support concurrency and distribution were proposed. Eiffel [MEY 93] is an influential proposal in this direction.

Also in the area of agent-oriented and component-based paradigms, combination proposals can be found. CompAA [ANI 08], SoSAA [DRA 09] and agent components [KRU 03] try to extend the agent-oriented paradigm with the concepts and mechanisms of the component-based paradigms. In CompAA, a component-based model is extended with adaptation points for services. These adaptation points allow for service selection at runtime according to the specifications of the functional and non-functional properties in the model. This flexibility is achieved by the addition of an agent for each component that is responsible for selecting the service at runtime. The SoSAA architecture consists of a base layer with a standard component system and a layer of agents that control the base layer to perform reconfigurations as an example of control. In Agent Components, the agents are slightly rendered as components connected using ports with predefined communication protocols.

Approaches that combine the agent-oriented paradigm with SOA are primarily motivated by the need for dynamic service composition where agents are used to dynamically search and select services during the execution. These approaches deal mainly with aspects linked to the semantic description and research of services, but do not aim at paradigm integration itself. As examples, we have the agent-oriented invocation of services using the web service integration gateway (WSIG)[4] component of the Java Agent

4 http://jade.tilab.com/.

DEvelopment framework (JADE) platform, or the code generation approach led by the PIM4agents model [ZIN 08] and workflow approaches such as WADE or JBees [EHR 05]. Agents are useful in achieving flexible and adaptable workflows using dynamic composition techniques based on negotiation and planning mechanisms.

There are also other approaches that combine the agent, component and object paradigms. ProActive [BAU 09] and AmbientTalk [VAN 07] are two recent approaches in this category, which provide strong conceptual foundations and a ready-to-use framework.

An approach in the context of software engineering has emerged under the name *service component architecture* (SCA) [MAR 09]. It was proposed by several major suppliers of the software industry, including IBM, Oracle and TIBCO. The SCA combines SOA with the component-based paradigms to provide SCA components that communicate via services.

Braubach and Pokahr [BRA 12] propose the concept of active components during the development of a distributed system project. The active component-based paradigm is proposed in the framework of an approach to reconcile ideas as well unifying the contributions of the object-oriented, component-based, service-oriented and agent-oriented concepts using a common conceptual perspective. The proposed paradigm is supported, on one the hand, by a programming model, which allows the development of systems with active components using XML and Java, and, on the other hand, by a *middleware* infrastructure, which directs a transparent distribution of the components and provides useful development tools. The active components are an upgrade of the SCA by adding the agent-oriented element in the SCA. The general idea is to transform passive components of the SCA to providers and service consumers, who act independently to better reflect real-world scenarios that are made up of different active stakeholders.

Aboud [ABO 12] proposes a metamodel combination approach called component agent service oriented model (CASOM), which allows the specification of applications composed of a set of interoperable agents, components and services in a coherent scheme.

Approaches and languages	Combined paradigms			
	Object	Component	Agent	Service
Programming languages, Java, C#, etc.	x			
Application server (JBOSS, Glassfish) Component specification by ADL		x		
Web service and business process specifications				x
FIPA agent specifications, agent-oriented platforms (JADE, Cougaar, etc.)			x	
Eiffel, active objects	x		x	
WSIG, WADE, PIM4Agents, JBees, etc.			x	x
Fractal, Java EE, OSGI, .Net	x	x		
Service component architecture (Passive SCA)		x		x
CompAA, SoSAA, agent components		x	x	
Active components [BRA 12], CASOM [ABO 12]		x	x	x

Table 1.3. *Approaches for integrating paradigms*

1.6. Summary and discussion

We recall that our purpose throughout this chapter has been to provide a cross-sectional view of the four paradigms, namely OOSE, CBSE, SOSE and AOSE.

The CBSE and the SOSE have two different points of view on the relationship between the customer and the supplier. The SOSE comes from certain functional requirements of specific application domains that have specific needs in terms of agility and adaptability, while the CBSE is defined for a larger purpose. The service- and component-oriented paradigms have a very high granularity; however, a service-oriented paradigm is generally of higher granularity than a component-based paradigm.

An *ad hoc* distinction between the agent-oriented and object-oriented paradigms is that:

– the agent-oriented paradigms are more independent than the object-oriented paradigms;

– the agent-oriented paradigms have flexible, reactive, proactive and social behavior;

– the agent-oriented paradigms have at least one control *thread* but may have more.

Agent-oriented paradigms can be considered as active objects that encapsulate both their state and behavior, and they can communicate by exchanging messages. The agent-oriented paradigms represent a mechanism of natural abstraction to decompose and organize complex systems, just as the object-oriented did before them. An agent-oriented paradigm is a system of rational decision-making: we need an agent to be able to have reactive and proactive behavior and to be able to perform the interweaving of these two types of behavior, if necessary.

OOPs are generally passive in nature: they need to receive a message before they become active. Although object-oriented paradigms encapsulate their state and behavior, they do not encapsulate behavioral activation. Thus, any object-oriented paradigm can call any other object's public method. Once the method is called, the corresponding actions are performed.

While this approach is sufficient for small applications in cooperative and well-controlled environments, it is not suitable for large, concurrent or competitive environments because the entire burden of invocation behavior will be charged to the customer. It would be better if the invocation action becomes a process of mutual consent.

According to these relevant observations, under the control of a single organization, software systems must move from one environment toward an open environment in which the system contains organisms that compete with each other.

The object-oriented paradigm fails to provide an adequate set of concepts and mechanisms for modeling complex systems. Individual objects have a fine-grained behavioral granularity and the invocation method is a mechanism too primitive to describe the different types of interactions that may occur.

An approach that is closely linked to that of the object-oriented approach is based on software components. The most important factor behind the component systems is the ultimate goal of software reuse. Essentially, a component-based model enables developers to create and combine software as units of deployment.

According to the description introduced for the component-based approach, we can say that it is a *top-down* approach to the object-oriented approach; therefore, it inherits all the properties of the object-oriented paradigms. The similarities between the object-oriented and agent-oriented paradigms are also present between the agent-oriented and component-based paradigms.

However, the components are not autonomous in the sense of the definition of independent agents; in addition, just as the object-oriented paradigms, the component-based paradigms do not have direct notions of responsiveness, pro-activity and social behavior. The service-oriented approach is considered an evolution of the component-based approach enriched by the principles of dynamicity, discovery and composition. To sketch the basic ideas of development, we propose a characterization tree shown in Figure 1.11.

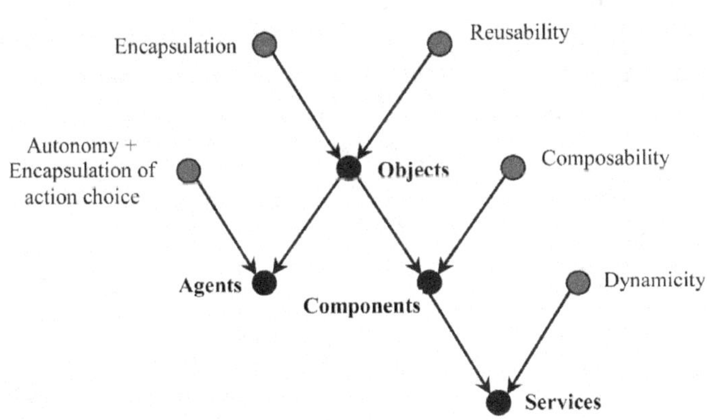

Figure 1.11. *Development of paradigms*

1.7. Conclusion

In this chapter, we have shown a conceptual comparison framework between the four software development paradigms (object-oriented, component-based, agent-oriented and service-oriented). The main objective of this chapter is to provide a clear specification of the conceptual differences between these paradigms and their contribution to the description of software architectures.

Our analysis is carried out through a *top-down* approach, which focuses first on the conceptual aspects of the different paradigms before developing the qualities that result from them. Decisions and choices on this comparison framework have a common goal to make it as generic as possible and independent of any description of software architecture paradigms. Therefore, we endeavor to increase its potential for reusability and ability to be applied to other areas of software engineering.

The proposed framework is based on two dimensions: quantitative and qualitative, where product and process represent the quantitative dimension. This dimension introduces the concepts defined by each paradigm required in the description of a software architecture. Meanwhile, the qualitative dimension defines eight properties, which group the elements that influence the quality of software architecture.

Finally, the qualitative dimension allows users to express their own quality factors using the eight selected quality criteria. This capacity to customize is provided by the notion of qualitative perspective that reflects the expertise of the user. In fact, a perspective allows him/her to communicate their understanding of a target quality through the way that they exploit and combine these properties.

1.8. Bibliography

[ABO 12] ABOUD N.A., Services-oriented integration of component and organizational multi-agents models, Doctoral Thesis, University of Pau and Pays de l'Adour, 2012.

[ALO 03] ALONSO G., CASATI F., KUNO H., *et al.*, *Web Services: Concepts, Architectures and Applications*, Springer, Berlin, 2003.

[AMI 09] AMIRAT A., OUSSALAH M., "First-class connectors to support systematic construction of hierarchical software architecture", *Journal of Object Technology*, vol. 8, no. 7, pp. 107–130, 2009.

[AND 08] ANDRÉ P., ARDOURE G., ATTIOGBÉ C., "Composing components with shared services in the KmeliaModel", *Software Composition*, vol. 4954, pp. 125–140, 2008.

[ANI 08] ANIORTÉ P., LACOUTURE J., "CompAA: a self-adaptable component model for open systems", *15th IEEE International Conference and Workshop on Engineering of Computer Based Systems (ECBS '08)*, pp. 19–25, 2008.

[BAR 06] BARBIER F., "An enhanced composition model for conversational enterprise JavaBeans", *Proceedings of the 9th International Conference on Component-Based Software Engineering (CBSE '06)*, pp. 344–351, 2006.

[BAU 09] BAUDE F., CAROMEL D., DALMASSO C., *et al.*, "Gcm: a grid extension to fractal for autonomous distributed components", *Annals of Telecommunications*, vol. 64, pp. 5–24, 2009.

[BEI 07] BEISIEGEL M., BOOZ D., EDWARDS M., *et al.*, "Software components: coarse-grained versus fine-grained", IBM Developer Works, 2007.

[BIA 07] BIANCO P., KOTERMANSKI R., MERSON P., Evaluating a services-oriented architecture, Technical Report, Software Engineering Institute, Carnegie Mellon University, 2007. Available at http://www.sei.cmu.edu/reports/07tr015.pdf

[BOU 92] BOURON M.T., Structures de communication et d'organisation pour la coopération dans un univers multi-agents, Doctoral Thesis, University of Paris 6, 1992.

[BRA 12] BRAUBACH L., POKAHR A., "Developing distributed systems with active components and Jadex", *Scalable Computing: Practice and Experience*, vol. 13, no. 2, pp. 100–119, 2012.

[BRE 07] BREIVOLD H.P., LARSSON M., "Component-based and services-oriented software engineering: key concepts and principles", *Proceedings of the 33rd EUROMICRO Conference on Software Engineering and Advanced Applications*, pp. 13–20, 2007.

[BRU 06] BRUNETON E., COUPAYE T., LECLERCQ M., *et al.*, "The FRACTAL component model and its support in Java", *Software Practice and Experience*, vol. 36, nos. 11–12, pp. 1257–1284, 2006.

[CAM 83] CAMMARATA S., MCARTHUR D., STEEB R., "Strategies of cooperation in distributed problem-solving", *International Joint Conference on Artificial Intelligence (IJCAI)*, pp. 767–770, 1983.

[CAV 09] CAVALLARO L., NITTO E.D., PRADELLA M., "An automatic approach to enable replacement of conversational services", *The 7th International Joint Conference on Service Oriented Computing*, Sweden, pp. 159–174, 2009.

[COX 91] COX B.J., NOVOBILSKI A.J., *Object-Oriented Programming: An Evolutionary Approach*, 2nd ed., Addison Wesley, Tahiti, Boston, 1991.

[CRN 06] CRNKOVIĆ I., CHAUDRON M., LARSSON S., "Component-based development process and component lifecycle", *International Conference on Software Engineering Advances*, Tahiti, p. 44, 2006.

[CRN 11] CRNKOVIĆ I., CHAUDRON M., SENTILLES S., *et al.*, "A classification framework for software component models", *Journal: IEEE Transactions on Software Engineering*, vol. 37, no. 5, pp. 593–615, 2011.

[DRA 09] DRAGONE M., LILLIS D., COLLIER R., *et al.*, "SoSAA: a framework for integrating components & agents", *Symposium on Applied Computing*, ACM Press, 2009.

[DUR 89] DURFEE E.H., *Coordination of Distributed Problem Solvers*, Kluwer Academic, Boston, 1989.

[DUS 05] DUSTDAR S., SCHREINER W., "A survey on web services composition", *International Journal of Web and Grid Services*, vol. 1, no. 1, pp. 1–30, 2005.

[EHR 05] EHRLER L., FLEURKE M., PURVIS M., *et al.*, "Agent-based workflow management systems", *Journal of Information Systems and e-Business Management*, vol. 4, pp. 5–23, 2005.

[ERI 08] ERICKSON J., SIAU K., "Web services, services-oriented computing, and services-oriented architecture: separating hype from reality", *Journal of Database Management (JDM)*, vol. 19, no. 3, pp. 42–54, 2008.

[FER 03] FERBER J., GUTKNECHT O., MICHEL F., "From agents to organizations: an organizational view of multi-agents systems", *Agent-Oriented Software Engineering (AOSE)*, vol. 2935, pp. 214–230, 2003.

[GAR 97] GARLAN D., MONROE R.T., WILE D., "Acme: an architecture description interchange language", *Proceedings of the 1997 Conference of the Centre for Advanced Studies on Collaborative Research (CASCON '97)*, Toronto, Canada, pp. 7–21, 1997.

[GAS 92] GASSER L., BRIOT J.P., "Object-based concurrent programming and distributed artificial intelligence", in AVOURIS N., GASSER L. (eds), *Distributed Artificial Intelligence: Theory and Praxis*, Kluwer, Norwell, pp. 81–107, 1992.

[GEE 08] GEEBELEN K., MICHIELS S., JOOSEN W., "Dynamic reconfiguration using template based web service composition", *Proceedings of the 3rd Workshop on Middleware for Service Oriented Computing (MW4SOC '08)*, pp. 49–54, 2008.

[GOL 83] GOLDBERG A., ROBSON D., *Smalltalk-80: The Language and its Implementation*, Addison-Wesley, Boston, 1983.

[HEI 01] HEINEMAN G.T., COUNCILL W.T., *Component-Based Software Engineering: Putting the Pieces Together*, Addision Wesley Professional, Boston, 2001.

[HEW 73] HEWITT C., BISHOP P., STEIGER R., "A universal modular actor formalism for artificial intelligence", *3rd International Joint Conference on Artificial Intelligence (IJCAI '73)*, 1973.

[HEW 77] HEWITT C., "Viewing control structures as patterns of passing messages", *Journal of Artificial Intelligence*, vol. 8, no.3, pp. 323–364, 1977.

[HEW 11] HEWITT C., "Actor model of computation: scalable robust information systems", *Proceedings of Inconsistency Robustness*, Stanford, 2011.

[HOC 11] HOCK-KOON A., Contribution à la compréhension et à la modélisation de la composition et du couplage faible de services dans les architectures orientées services, Doctoral Thesis, University of Nantes, 2011.

[HYA 96] HYACINTH S.N., "Software agents: an overview", *Knowledge Engineering Review*, vol. 11, no. 3, pp. 205–244, 1996.

[JAC 05] JACOB D., "Enterprise software as service", *Queue - Enterprise Distributed Computing*, vol. 3, no. 6, pp. 36–42, 2005.

[JEN 01] JENNINGS N.R., "An agent-based approach for building complex software systems", *Communications of the ACM*, vol. 44, no. 4, pp. 35–41, 2001.

[KAY 93] KAY A.C., "The early history of Smalltalk", *ACM SIGPLAN Notices*, vol. 28, no. 3, pp. 69–95, 1993.

[KIT 96] KITCHENHAM B., PFLEEGER S.L., Software quality: the elusive target, *IEEE Software*, special issues section, vol. 13, no. 1, pp. 12–21, 1996.

[KRU 03] KRUTISCH R., MEIER P., WIRSING M., "The agent component approach, combining agents, and components", *1st German Conference on Multi-Agent System Technologies (MATES)*, Springer, Berlin, pp. 1–12, 2003.

[MAR 09] MARINO J., ROWLEY M., *Understanding SCA (Service Component Architecture)*, 1st ed., Addison Wesley Professional, Boston, 2009.

[MCI 68] MCILROY D., "Mass-produced software components", in BUXTON J.M., NAUR P., RANDELL B. (eds), *Software Engineering Concepts and Techniques*, NATO Science Committee, pp. 88–98, 1968.

[MEY 93] MEYER B., "Systematic concurrent object-oriented programming", *Communication ACM*, vol. 36, pp. 56–80, 1993.

[MIC 13] MICROSOFT COM (COMPONENT OBJECT MODEL) TECHNOLOGY, 2013. Available at www.micro-soft.com/com/default.mspx.

[MOH 08] MOHAMED A., ZULKERNINE M., "At what level of granularity should we be componentizing for software reliability?", *11th IEEE High Assurance Systems Engineering Symposium (HASE '08)*, pp. 273–282, 2008.

[NIT 08] NITTO E.D., GHEZZI C., METZGER A., *et al.*, "A journey to highly dynamic, self-adaptive service-based applications", *Automated Software Engineering*, vol. 15, nos. 3–4, pp. 313–341, 2008.

[OAS 08] OAS, "Reference architecture for service oriented architecture, version 1.0", 2008. Available at http://docs.oasis-open.org/wsbpel/2.0/OS/wsbpel-v2.0-OS.html.

[OAS 09] OAS, "Service component architecture assembly model specification, version 1.1, 2009". Available at http://docs.oasis-opensa.org.

[OMG 12] OMG, "Common object request broker architecture (CORBA)", 2012. Available at www.omg.org/spec/CORBA/.

[OUS 99] OUSSALAH M., *et al.*, *Génie Objet*, Hermes, Paris, 1999.

[OUS 05] OUSSALAH M., *et al.*, *Ingénierie des Composants: Concepts, Techniques et Outils*, Vuibert, Paris, 2005.

[PAP 07] PAPAZOGLOU M.P., HEUVEL W.J., "Service-oriented architectures: approaches, technologies and research issues", *The VLDB Journal*, vol. 16, pp. 389–415, 2007.

[PES 00] PESCHANSKI F., MEURISSE T., BRIOT J.P., "Les composants logiciels: évolution technologique ou nouveau paradigme?", *Proceedings of the Conference on Objects, Components and Models (OCM '00)*, Nantes, France, pp. 53–65, 2000.

[SMI 81] SMITH R.G., DAVIS R., "Frameworks for cooperation in distributed problem-solving", *IEEE Transactions on Systems, Man and Cybernetics*, vol. 11, no. 1, pp. 61–70, 1981.

[SOM 04] SOMMERVILLE I., *Software Engineering*, 7th ed., Addison Wesley, Harlow, 2004.

[SUT 05] SUTTER H., LARUS J., "Software and the concurrency revolution", *ACM Queue*, vol. 3, no. 7, pp. 54–62, 2005.

[STO 05] STOJANOVIC Z., DAHANAYAKE A., *Services-Oriented Software System Engineering: Challenges and Practices*, IGI Publishing, Hershey, PA, 2005.

[SZY 02] SZYPERSKI C., *Component Software: Beyond Object-Oriented Programming*, Addison-Wesley Professional, Harlow, 2002.

[TAY 09] TAYLOR R.N., MEDVIDOVIC N., DASHOFY E., *Software Architecture: Foundations, Theory, and Practice*, Wiley-Blackwell, Chichester, 2009.

[THE 08] THE SECSE TEAM, "Service centric system engineering", EU Integrated Project, 2008. Available at www.secse-project.eu/.

[VAN 07] VAN CUTSEM T., MOSTINCKX S., BOIX E.G., *et al.*, "Ambienttalk: object-oriented event-driven programming in mobile ad hoc networks", *Proceedings of the XXVI International Conference of the Chilean Society of Computer Science*, Chile, pp. 3–12, 2007.

[VIN 97] VINOSKI S., "CORBA: integrating diverse applications within distributed heterogeneous environments", *IEEE Communications Magazine*, vol. 14, pp. 46–55, 1997.

[WEI 91] WEISER M., *The Computer for the 21st Century*, Scientific American, New York, 1991.

[WOO 09] WOOLDRIDGE M., *An Introduction to Multiagent Systems*, 2nd ed., John Wiley & Sons, New York, 2009.

[ZEN 03] ZENG L., BENATALLAH B., DUMAS M., *et al.*, "Quality driven web services composition", *Proceedings of the 12th International Conference on World Wide Web (WWW '03)*, pp. 411–421, 2003.

[ZIN 08] ZINNIKUS I., HAHN C., FISCHER K., "A model-driven, agent-based approach for the integration of services into a collaborative business process", *Proceeding of AAMAS (IFAAMAS '08)*, pp. 241–248, 2008.

Chapter 2

Reference Architectures

2.1. Introduction

Reference architectures (or reference software architectures) refer to a special type of software architecture that captures the essence of the architectures of a set of systems in a given domain. The purpose of a reference architecture is mainly to provide guidance for the development, standardization and evolution of system architectures. Designed for various domains and purposes, they have increasingly impacted important aspects of software system development, such as productivity and quality of the systems. Thus, it is observed that there is real evidence of the importance of reference architectures for the software development and they could therefore be considered as one of the most promising disciplines in the near future.

From this perspective, the establishment of reference architectures is interesting when a set of knowledge and experience of how to design a set of similar software systems, sometimes gained through past projects, is available and a means to communicate or reuse this knowledge and experience is necessary. Thus, individuals, research groups, companies, consortiums and any interested parties can propose reference architectures. To be effective, a reference architecture should also be continually updated with new experience and knowledge.

Chapter written by Elisa Yumi NAKAGAWA, Flavio OQUENDO and José Carlos MALDONADO.

In this chapter, we first discuss definitions given to reference architectures; besides this, we clarify the differences between the reference architecture and reference model, as well as between the reference architecture and product line architecture (i.e. the architecture of software product line). Following this, we present a model that describes the set of elements that could be found in reference architectures. Aiming at systematizing reference architecture engineering, we present a process for that. Various perspectives of applying these architectures are also discussed. This chapter ends with examples of these architectures and future perspectives for them.

2.2. Definition of reference architecture

A study of the main works in the software architecture literature allows us to identify some important definitions for reference architecture. One of the first definitions was stated by Kruchten [KRU 00]: "A reference architecture is, in essence, a predefined architectural pattern, or set of patterns, possibly partially or completely instantiated, designed and proven for use in particular business and technical contexts, together with supporting artifacts to enable their use. Often, these artifacts are harvested from previous projects". From the perspective of a specific domain, Rosen *et al.* [ROS 07] stated that "A reference architecture is a working example of a critical aspect of your enterprise architecture, such as [...] how to work with your organization's message bus or [...] how to work with your business rules engine". From the same perspective, Angelov *et al.* [ANG 09] stated that "A reference architecture is a generic architecture for a class of information systems that is used as a foundation for the design of concrete architectures from this class". To complete these definitions, Reed thinks that "A reference architecture consists of information accessible to all project team members that provides a consistent set of architectural best practices". Even though syntactically different, these definitions present the same essence: the reuse of knowledge about software development in a given domain, in particular, with regard to architectural design. Other definitions are also found, but the ones presented above are sufficient for our purpose. Based on these works, we believe that:

"A reference architecture refers to an architecture that encompasses the knowledge about how to design concrete architectures of systems of a given application domain; therefore, it must address the business rules, architectural styles (sometimes also defined as architectural patterns that can also address quality attributes in the reference architecture), best practices of software development (for instance, architectural decisions, domain constraints, legislation and standards), and the software elements that support development of systems for that domain. All of this must be supported by a unified, unambiguous and widely understood domain terminology".

2.2.1. *Reference architecture versus reference model*

Sometimes the terms "reference architecture" and "reference model" have been used interchangeably. However, it is interesting to clarify the difference between them as it is sometimes desirable to build a reference model while other times intended to have a reference architecture. A reference model can be considered an abstract framework that presents a set of unifying concepts, axioms and relationships within a particular problem domain, independent of specific standards, technologies, implementations or other concrete details [BAS 03]. Conceptual models that present concepts and their relationships, as well as ontologies of a given domain, can be considered as a reference model. According to Bass *et al.* [BAS 03], a reference model mapped onto software elements (that cooperatively implement the functionality defined in the reference model) and the data flows between them can be considered a reference architecture.

Figure 2.1 presents the relationship between a reference model and a reference architecture. Based on one or more existing reference models together with other elements, such as domain expert knowledge, architectural styles and software elements, a reference architecture can be created. Using this architecture as the basis, concrete architectures can be created. However, it is worth mentioning that it is not necessary to previously have these models in order to create these architectures. As presented in section 2.4, we have several other sources of information that can be used to create reference architectures.

2.2.2. *Reference architecture versus product line architecture*

Various synonyms are used for the term "product line architecture", such as software product line architecture, domain-specific software architecture, domain architecture and even reference architecture in [POH 05, DEB 98]. However, "product line architecture" seems to be the term that fits best into the Software Product Line (SPL) context. In parallel, there are also different definitions of this term. DeBaud *et al.* [DEB 98] say that it is an architecture with a required degree of flexibility and is shared by all the members of a product line, ensuring their conceptual integrity. According to Pohl *et al.* [POH 05], "product line architecture is a core architecture that captures the high-level design for the products of the SPL, including the variation points and variants documented in the variability model". From the same perspective, Gomaa [GOM 04] stated that "product line architecture is an architecture for a family of products, which describes the kernel, optional and variable components in the SPL, and their interconnections". In a more complete definition, *Software Engineering Institute* (SEI) [SEI 13] declared that "The product line architecture is an early and prominent member in the collection of core assets. [...] The architecture defines the set of software components [...] that populates the core asset base. The product line architecture – together with the production plan – provides the prescription [...] for how products are built from core assets". It is worth emphasizing that, in general, other definitions are derivations of those presented herein. Moreover, it is important to observe that the common essence in these definitions is "variability on a common core". In this scenario, we can define product line architecture as a special type of software architecture used to build a product line; it explicitly describes commonality and variability and is the basis for the architectures of all product line members.

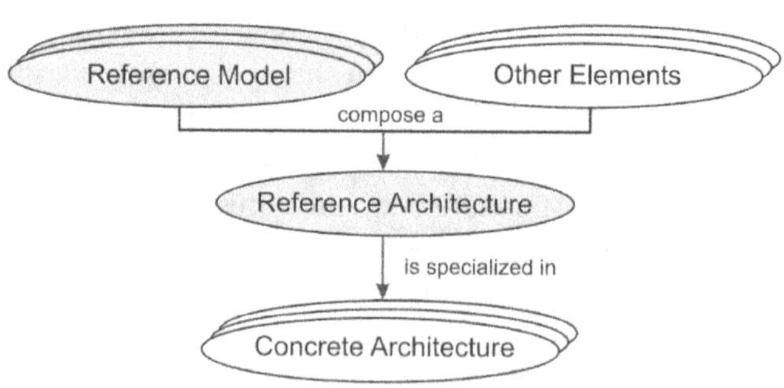

Figure 2.1. *Relationship between reference model and reference architecture*

While reference architectures deal with the range of knowledge of an application domain, providing standardized solutions for a broader domain, product line architectures are more specialized, focusing sometimes on a specific subset of the software systems of a domain and providing standardized solutions for a smaller family of systems. Another essential difference is that product line architectures are concerned with the variabilities among products. Furthermore, reference architectures are generally on a higher level of abstraction compared to product line architectures.

As illustrated in Figure 2.2, we have proposed to consider reference architectures as a basis for product line architectures. A reference architecture can be specialized to different product line architectures, each for a specific SPL. Besides product line architectures, reference architectures can be used as the basis of other elements of the core assets of SPL [NAK 11a]. For example, the variability model, products feature list, products description and product line components can be created using the knowledge contained in the reference architectures [NAK 11a].

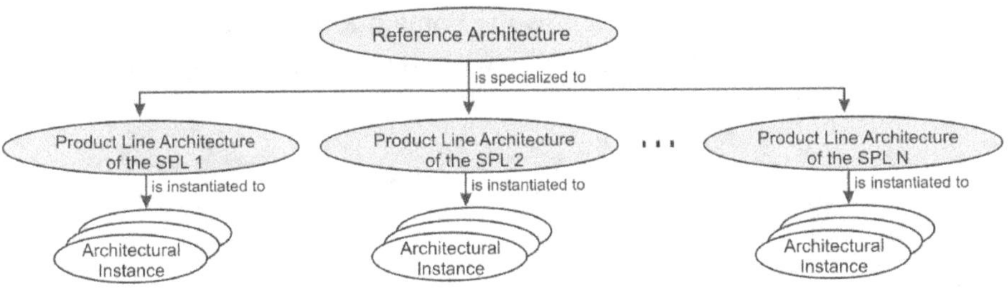

Figure 2.2. *Relationship between reference architecture and product line architecture*

2.3. A model for reference architectures

To facilitate the interaction of reference architectures, a better understanding of their elements or components is essential to adequately build, use and even evolve such architectures. RAModel is a reference model for reference architectures, providing information on the elements and their relationships that could be contained in the reference architectures, independently of the application domains or purpose of such architectures. As illustrated in Figure 2.3, RAModel is composed of four groups of elements:

– Domain: it contains elements related to self-contained, specific information of the space of human action in the real world, such as domain legislations, standards and certification processes, which impact systems and related reference architectures of that domain.

– Application: it contains elements that provide a good understanding about the reference architecture, its capabilities and limitations. It also contains elements related to the business rules (or functionalities) that can be present in software systems built from the reference architecture.

– Infrastructure: it refers to elements that can be used to build the software systems based on the reference architecture. These elements are responsible for enabling these systems to automate, for instance, processes, activities and tasks of a given domain.

– Crosscutting elements: it aggregates a set of elements that are usually spread across and/or tangled with elements of the other three groups (domain, application and infrastructure). We have observed that communication (which we have identified as internal and external) in the software systems built from the reference architecture, as well as the domain terminology and decisions, are present in a spread and tangled way when describing other groups and are, therefore, crosscutting elements.

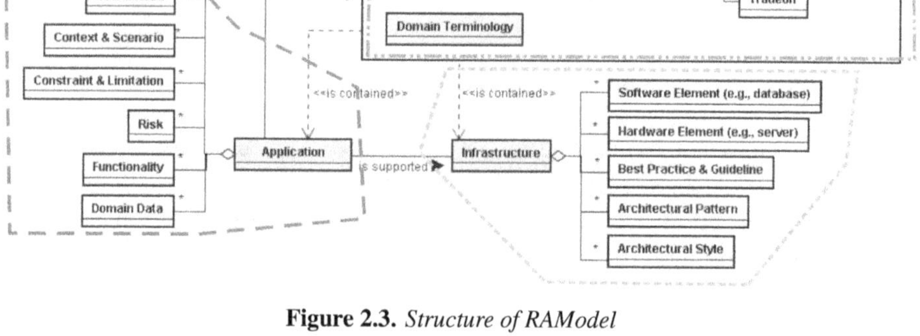

Figure 2.3. *Structure of RAModel*

This structure together with the common elements, as presented in Table 2.1, composes the reference model for reference architectures.

Considering that the RAModel contains possibly all the important elements in reference architectures, four main perspectives exist to use this:

Elements of the group domain	
Element	itemize
Legislations, standards and regulations	Laws, standards and regulations existing in the domain that should be present in systems resulted from the reference architecture.
Quality attributes	Quality attributes, for instance, maintainability, portability and scalability, that are desired in systems resulted from the reference architecture.
System compliance	Means to verify whether systems developed from the reference architecture follow existing legislations, standards and regulations.
Elements of the group Application	
Element	Description
Constraints	Constraints presented by the reference architecture and/or constraints in specific part of a reference architecture.
Domain data	Common data found in systems of the domain. These data are presented in a higher level of abstraction, considering the higher level of abstraction of the reference architecture.
Functional requirements	Set of functional requirements that are common in systems developed using this architecture.
Goal and needs	Intention of the reference architecture and needs are covered by the reference architecture.
Limitations	Limitations presented by the reference architecture and/or limitations in specific part of a reference architecture.
Risks	Risks in using the reference architecture and/or risks in using some part of such architecture.
Scope	Scope that is covered by the reference architecture, i.e. the set of systems developed on the basis of the reference architecture.
Elements of the group Infrastructure	
Element	itemize
Best practices and guidelines	Well-experimented practices to develop systems of the domain, These practices are accompanied by guidelines which describe how to apply these practices.
General structure	General structure of the reference architecture, represented sometimes by using existing architectural styles.
Hardware elements	Elements of hardware, such as server and devices, which host systems resulted from the reference architecture.
Software elements	Elements of software present in the reference architecture, e.g. subsystems and classes, which are used to develop software systems.
Elements of the group Crosscutting Elements	
Element	Description
Decisions	Decisions, including description of the decision, options (alternatives), rationale and trade-offs, must be reported during the development of the reference architecture.
Domain terminology	The set of terms of the domain that is widely accepted by the community related to that domain and is, therefore, used in the description of the reference architecture.
External communication	Means through which exchange of information between the systems resulted from the reference architecture and the external environment occurs.
Internal communication	Means through which exchange of information among internal parts of the systems resulted from the reference architecture occurs.

Table 2.1. *Groups of elements*

– Analysis of reference architectures: as stated before, a considerable number of reference architectures have been proposed in recent years; however, they have sometimes been developed without concern or conscience about what they should contain. These architectures can then be analyzed and confronted with RAModel, aiming at identifying the elements that are missing and, if significant, then these elements could be inserted into these architectures. For instance, the RAModel establishes that "decision" is an element that could be present in reference architectures, since decisions can make easier to understand why things are as they are. However, reference architectures usually do not present such information; thus, information about decisions should be inserted into these architectures.

– Comparative analysis of reference architectures: the RAModel can be used to conduct comparative analysis of reference architectures, when it is necessary to select reference architectures among a set of them, intending to use them in a new software system project. The RAModel can be used as a guideline to observe which elements each reference architecture contains, i.e. it can be used to better understand each architecture, supporting more adequately the decision about which architecture or which part of the architecture should be adopted. This comparative analysis is quite relevant in domains that present several reference architectures, such as ambient assisted living (AAL) [ANT 11, UNI 13, WIC 10].

– Support to the design of SPL (Software Product Line): there is a close relationship between the reference architecture and the SPL, in particular, the product line architectures (PLA), which is the core asset of an SPL. Thus, we have explored the use of reference architectures as a basis to build the artifacts of SPL.

– Basis for the establishment of reference architectures: the RAModel can also be used to gain information about which elements could be inserted into new reference architectures. By using the RAModel, designers of reference architectures have a guide to follow and ideally, as a result, time and effort to establish such architectures could be reduced. Moreover, since the RAModel provides a comprehensive set of elements, the intention is to achieve more complete architectures. Thus, these architectures will have more chances to effectively contribute to the development of systems. Therefore, this model can be used during the reference architecture engineering, discussed in section 2.4.

It is important to say that depending on the intention of a reference architecture, the presence of certain elements proposed by the RAModel is more important or interesting than others.

2.4. Reference architecture engineering

In general, reference architectures have been built using an *ad hoc* approach, i.e. without following a systematic process. However, systematizing their building is certainly interesting and aims at achieving more effective reference architectures, i.e. architectures that could more completely attempt their purpose. In spite of the relevance of this systematization, there is a lack of processes and methods. However, recommendations can be found. Muller [MUL 08] has proposed a set of recommendations in order to create and maintain reference architectures; briefly, reference architectures must be understandable, up-to-date and maintainable. Trienekens *et al.* [TRI 11] proposed a set of quality attributes for reference architectures – completeness, acceptability, buildability, applicability and understandability – that could be considered during the development of reference architectures.

In this context, ProSA-RA is a process that systematizes the design, representation and evaluation of reference architectures. Notably, it is a result of our experience in the establishment of architectures for several domains, such as software engineering [NAK 11b, NAK 07, OLI 11a] and embedded systems [BOR 11, DUA 12, FEI 13]. To adequately apply this process, first, it is important to establish the scope of the reference architecture, i.e. the target domain of the reference architecture. This scope can be defined by considering the set of systems that are intended to be produced on the basis of the reference architecture.

The outline structure of ProSA-RA is illustrated in Figure 2.4. Briefly, four basic steps need to be performed in order to build a reference architecture by using ProSA-RA. First, information sources are selected and investigated (step RA-1). Second, the architectural requirements of the reference architecture are identified (step RA-2), describing the common functionalities and configurations present in the systems of the target domain. Third, the architectural description of the reference architecture is established (step RA-3) and, finally, an evaluation of the resulting architecture is conducted (step RA-4). Analysts, software architects and domain experts should be involved in performing all the steps of ProSA-RA. In the following sections, each step is discussed in detail.

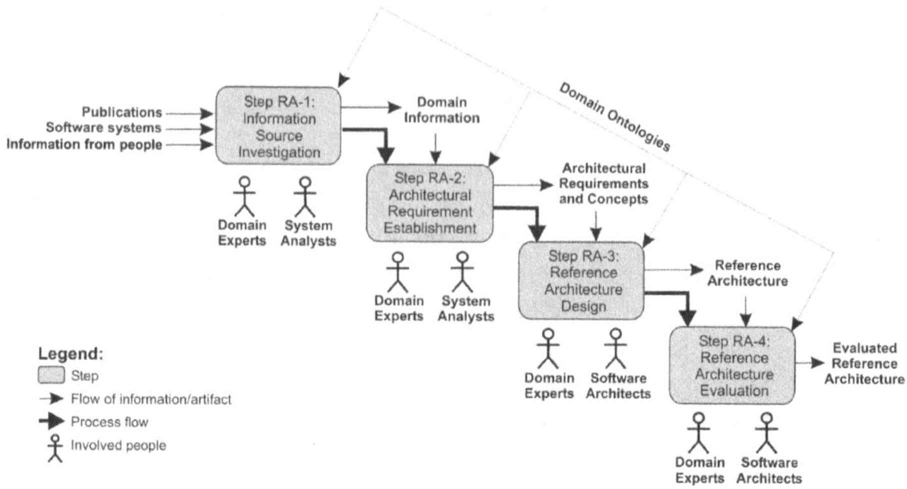

Figure 2.4. *Overall structure of ProSA-RA*

2.4.1. *Information source investigation*

In this step, the main information sources are selected. These sources must provide information about the processes, activities and tasks that could be supported by software systems of the target application domain. Since reference architectures are the basis of a set of software systems of a given domain, these information sources must involve a more comprehensive knowledge about the domain, if compared with information sources when developing the architecture of a specific software system. From this perspective, as the most relevant information sources, ProSA-RA highlights the following:

– People: customers, users, researchers and system developers of the application domain are considered as relevant information sources. To get information from these people, techniques for requirements elicitation, such as interviews and questionnaires, can be used. Besides that, it is also important to concentrate on the identification of needs and limitations that are generally found in the application domain. Examples include functionalities that might be available in systems of that domain or new legislations and standards that will come into force for that domain and, as a result, it will be a need in new systems.

– Software systems: the main systems related to the domain are selected and investigated through their use (when available) and related documentation. Their architectures are also investigated, focusing on the capabilities for evolution and adaptation. Besides that, the architectural styles and architectural patterns commonly found in the architectures of such systems are also identified.

– Publications: information related to the processes/activities/tasks of the application domain are identified from publications, such as articles, books and technical reports. To identify the relevant information required, either an informal or a more systematic approach can be used. For instance, considering the latter perspective, the systematic review technique [KIT 04] can be used. Proposed by Evidence-Based Software Engineering (EBSE) [DYB 05], the systematic review technique intends to identify, evaluate and interpret all the significant available works related to a particular domain by using a trustworthy, rigorous and auditable review methodology [KIT 04]. Thus, the systematic review can be considered a relevant mechanism to find a set of publications/documents about a specific domain, aiming at contributing to get knowledge about what can be considered in the intended reference architecture. For instance, we have successfully applied a systematic review in order to establish a service-oriented reference architecture for the software testing domain [NAK 11c, OLI 11b].

– Domain ontologies: ontologies represent the domain terminology (i.e. concepts/terms of the domain and the relationships among them, as well as their definitions, properties and constraints expressed by means of axioms) in a well-structured format [USC 96]. During the establishment of reference architectures, the use of a common, well-known terminology for the elements that compose the architectures is very important, aiming at facilitating their further understanding [NAK 09]. Thus, investigation and selection of domain ontologies must also be conducted. Besides ontologies, controlled vocabularies, taxonomies, thesauri and concept maps, among others, can also be used. As stated before, from this perspective, reference models for the target domain can also be adopted.

To perform this step, the direct involvement of domain experts and system analysts is required. The domain experts must be responsible for contributing with their specialist knowledge or skills in the application domain. Otherwise, the system analysts must be responsible for managing all information sources that were identified and for interacting with all people involved in this step at the end of step RA-1, a set of information sources is obtained.

2.4.2. *Architectural requirements establishment*

Based on the selected sources, in this step (step RA-2), information related to the application domain is identified, resulting in a set of requirements and a set of concepts that must be considered in the reference architecture. For this, four main tasks are performed:

– Identification of the system requirements: functional and non-functional requirements of existing or envisioned systems in the application domain are identified. Such requirements must reflect the processes/activities/tasks that must be automated by the systems to be built from the reference architecture. Techniques traditionally used to describe requirements of software systems, such as natural language sentences supplemented with diagrams and tables of detailed information, can be used for that.

– Establishment of the reference architecture requirements: based on the system requirements, a set of architectural requirements for the reference architecture is established. Probably, one or more system requirements will be aggregated in an architectural requirement. Note that these architectural requirements must be more comprehensive than the system requirements, since they describe the requirements, both functional and non-functional, of a set of systems of a domain and they are related to a reference architecture that is in a higher abstraction level.

– Identification of the domain concepts: each architectural requirement is mapped to a domain concept (i.e. each requirement is associated with a concept that better addresses it). More than one requirement can be mapped to a unique concept. Since ontologies usually embrace all concepts of a given domain, they can be used to identify the concepts used in this task. When ontologies are not available, knowledge and experience, mainly from domain experts, can be used for that. The domain concepts identified in this task will be further used as an input to the architectural design of the reference architecture.

Domain experts and system analysts are also directly involved in this step. System analysts, supported by domain experts, manage the requirements of the systems and the reference architecture, as well as the concepts. In summary, the outputs of this step are the set of requirements of the reference architecture and the set of concepts.

2.4.3. *Reference architecture design*

The main objective of this step is to adequately design and represent reference architectures. In this scenario, the effective reuse of the knowledge contained in the reference architectures depends not only on raising the domain knowledge but also on efficiently documenting this knowledge through an adequate architectural description. Representation of reference architectures, i.e. their architectural description, in order to make them understandable for a wide variety of stakeholders (such as customers, product managers, project managers and engineers) consists of an activity essential for their success. From this perspective, although most architectures are represented in an informal way (for instance, using box-and-lines), initiatives that propose a means to more adequately document reference architectures can be identified [GUE 11].

Considering the effectiveness of using architectural views to represent software architectures [BAY 06, CLE 03], architectural views can also be adopted to describe reference architectures [GUE 11, NAK 08]. Lopez *et al.* [LOP 09] propose to use enterprise view, computational view and information view. Meland *et al.* [MEL 09] suggest using a component and connector view, and information view. To represent these views, different Unified Modeling Language (UML) diagrams, such as the use case diagram, component diagram, class diagram and deployment diagram, have been adopted [LOP 09, MEL 09]. Besides semi-formal techniques of UML, reference architectures can also be represented using formal architectural descriptions languages (ADLs), such as ADLARS [BAS 05], *pi*-ADL [CHE 10] and WRIGHT [FRI 99].

To build this architectural description, well-known architectural styles and patterns (for instance, client-server [EDE 94], three-tier architecture [ECK 95] and Model-View-Controller (MVC) [BUS 96]), as well as a combination of these and other styles, should be adopted. Furthermore, if architectural styles and/or architectural patterns were identified in step RA-1, they must also be considered. These styles and patterns are the basis on which concepts previously identified are organized. For instance, if a three-tier architecture is used as an architectural style of the reference architecture, the concepts related to the business rules and identified in step RA-2 should be organized into the application tier, since this tier usually contains the business rules.

To represent reference architectures, the main architectural views proposed by ProSA-RA, as also discussed in [NAK 08], are module view, runtime view, deployment view and conceptual view. Besides that, to represent these views, ProSA-RA suggests the use of UML techniques [OMG 13]. The main architectural views, UML techniques and required extensions to represent these architectures are the following:

– Module view: it shows the structure of the architecture in terms of packages, classes, containment, specialization/generalization and relationships. To represent this view, UML class diagram can be used.

– Runtime view: it shows the structure of the systems, which will be built on the basis of reference architecture, when these systems are executing. Since this view refers to a view of the reference architecture, it should show the behavior of all the systems derived from the architecture in a higher level of abstraction. This view can present the subsystems, components, packages, objects, provided and required interfaces, ports and connectors. UML component diagram can be used to represent this view.

– Deployment view: it describes the hardware (such as, server machines, database servers and client machines), the software system or subsystems that are installed on that hardware, and the network connections if they exist. An adequate technique to represent this view is the UML deployment diagram.

– Conceptual view: it aims at describing and supporting the understanding of each domain concept or term used in the reference architecture. For describing this view, ontologies, controlled vocabularies, taxonomies, thesauri and concept maps, among others, can be used. Regarding ontology, it basically consists of concepts and relations, as well as their definitions, properties and constraints expressed by means of axioms [USC 96]. ProSA-RA proposes to use ontologies to represent this view [NAK 07].

Our experience has shown that these views are sufficient to represent reference architectures; however, other architectural views can also be adopted. For instance, an enterprise view can be adopted if it is required to represent the scope, purpose and policies of the architecture [LOP 09]; UML can also be adopted to describe this view. Furthermore, when establishing reference architectures for critical domains, such as critical embedded systems, safety-critical systems and hard real-time systems, a formal representation of these architectures is interesting. For this, formal ADLs can be adopted [BAS 05, CHE 10, FRI 99]; however, they must be investigated and possibly adapted to represent the reference architectures.

In order to conduct this step, software architects, supported by domain experts, build the architectural views using their experience in architectural design. At the end, this step results in an architectural description composed of a set of architectural views of the reference architecture.

2.4.4. *Reference architecture evaluation*

The quality of reference architectures is important, since such architectures will be used as the main basis of a set of systems of the given application domain. Thus, if these architectures have quality, the systems resulted from them probably have more quality as well. Quality in reference architecture refers to a set of quality attributes, such as completeness, applicability and understandability [TRI 11]. From this perspective, several initiatives can be pointed out to conduct the evaluation of reference architectures, for instance, adaptation of Software Architecture Analysis Method (SAAM) [GRA 05] and Architecture Tradeoff Analysis Method (ATAM) [GAL 00]. These methods can also be adopted to evaluate architectures in the context of ProSA-RA.

In another direction, ProSA-RA proposes the use of a checklist-based inspection approach, named Framework for Evaluation of Reference Architectures (FERA) [SAN 13], in order to evaluate the reference architectures. FERA was also proposed based on RAModel, which, as stated before, proposes a large set of elements that can be used to describe the reference architectures. In brief, a checklist corresponds to a list of questions that guide reviewers on detecting defects in documents and, specifically in our work, defects in documents related to the reference architecture design. Our checklist is composed of 78 multiple choice questions, whose answers vary from “fully satisfactory” to “totally unsatisfactory” (and a field for adding comments) and which are supposed to be answered by eight types of stakeholders (namely, architects, domain experts, analysts, software project managers, designers/developers/implementers, integrators, testers and quality assurance stakeholders). In particular, the main intention during evaluation of reference architectures using FERA is to get information on (1) whether the reference architectures are adequately represented, i.e. they provide general information (such as the change history, potential risk, constraints and scope) and they use an adequate set of architectural viewpoints, views and models; (2) whether the documentation related to the reference architectures contains important information, such as architectural decisions, best practices and guidelines, policies and rules, international standards and interfaces among modules; (3) whether the reference architectures considered quality attributes, such as interoperability, security and scalability; (4) whether the reference architectures can be easily instantiated; and (5) what could be changed, if necessary, in order to improve the reference architecture documentation.

It is important to highlight that this step of ProSA-RA involves several stakeholders, including, for instance, software architects and testers, who sometimes do not have in-depth knowledge about the application domain; thus, the support of domain experts is relevant. Besides that, ontologies can play an essential role in the scenario, since they support the understanding of concepts and terms contained in the reference architecture and, as a result, support the conduction of the evaluation.

2.5. Uses of reference architectures

As reference architectures usually contain important knowledge about how to organize architectures of software systems of a given domain, they present several possibilities of use. Various purposes have guided their adoption and use, such as:

– Building software systems: reference architectures can be considered an important basis on which concrete architectures of software systems are built. For this, the activity of reference architecture instantiation is conduced. In brief, instantiation of reference architectures refers to the following tasks: (1) reading and understanding the documentation related to the reference architecture; (2) selecting the whole architecture or their parts that are interesting to be present in the software system to be developed; (3) refining and adapting the architecture or their parts, using the specification of the software system, including requirements, constraints, context of applications and so on; (4) documenting the architectural instance; (5) evaluating the architectural instance; and (6) concreting the architectural instance through implementation. Note that instantiation is not a trivial task; therefore, processes and methods that systematize such a task are necessary. Furthermore, the inclusion of reference architectures in the current software processes of an organization is also not trivial. Therefore, software processes need to be adequate to cover these new additional elements. Moreover, process models, such as Rational Unified Process (RUP), need to be remodeled, covering the tasks related to the reference architecture management. By adopting these new processes and using reference architectures, a project team can potentially reduce the time, effort and mistakes, and thus can improve the productivity.

– Domain standardization: reference architectures have been adopted as a means to standard software systems of a given domain. This standardization has occurred in the interfaces among subsystems that must establish communications, composing a more complex, large system. Moreover, reference architectures have also established the external interfaces of systems that are built based on these architectures, facilitating the integration of these systems with other ones. Therefore, reference architectures have promoted internal and external interoperability in software systems.

Reference architectures have also standardized the internal structure of software systems, i.e. they have established the set of modules and relationship and distribution of these modules based on architectural styles and patterns. This knowledge contained in such architectures can possibly reduce the efforts to design new systems as well as their internal and external interfaces.

– Evolution of existing software systems: the most software systems present evolution as a natural, needed process, mainly in successful systems. These systems evolve for several purposes, for instance, to adapt to new contexts, modify their functionalities, improve their quality and so on. During this process, the reuse of knowledge about how to evolve them is certainly important. Reference architectures can be used in this context. In general, the following are necessary: (1) the selection of one or more reference architectures if they were not selected before, (2) the study of related documentation of these architectures, (3) the investigation of parts/elements contained in the reference architectures that could comply with the requirements of the required evolution, (4) the instantiation of these parts/elements through refinements and adequation and (5) the implementation of such parts/elements.

The successful use of a reference architecture in this context depends mainly on whether this architecture matches with the domain of the system to be evolved and also on the quality of such architecture. It is also interesting to note that this architecture has been proved successful in building software systems.

– Deriving new reference architectures: existing reference architectures can be used as a basis to derive new reference architectures, in particular, for the same domain or neighboring domains. For instance, a reference architecture that has as a basis a specific architectural style (such as client-server) can be derived to an architecture that has the service-oriented architectural style. In this case, modules must probably be mapped to services and other issues that appear with service orientation must be solved, such as the Quality of Service (QoS), orchestration and choreography, publication and discovery of services. Note that elements contained in previous architectures can be reused and adapted to the new architectures. Reduction in efforts can also be achieved with this approach, mainly when the previous architectures are more mature and have already been successfully used. An example is the establishment of a service-oriented reference architecture for software testing tools [OLI 11b] derived from a previous architecture for testing tools [NAK 07], which was based on two architectural styles: three-tier architecture and MVC.

– Supporting the building of SPL: reuse in large numbers is an important concern in software product line engineering (SPLE) and, at the same time, in fact, reference architectures have presented a considerable, valuable body of knowledge about how to structure systems of a domain and, therefore, they can be considered as important elements to be reused. In this scenario, the combination of reference architectures and SPL is interesting. In particular, the use of existing reference architectures as the basis of SPL can be explored. Reusing knowledge contained in these architectures can contribute to reduce the effort required to build SPL artifacts, such as the variability model and the PL architecture, and, therefore, to improve the productivity during SPLE.

In [NAK 13], a process to design product line architectures based on reference architectures is presented. This process, named ProSA-RA2PLA, is an iterative process that systematizes the steps to build product line architectures using the knowledge and elements contained in the reference architectures. As illustrated in Figure. 2.5, during the SPLE, in particular, the *family engineering* (when product line architectures are usually developed), ProSA-RA2PLA is responsible for supporting the product line architectures design. For this, ProSA-RA2PLA has as its main input existing references architectures and these architectures are specialized to the product line architecture of an SPL.

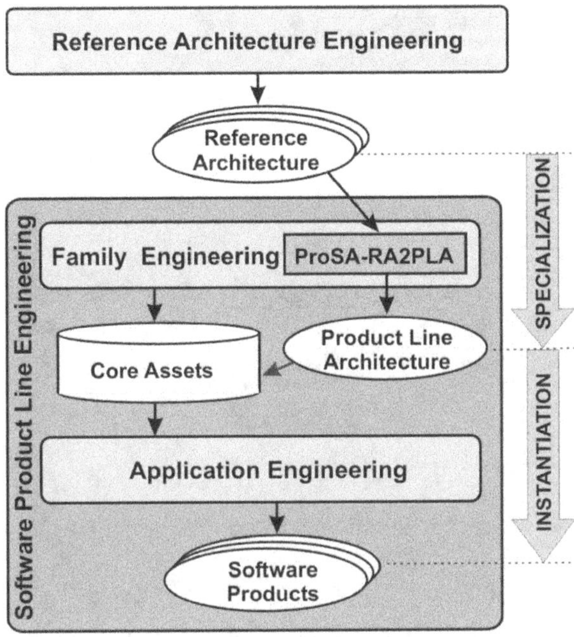

Figure 2.5. *Application context of ProSA-RA*

Basically, when using ProSA-RA2PLA, one or more reference architectures are first identified and selected. As they reflect, perhaps, the best design principles in the overall domain and include the respective design rationale, they are used as the starting point for the iterative product line architecture design activity. ProSA-RA2PLA first builds the general structure of the product line architecture, based on the main, higher level structure of the reference architectures. Then, this process selects and prioritizes the elements contained in the reference architectures and uses these elements, together with other pertinent artifacts in the SPLE, to iteratively refine the structure of the PLA and to build the variability model. The commonality and, especially, the variability are refined and modeled, e.g. with adequate decision. The idea is that reference architectures are concretized and enhanced to support the predicted variability in the family of systems in a suitable manner. ProSA-RA2PLA uses a top-down, iterative approach of planning, building and assessment in order to establish product line architecture, as illustrated in Figure 2.6.

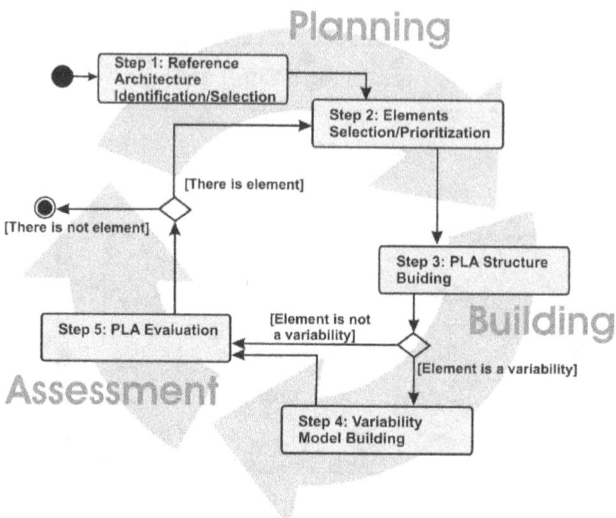

Figure 2.6. *Overall structure of ProSA-RA2PLA*

In particular, in the last two situations (deriving new reference architectures and supporting the building of SPL), as stated before, the use of RAModel is quite interesting.

2.6. Examples of reference architectures

Considering their relevance, it is observed that different domains have already understood the need for encapsulating knowledge in reference architectures, with the aim of disseminating and reusing this knowledge and standardizing the systems as well. Some good examples are AUTomotive Open System Architecture (AUTOSAR) [AUT 13], for the automotive domain, and Continua [CON 13] and UniversAAL [UNI 13], for AAL [BRO 10]. In particular, these architectures have been developed by consortiums that involve major industrial players (such as manufacturers and suppliers) and researchers.

Besides, platform-oriented architectures, i.e. architectures not related to the specific application domain, but to a specific architectural style or technology, have also been proposed and widely used as reference architectures. Some good examples are OASIS [OAS 08] and S3 [ARS 07], for software systems based on Service-Oriented Architecture (SOA) [PAP 08], and Open Services Gateway initiative framework (OSGi) [OSG 13], a set of specifications and a layered architecture that define dynamic component systems for Java.

2.7. Future perspectives of reference architectures

Currently, reference architectures are the focus of attention of academies and industries. Important contributions in the area of reference architectures can be found; however, it is too early to say that this area is already matured and consolidated. For the future, on-going research needs to progress and consolidate. Furthermore, there are several other research perspectives for reference architectures. In this section, we will briefly discuss reference architectures in Systems-of-Systems (SoS), SOA, dynamic software architectures, Multi-Software Product Line (MSPL or simply Multi-Product Line – MPL) and variability in reference architectures.

Currently, SoS, a new class of software systems, have arisen and become increasingly ubiquitous, larger and more complex. These systems have sometimes arisen as a result of the integration of various operationally independent systems, even developed with different technologies and for various platforms. An adequate integration has been increasingly necessary to promote the cooperation among these independent systems in order to provide more complex functions, which could not be provided by any system working separately. There are various systems that can be classified as SoS. An example is a medical system that integrates systems for the diagnosis, treatment and management of patients [HAT 07]. Examples involving critical embedded systems can also be found, such as airport systems [JAM 08], automotive [AOY 11], avionics [FAR 10] and robotics [BOW 10]. The main characteristics of SoS are [MAI 99] operational/managerial independence of constituents of an SoS, evolutionary development, emergent behavior and geographic distribution. In this scenario, reference architectures could have an essential role to improve the interoperability among constituent systems of an SoS. For this, these architectures must establish the external interfaces of these constituents, aiming at facilitating the communication and integration with others.

In the context of software architecture, an architectural style has gained attention in the past few years: the SOA. This style makes it possible to improve integration, scalability and reuse, since systems based on this style present independence regarding programming language and execution platforms. Considering the advantages of SOA, it has been widely investigated and used as an architectural style of diverse types of software systems. It has also been the main architectural style of SoS. Therefore, reference architectures are also quite important when service-oriented systems need to be developed. Information about how to organize the services and their external interfaces can be set by the reference architecture.

From another perspective, dynamic software architectures are characterized by architectures that can evolve/modify during the execution of the system, i.e. components or connectors can be created, deleted or reconfigured at runtime [OQU 08]. For this, these architectures must provide a specification of modifications at runtime. Currently, many application domains have presented software systems with dynamic architectures, such as robotics, automatic guided vehicles, unmanned vehicle and intelligent cameras. There are also several initiatives of reference architectures, reference models and domain-oriented software architectures for systems with dynamic architectures. However, research in this topic is quite recent and more investigation must be developed regarding design, representation, evaluation and evolution of such architectures.

From another perspective, MPL has recently emerged as a special type of SPL [ROS 10]. MPL refers to a new approach for the software development where software products are the result of components developed from independent SPLs, sometimes, by various organizations, using various approaches and even technologies. MPL must then make it possible to manage a set of interacting, interdependent SPLs. In this context, we can foresee several perspectives of exploring reference architectures in the context of MPL. Figure 2.7 illustrates the panorama involving reference architectures and MPL. Note that one or more reference architectures could be used as the basis of MPL. Then, we list the main perspectives: (1) the use of reference architectures for the establishment of interfaces, (2) the use of reference architectures for communication improvement among various development teams, (3) the evolution and refinement of existing reference architectures for MPL and (4) the establishment of new reference architectures for MPL.

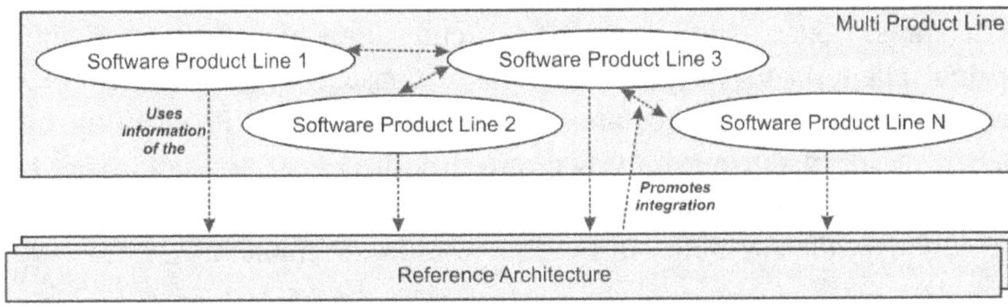

Figure 2.7. *Relationship between reference architecture and MPL*

In a similar scenario, variability has arisen as an important concept, since the development of a set of similar systems is a very common situation. Therefore, this concept has been developing in the context of several research topics, such as SPL, self-adaptive systems, configurable interfaces of software components and service-based systems with dynamic runtime composition. According to Galster *et al.* [GAL 11], variability is the ability of a software artifact to be adapted for a specific context in a preplanned manner. From this perspective, the main element that could promote variability is the software architecture; thus, variability should be treated as a first-class, crosscutting concern in the software architecture [GAL 11]. Therefore, software architectures that were built considering variability have certainly more chances of developing successful systems. For instance, in the context of SPL, the product line architecture has explicitly considered variabilities and variability management has been considered as an essential activity for the SPL engineering. Variability management explicitly represents software artifact variations for managing dependencies among SPL variants and supports their instantiations throughout the SPL lifecycle [BAB 10]. Besides SPL, variability management is also a challenge in the development, maintenance and evolution of software-intensive systems.

Regarding reference architectures, there is not a clear understanding about what is variability in such architectures. According to Galster *et al.* [GAL 11], variability in reference architectures is the ability of a software artifact built from such architectures to easily be adapted for a specific context in a preplanned manner. In spite of the considerable relevance and amount of reference architectures available for various application domains and, at the same time, the relevance of the concept of variability in software development, in general, reference architecture engineering has not specifically concerned itself with variability during the establishment of such architectures. Hence, existing reference architectures have been built without a special attention to variability and, as a consequence, software systems resulting from these architectures could have difficulty in adapting or in evolving to suit new contexts. Therefore, it is necessary to think about how reference architectures can be better designed, represented and evaluated in order to satisfy the variability in systems resulting from them.

2.8. Final remarks

Note that reference architecture *per se* is a relatively new research area. Important contributions have been made in the past decade and are concentrated mainly in the past few years. However, there are several areas, such as avionics, automotive, robotics and web systems, that have proposed reference architectures, including those with diverse purposes. In general, most of these architectures have been designed using *ad hoc* approaches, represented using informal techniques and used without a previous evaluation.

Considering the relevance and impact of reference architectures, currently, in systems development contributions in four subjects are found: design, representation, evaluation and use of reference architectures. There is, however, a lack of work dealing specifically with evolution of reference architectures.

There are also several lines of investigation that still need to be developed. The evolution of this area is extremely important as software systems, technologies and development approaches are constantly changing. Reference architectures must follow these new tendencies if they intend to be updated and continue contributing effectively to the development of software systems.

2.9. Bibliography

[ANG 09] ANGELOV S., GREFEN P., GREEFHORST D., "A classification of software reference architectures: analyzing their success and effectiveness", *8th Working IEEE/IFIP Conference on Software Architecture (WICSA 2009)*, Cambridge, UK, pp. 141–150, 2009.

[ANT 11] ANTONINO P.O., SCHNEIDER D., HOFMANN C., *et al.*, "Evaluation of AAL platforms according to architecture-based quality attributes", *International Joint Conference on Ambient Intelligence (AmI 2011) (LNCS 7040)*, Amsterdam, Netherlands, pp. 264–274, 2011.

[AOY 11] AOYAMA M., TANABE H., "A design methodology for real-time distributed software architecture based on the behavioral properties and its application to advanced automotive software", *18th Asia Pacific Software Engineering Conference (APSEC 2011)*, Ho Chi Minh, Vietnam, pp. 211–218, 2011.

[ARS 07] ARSANJANI A., ZHANG L.-J., ELLIS M., *et al.*, "S3: A service-oriented reference architecture", *Information Technology Professional*, vol. 9, no. 3, pp. 10–17, 2007.

[AUT 13] AUTOSAR, AUTOSAR (automotive open system architecture), 2013. Available at http://www.autosar.org/.

[BAB 10] BABAR M.A., CHEN L., SHULL F., "Managing variability in software product lines", *IEEE Software*, vol. 27, no. 3, pp. 89–91, 94, 2010.

[BAS 03] BASS L., CLEMENTS P., KAZMAN R., *Software Architecture in Practice*, Addison-Wesley, 2003.

[BAS 05] BASHROUSH R., BROWN T.J., SPENCE I., *et al.*, "ADLARS: an architecture description language for software product lines", *29th Annual IEEE/NASA on Software Engineering Workshop (SEW 2005)*, Greenbelt, MD, pp. 163–173, 2005.

[BAY 06] BAYER J., MUTHIG D., "A view-based approach for improving software documentation practices", *13th Annual IEEE International Symposium and Workshop on Engineering of Computer Based Systems (ECBS 2006)*, Los Alamitos, CA, pp. 269–278, 2006.

[BOR 11] BORG Z., A reference architecture for marine systems, Master's Thesis, University of Kaiserslautern and Fraunhofer Institute for Experimental Software Engineering (IESE), Kaiserslautern, Germany, 2011.

[BOW 10] BOWEN R., SAHIN F., "A net-centric XML based system of systems architecture for human tracking", *5th International Conference on System of Systems Engineering (SoSE 2010)*, Loughborough, UK, pp. 1–6, 2010.

[BRO 10] BROEK G.V.D., CAVALLO F., WEHRMANN C., *AALIANCE Ambient Assisted Living Roadmap*, IOS Press, Amsterdam, Netherlands, 2010.

[BUS 96] BUSCHMANN F., MEUNIER R., ROHNERT H., *et al.*, *Pattern-Oriented Software Architecture: A System of Patterns*, vol. 1, John Wiley & Sons, 1996.

[CHE 10] CHEN J., WU D., ZHANG J., *et al.*, "Formal modelling and analysis of HLA architectural style", *International Journal of Modelling, Identification and Control*, vol. 9, no. 1–2, pp. 71–82, 2010.

[CLE 03] CLEMENTS P., BACHMANN F., BASS L., *et al.*, *Documenting Software Architecture: Views and Beyond*, 3rd ed., Addison-Wesley, Boston, MA, 2003.

[CON 13] CONTINUA HEALTH ALLIANCE, "Continua Health Alliance", *World Wide Web*, 2013. Available at http://www.continuaalliance.org/.

[DEB 98] DEBAUD J.-M., FLEGE O., KNAUBER P., "PuLSE-DSSA – a method for the development of software reference architectures", *3rd International Workshop on Software architecture (ISA 1998)*, Orlando, FL, pp. 25–28, 1998.

[DUA 12] DUARTE L.S., Establishment of a reference architecture for digital television applications, Master's Thesis, University of São Paulo, São Carlos, Brazil, 2012.

[DYB 05] DYBÅ T., KITCHENHAM B., JORGENSEN M., "Evidence-based software engineering for practitioners", *IEEE Software*, vol. 22, no. 1, pp. 5865, 2005.

[ECK 95] ECKERSON W.W., "Three tier client/server architecture: achieving scalability, performance, and efficiency in client server applications", *Open Information Systems Journal*, vol. 10, no. 1, pp. 46–50, January 1995.

[EDE 94] EDELSTEIN H., "Unraveling client/server architecture", *DBMS Magazine*, vol. 34, no. 7, pp. 34–41, May 1994.

[FAR 10] FARCAS C., FARCAS E., KRUEGER I., *et al.*, "Addressing the integration challenge for avionics and automotive systems: from components to rich services", *Proceedings of the IEEE*, vol. 98, no. 4, pp. 562–583, 2010.

[FEI 13] FEITOSA D., SIMuS – reference architecture for service multirobotics systems, Master's Thesis, University of São Paulo, São Carlos, Brazil, January 2013.

[FRI 99] FRITSCHI H., GATZIU S., A reusable architecture to construct active database systems, Technical Report no. IFI-99.02, University of Zurich, Switzerland, 1999.

[GAL 00] GALLAGHER B.P., Using the architecture tradeoff analysis method to evaluate a reference architecture: a case study, Report no. CMU/SEI-2000-TN-007, 2000.

[GAL 11] GALSTER M., AVGERIOU P., WEYNS D., *et al.*, "Variability in software architecture: current practice and challenges", *SIGSOFT Software Engineering Notes*, vol. 36, no. 5, pp. 30–32, 2011.

[GOM 04] GOMAA H., *Designing Software Product Lines with UML*, Object Technology Series, Addison-Wesley, July 2004.

[GRA 05] GRAAF B., VAN DIJK H., VAN DEURSEN A., "Evaluating an embedded software reference architecture – industrial experience report", *9th European Conference on Software Maintenance and Reengineering (CSMR 2005)*, Manchester, UK, pp. 354–363, March 2005.

[GUE 11] GUESSI M., DE OLIVEIRA L.B.R., NAKAGAWA E.Y., "Representation of reference architectures: a systematic review", *23nd International Conference on Software Engineering and Knowledge Engineering (SEKE 2011)*, Miami Beach, pp. 782–785, July 2011.

[HAT 07] HATA Y., KAMOZAKI Y., SAWAYAMA T., *et al.*, "A heart pulse monitoring system by air pressure and ultrasonic sensor systems", *2nd IEEE International Conference on System of Systems Engineering (SoSE 2007)*, Loughborough, UK, pp. 1–5, 2007.

[JAM 08] JAMSHIDI M., *System of Systems Engineering – Innovations for the 21st Century*, John Wiley & Sons, New York, 2008.

[KIT 04] KITCHENHAM B., Procedures for performing systematic reviews, Report no. TR/SE-0401, Keele University, July 2004.

[KRU 00] KRUCHTEN P., *The Rational Unified Process: An Introduction*, 2nd ed., edition, The Addison-Wesley Object Technology Series, Addison-Wesley, 2000.

[LOP 09] LOPEZ D.M., BLOBEL B.G., "A development framework for semantically interoperable health information systems", *International Journal of Medical Informatics*, vol. 78, no. 2, pp. 83–103, 2009.

[MAI 99] MAIER M.W., "Architecting principles for systems-of-systems", *Systems Engineering*, vol. 1, no. 4, pp. 267–284, 1999.

[MEL 09] MELAND P.H., ARDI S., JENSEN J., *et al.*, "An architectural foundation for security model sharing and reuse", *International Conference on Availability, Reliability and Security (ARES 2009)*, Fukuoka, Japan, vol. 1–2, pp. 823–828, 2009.

[MUL 08] MULLER G., "A reference architecture primer", *World Wide Web*, 2008. Available at http://www.gaudisite.nl/.

[NAK 07] NAKAGAWA E.Y., SIMAO A.S., FERRARI F., *et al.*, "Towards a reference architecture for software testing tools", *19th International Conference on Software Engineering and Knowledge Engineering (SEKE 2007)*, Boston, MA, pp. 1–6, July 2007.

[NAK 08] NAKAGAWA E.Y., MALDONADO J.C., "Reference architecture knowledge representation: an experience", *3rd Workshop on SHAring and Reusing architectural Knowledge (SHARK 2008) at 30th International Conference on Software Engineering (ICSE 2008)*, Leipzig, Germany, pp. 51–54, May 2008.

[NAK 09] NAKAGAWA E.Y., BARBOSA E.F., MALDONADO J.C., "Exploring ontologies to support the establishment of reference architecture: an example on software testing", *IEEE/IFIP Conference on Software Architecture 2009, European Conference on Software Architecture 2009 (WICSA/ECSA 2009)*, Cambridge, UK, pp. 249–252, 2009.

[NAK 11a] NAKAGAWA E.Y., ANTONINO P.O., BECKER M., "Exploring the use of reference architectures in the development of product line artifacts", *2nd International Workshop on Knowledge-Oriented Product Line Engineering (KOPLE 2011) at 15th International Software Product Line Conference (SPLC 2011)*, Munchen, Germany, pp. 1–8, August 2011.

[NAK 11b] NAKAGAWA E.Y., FERRARI F., SASAKI M.M.F., *et al.*, "An aspect-oriented reference architecture for software engineering environments", *Journal of Systems and Software*, vol. 84, no. 10, pp. 1670–1684, 2011.

[NAK 11c] NAKAGAWA E.Y., OLIVEIRA L.B.R., "Using systematic review to elicit requirements of reference architectures", *14th Workshop on Requirements Engineering (WER 2011)*, Rio de Janeiro, Brazil, pp. 273–284, 2011.

[NAK 13] NAKAGAWA E.Y., BECKER M., MALDONADO J.C., "Towards a process to design product line architectures based on reference architectures", *17th International Software Product Line Conference (SPLC 2013)*, Tokyo, Japan, pp. 1–5, 2013.

[OAS 08] OASIS, Reference architecture for service oriented architecture version 1.0, Report, OASIS Standard, April 2008.

[OLI 11a] OLIVEIRA L.B.R., Establishment of a service-oriented reference architecture for software testing tools, Master's Dissertation, Institute of Mathematics and Computer Sciences, University of São Paulo, São Carlos, SP, Brazil, January 2011.

[OLI 11b] OLIVEIRA L.B.R., NAKAGAWA E.Y., "A service-oriented reference architecture for the software testing domain", *5th European Conference on Software Architecture (ECSA 2011)*, Essen, Germany, pp. 405–421, 2011.

[OMG 13] OMG, "Unified modeling language version 2.2", *World Wide Web*, 2013. Available at http://www.omg.org/spec/UML/2.2/.

[OQU 08] OQUENDO F., "Dynamic software architectures: formally modelling structure and behaviour with Pi-ADL", *3rd International Conference on Software Engineering Advances (ICSEA 2008)*, Sliema, Malta, pp. 352–359, 2008.

[OSG 13] OSGI ALLIANCE, "OSGi Alliance specifications", *World Wide Web*, 2013. Available at http://www.osgi.org/Specifications/.

[PAP 08] PAPAZOGLOU M.P., TRAVERSO P., DUSTDAR S., *et al.*, "Service-oriented computing: a research roadmap", *International Journal of Cooperative Information Systems*, vol. 17, no. 2, pp. 223–255, 2008.

[POH 05] POHL K., BÖCKLE G., VAN DER LINDEN F., *Software Product Line Engineering: Foundations, Principles, and Techniques*, Springer-Verlag, Berlin, 2005.

[ROS 07] ROSEN M., AMBLER S.W., HAZRA T.K., *et al.*, "Enterprise architecture trends", *Enterprise Architecture*, vol. 10, no. 1, 2007.

[ROS 10] ROSENMÜLLER M., SIEGMUND N., "Automating the configuration of multi software product lines", *4th International Workshop on Variability Modelling of Software-Intensive Systems (VAMOS 2010)*, Linz, Austria, pp. 123–130, 2010.

[SAN 13] SANTOS J.F.M., GUESSI M., GALSTER M., *et al.*, "A checklist for evaluation of reference architectures for embedded systems", *25th International Conference on Software Engineering and Knowledge Engineering (SEKE 2013)*, Boston, MA, pp. 1–4, 2013.

[SEI 13] SEI, "A framework for software product line practice, version 5.0", *World Wide Web*, 2013. Available at http://www.sei.cmu.edu/productlines/framereport/index.html.

[TRI 11] TRIENEKENS J., ANGELOV S., GREFEN P., *et al.*, "Quality of software reference architectures", *IADIS International Conference Information Systems 2011 (IADIS IS 2011)*, Avila, Spain, pp. 145–151, 2011.

[UNI 13] UNIVERS AAL PROJECT, "The Univers AAL reference architecture", *World Wide Web*, 2013. Available at http://www.universaal.org/.

[USC 96] USCHOLD M., GRÜNINGER M., "Ontologies: principles, methods, and applications", *Knowledge Engineering Review*, vol. 11, no. 2, pp. 93–155, 1996.

[WIC 10] WICHERT R., "Challenges and limitations of intelligent ambient assisted living environments", *1st international joint conference on Ambient intelligence (AmI 2010)*, Malaga, Spain, Springer-Verlag, pp. 304–309, 2010.

Chapter 3

Multihierarchy/Multiview Software Architectures

On the basis of a broad study of approaches and notation languages or description languages of the views of complex systems, in this chapter, we have identified the basic concepts brought by the views, from their definition to their integration through their decomposition into multiple hierarchies of abstraction, description, conceptualization and modeling.

3.1. Introduction

Software architectures have made a real contribution to the development of complex distributed systems. On the one hand, their main characteristics come from their power to manage abstractions and levels of expression of a system and, on the other hand, in their ability to take into account the modeling of the structure and behavior of a system. Nowadays, it is widely accepted that one of the critical issues in the design and development of any complex software system is its architecture, i.e. the organization of the architectural elements that constitute it. Good architecture can help produce the critical properties of a system (reliability, portability, interoperability, etc.). However, bad architecture can have disastrous consequences on the system. Moreover, good architecture can serve as a system's "conscience" during its development. In fact, it guides the process of a system's evolution,

Chapter written by Ahmad KHEIR, Hala NAJA and Mourad Chabane OUSSALAH.

for example by indicating which aspects of the system can be modified without compromising its integrity.

Nowadays, new engineering applications, in particular those dedicated to the design and development of complex distributed systems, have highlighted the need for manipulating multiple views of the same architectural element. The sustainability, adaptability and scalability of such systems become a very important economic issue. In fact, having often needed several years of development and maintenance (human resources / months), it becomes imperative for these systems to allow for a consequent life and especially to respond to the changing needs of the different categories of users involved in modeling these systems. In this chapter, we discuss, in general, various existing approaches to the views of a system and, in particular, in software architectures, while stressing the key indispensable concepts for taking these views, and the different levels of hierarchy carried by these views, into account.

3.2. Existing viewpoint approaches

3.2.1. *Introduction*

The viewpoint concept, also called view, takes various meanings across the field of computer science. In general, we are interested in the views as soon as we model complex systems involving a large amount of data that requires the cooperation of several experts from different fields of knowledge and different points of interest, and addressing a wide range of users. As discussed in [NAJ 98], a viewpoint links a designer, a universe of discourse (i.e. the system model) and the goal that the designer is trying to achieve. The viewpoint enables a partial representation of the system to be modeled, while highlighting one or more aspects of the latter and concealing others.

The first work on viewpoints falls within the field of knowledge representation in artificial intelligence. Here, we can mention the work of Minsky [MIN 75] followed by KRL languages [BOB 77], LOOPS languages [BOB 83] and ROME languages [CAR 90], which have all highlighted the need to bestow several representations to the same object.

In databases, the viewpoint concept was introduced in 1975 for the first time in Ansi/Sparc's report under the name *external schema*. An external schema represents the unique point from which users can access data from the database. This is a part of the base, which interests a user or group of users and incorporates the concept of access rights. A viewpoint restricts the visibility of data and/or adapts their structure to the application requirements. It helps solve problems related to the configuration of the user interface for the data protection, for the evolution of data organization needs without disrupting the existing organization as well as for the query optimization.

In software engineering, the motivation of the viewpoint is the separation of concerns. Thus, points of views are introduced as construction elements for the management of the complexities of artifacts products (such as requirements specifications, design models and programs). In the following, we conduct a survey on views in four areas of software engineering, which are requirements specifications, system modeling, system implementation and software engineering architectures. We extend the review to software architecture as it is closely connected with the purpose of our study.

3.2.2. *Views in requirements specifications*

In 1979, Mullery developed a formal method for the specification and modeling of complex computer systems called CORE [MUL 79]. In this method, he proposed to break down the modeling process into several steps and, for each of them, to identify the viewpoints associated with them, so as to finally achieve a schematic representation of the system while taking into account all viewpoints of this system.

Finkelstein *et al.* [FIN 89] and Robinson *et al.* [ROB 90] developed methods and tools for the derivation of the computer systems specifications from a dialogue between different points of view. Delugash *et al.* [DEL 90] represented the needs associated with each viewpoint in a conceptual graph. Then, an integration of the different graphs into a single graph is carried out. The graph achieved specifies the requirements for the entire system. Nuseibeh *et al.* [NUS 94] represent the links and relationships that can exist between the points of view through a given platform. Finally, in 1997, Sommerville proposed his *Preview* approach [SOM 97], which gives architects of computer systems a method and the tools to discover and analyze the requirements of different viewpoints.

3.2.3. *Views in systems modeling*

In terms of systems modeling, the UML symbol proves that it embodies the broader concept of the viewpoint. In fact, in its current standard, the

UML proposes 13 types of diagrams where each type bestows an implied viewpoint, from which a complex system will be approached, thus allowing the decomposition of a complex system model into several less complex, more easily affordable and intelligible supplementary submodels. In addition, the UML proposes an extension mechanism that allows users to add or customize the predefined types of diagrams and thus to add points of views.

In the VUML approach [ANW 10, ANW 11, NAS 03, NAS 09], a given extension of the UML is proposed. It is based on the ability to make more than one class diagram for the same system to coexist, and then to proceed to an integration of these diagrams into a single one, consistent with the proposed VUML metamodel.

Also, Dijkman *et al.* [DIJ 08] presented a platform in which the computer system architect can model different viewpoints of the system by determining a collection of basic concepts that are common to all, and then associating each viewpoint with a suitable level of abstraction and defining the relationships that may exist between the viewpoints.

Still in modeling, in [NAJ 98], the author defines five properties that an object-oriented model should have in order to make it a multiview object-oriented model. These properties are:

– a range of one viewpoint at various levels;

– multiple representation has a repository;

– multiple representation is decentralized;

– partial representations exchange information between them;

– multiple representations are consistent.

3.2.4. *Views within programming*

In the history of programming languages, the terms “decomposition” and “modularity” have always been keywords to reduce the complexity of programs. Thus, we obtain less complex, loosely coupled and easily reusable modules.

The separation of concerns aims to carry out a modularization of programs based on various concerns. The idea is to consider a system as a core with extensions. The core is the set of basic functional requirements for which the system is primarily designed and the extensions are additional secondary requirements, which add functionalities to the core. An extension is a concern that cross-cuts several basic functional requirements. The implementation of a concern gives rise to an aspect; hence, the programming called "Aspect Oriented Development" [MCH 06, MIL 99]. Other paradigms exist based on the same principle; however, they diverge for several reasons, such as subject-oriented programming [DIJ 08] or view-oriented programming [MIL 99]. We do not extend the comparison between these different paradigms. The interested reader can refer to [MCH 06] for such a comparison.

3.3. Views in software architecture

Within software architecture, it is almost impossible to capture the architecture of a complex system in a single model that is understood by all stakeholders. By stakeholder, we include both the user of the future system and the manufacturer of the latter. A manufacturer is a person or a group of people that designs, develops, tests, deploys or maintains the future system.

In each of these activities, each stakeholder has its own needs, interests, requirements and wishes that the system takes into account. Understanding the role and aspirations of each stakeholder is the role of the architect during the development of the system.

The recommended solution for an architectural description (AD) is to partition it into a number of separate and interdependent points of views, which collectively describe the functional and non-functional aspects (such as performance, robustness, availability, competition and distribution) of the system. This solution is not new; in fact, it goes back to the work of Parnas in [PAR 71] and most recently, in [PER 92], to that of Perry and Wolf.

3.3.1. *Contributions of the views in software architecture*

The introduction of viewpoints in software architecture contributed to the improvement of the process of describing architecture in several ways [ROZ 11]:

– Separation of concerns: the separation of multiple aspects of a system using several different models during the design process, analysis, etc., helps a particular aspect while being able to focus on each step.

– Communication with viewpoint groups: communication between viewpoint groups with various concerns is a challenge for the architect. Approaches based on views provide an opportunity for stakeholders to converge relatively quickly toward the ADs that interest them and that respond to their concerns.

– Managing complexity: all aspects of a system, considered simultaneously in the same model, result into a complexity that a human being cannot handle. The thought of breaking down the model into models according to different views notably reduces the complexity.

In what follows, we describe three approaches, which have provided satisfactory solutions to this problem. We quote:

– in 1995, P. Kruchten's "4 +1" View Model (section 3.3.2);

– in 1996, the ISO/IEC/IEEE 42010 (section 3.3.3) IEEE Architecture Planning Group (APG), which was approved in 2000 by the IEEE -SA Standards Board and coded IEEE 1471-2000. In 2007, this standard was taken by the ISO/IEC JTC1/SC7 and named ISO/IEC 42010:2007;

– views and beyond (V&B) approach (section 3.3.4) for the documentation of software architectures developed by the Carnegie Mellon Software Engineering Institute (SEI).

3.3.2. *"4+1" view model*

The "4+1" model [KRU 95] was proposed by P. Kruchten of the Rational Software Corp. This model is based on five main views, shown in Figure 3.1, which are as follows:

– The logical view covers mainly the functional requirements of the system, or in other words, what the system provides as services to users. The logical view shows the system objects and the relationships between them.

– The process view represents a non-functional aspect of the system requirements such as performance, availability, concurrence, distribution and integrity. This view divides the system into a set of processes and represents the interactions that will take place between these processes.

– The development view focuses on the modular organization of the system. Thus, in this view, the system is broken down into several libraries or subsystems that can each be implemented by a developer or a small team of developers. This view covers the internal requirements of the implementation such as reusability, compliance with implementation standards, compliance with constraints imposed by the tools used, etc.

– The physical view mainly takes the non-functional system requirements, such as availability, reliability, performance and scalability, into account. In the physical view, software elements, such as processes and objects, will be associated with different physical components such as processors and hard disks.

– Scenarios represent the integration of elements of the previous four views using a small set of scenarios that seem important.

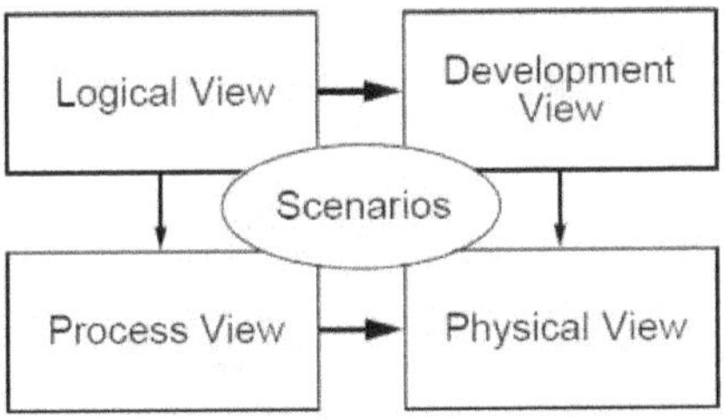

Figure 3.1. *Kruchten's "4+1" model*

The views offered in this model are not completely independent. In fact, matches can be seen between these views, for example as a match practice between a small class or set of classes, which will normally be represented as a module or a set of modules in the development view, or the process for the process view, which will be associated with the physical media of the physical view to be performed.

It should be noted that this model has been adopted in the iterative development process called rational unified process (RUP).

3.3.3. *ISO/IEC/IEEE 42010*

ISO/IEC/IEEE 42010 [ISO 11] was designed by the IEEE APG in order to formalize the definition of software architecture and its main elements, and also in order to provide a common standard for the incorporation and embodiment of the efforts made in this field.

IEEE 42010 defined an architecture or AD as being the organization of a system, structured by a collection of components (i.e. units) and software links or relationships defined between these components.

Figure 3.2 illustrates the proposed IEEE 42010 model.

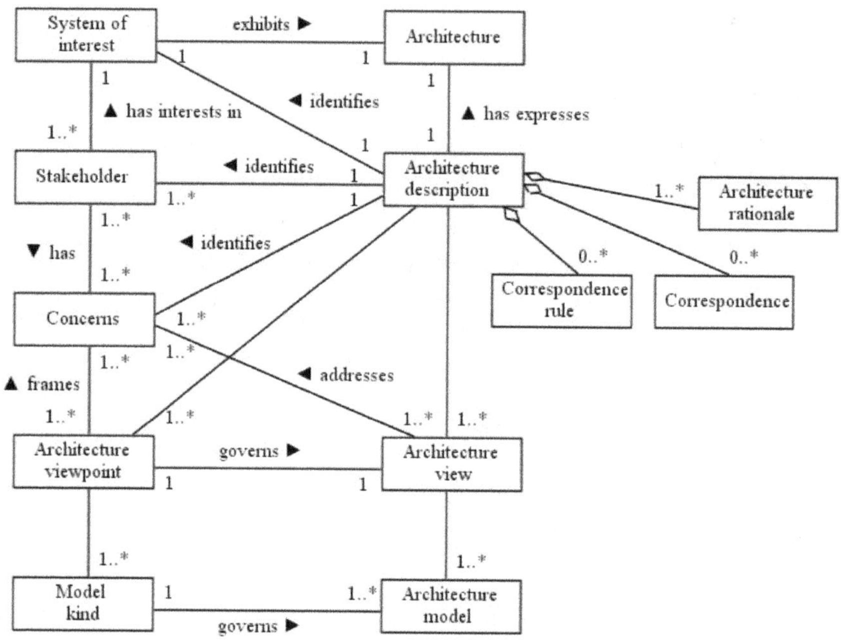

Figure 3.2. *The proposed model in IEEE 42010*

According to the proposed model in IEEE 42010:

– an AD addresses a broad array of stakeholders who have concerns. A concern may be covered by viewpoints:

- a viewpoint is a specification of the construction agreements of its own views. These agreements may be defined in the architecture itself or imported from an external entity called Model kind;

- a view is consistent with a viewpoint and consists of a set of models;

- an AD is made up of a set of views, so that each one complies with a viewpoint and consists of a set of models that describe the architecture.

3.3.4. *The views and beyond approach*

Within the SEI (Carnegie Mellon), Clements *et al.* developed the V&B approach [CLE 02] for documenting software architectures. This approach, as its name suggests, uses views to achieve a fundamental organization of software architectures. In fact, V&B approach is based on the principle that the documentation of a software architecture begins with the documentation of its relevant views and, thereafter, documenting the information linking these views together.

As in the case of IEEE 42010, the V&B approach is for all viewpoints in the development process of the computer system, and aims to provide documentation of a software architecture that is decomposed into several views for the different stakeholders and that meets their requirements.

In this approach, a three-level hierarchy is defined as follows:

– The viewtypes: like the viewpoints defined in IEEE 42010, a viewtype represents a category of views and is for one or a set of stakeholders. There are three viewtypes:

- the module viewtype represents the structure of the system in terms of a set of units of code;

- the component and connector (C&C) viewtype represents a set of elements that interact during the execution;

- the allocation viewtype represents the relationship between the software components and non-software components such as machinery and processing elements.

– The styles: an architectural style also known as an architectural pattern is a high-level pattern that assists to specify the basic structure of an application. Any style helps to achieve an overall property of the system, such as the adaptability of the user interface or distribution. Styles are grouped in viewtypes, which are considered as categories of styles. For example, the client-server model is a style for the C&C viewtype. The list of styles defined for each viewtype is illustrated in Table 3.1. It should be noted that the concepts of style and category of style are not specific to the V&B

approach but have already been proposed and widely reported in other works in software architecture, especially in the book of Buschmann *et al.* [BUS 96].

– The views: it represents collections of system elements and relationships that link them. Note that the architectural views are documented in a template defined by the designers of this approach. In fact, an architectural view is always consistent to a style of a viewtype.

Viewtypes	Styles	Views
Module	Decomposition	Styles applied to particular systems
	Generalization	
	Uses	
	Layers	
	Pipe-and-filter	
Component and connector	Shared data	
	Communicating-processes	
	Peer-to-peer	
	Client-server	
	Work assignment	
Allocation	Deployment	
	Implementation	

Table 3.1. *Viewtypes, styles and views in V&B approach*

V&B approach offers a three-step guide for the selection of relevant views necessary to document the architecture of a system:

1) Produce a list of candidate views: this step is to construct a two-dimensional array (row-column). The rows represent the stakeholders that the architect considers relevant to the current project and the columns denote grouped views into viewtypes and the styles that can be applied. Then, fill in the boxes of the table with values describing the level of information required for each stakeholder and each style. The level of information can be: *d* for detailed information, *s* for some detail and *o* for overview information.

2) Combine the views: this step aims to minimize the number of views obtained in step 1 by ignoring the views whose architectural value is covered in other views and by combining other views. Combining the views will produce a view from other views called a combined view; it amounts to combining elements from two or more views into one. For example, in small

or medium projects, work assignment and implementation views may overlap with the module decomposition view.

3) Triaging views: triaging the remaining views will be carried out in the order of priority of the documentation, depending on the specific details of the project.

The last phase of the documentation of a proposed architecture by the V&B approach is the documentation of inter-views information that are applied to multiple views. This phase has been proposed to link the views of the architecture together and give an overall picture facilitating the understanding of the stakeholders. In fact, this phase can be divided into the following three steps:

– the specification of the overall organization by providing a map of the entire documentation;

– the description of the architecture by giving an overview of the system, an index of all the elements of the architecture, a glossary and a list of acronyms;

– the justification of the final architecture and the decisions taken to achieve this architecture.

3.3.5. *Summary*

Following the previously discussed study, we make a comparative summary (see Table 3.2) between the three approaches based on the following seven criteria:

– Area covered:

- the area covered by the "4+1" View Model is the AD of a software-intensive system guided by scenarios and agreeing with incremental development processes such as RUP,

- IEEE 42010 refers to the standardization of concepts and practices related to the description of a software-intensive system architectural design,

- the V&B approach is the documentation of an AD that is decomposed into several views for the various stakeholders and that meet their requirements.

– Approach focused on:

- IEEE 42010 and the V&B approach is based on the requirements of various stakeholders of the system being built,

- the “4+1” View Model is rather focused on the different phases of system development.

– Status/number of views: by status, we mean if the views are fixed and predefined by the approaches or if they can be created by the architect (by instantiating a metaconcept):

- in the “4+1” view model: the views are fixed and their number is 5. Notwithstanding this, all projects are not required to specify the five views but possibly a subset of them. The architect chooses this subset,

- in the V&B approach, combining existing views can create new views but the architect cannot introduce new styles and new categories of styles (viewtypes).

– Categorization of views:

- in the IEEE 42010, architectural views are categorized in viewpoints. A viewpoint is a specification of the construction agreements and the use of a view. A view must conform to a viewpoint,

- in the V&B approach, views are organized in viewtypes. A viewtype represents the structure of the system in terms of a set of elements and relationships between them according to agreements and notations defined in different styles,

- the “4+1” view model has not defined a clear organizing principle for its five views.

– Architectural styles associated with views:

- in the “4+1” view model, Kruchten noted the possibility of applying styles to different architectural views as, for instance, the object-oriented style for the logical view and the Pipes and Filters styles for the process view, etc. However, he did not formalize the application of these styles and he gave the designer complete flexibility to choose the architectural styles for the views,

- in the V&B approach, architectural styles are explicitly and formally associated with different viewtypes like the Pipes and Filters style associated with the C&C viewtype,

- IEEE 42010 did not consider architectural styles for views.

– Integration of views:

- within the "4+1" view model, the four main views (logical, development, process and physical) are integrated through a fifth view, which is the "scenario" view, whereby the notation "4+1" view model emanates;

- in the V&B approach, the view integration is considered in the second stage of the guide, where the designer combines the views which, according to him, seem close to one another and neglects the other views that focus on the details included in the other views.

– Levels of abstraction associated with views: to our knowledge, the V&B approach is the only approach that (implicitly) introduced levels of abstraction or information. These levels are considered in the first step of the process during which the designer must specify the level of information for each cell of the table built (detailed information, some information and overview information).

	"4+1" View model	ISO/IEC/IEEE 42010	V&B
Area targeted	Software design	Architectural description	Architectural documentation
Approach centered on	Different design phases	Stakeholders	Stakeholders
Status/number of views	Fixed/five views	Variable/number defined by the architect	Variable/number defined by the architect
Categorization of views	Informal	*Viewpoint*	*Viewtype*
Architectural styles associated with views	Yes	--	Yes
Integration of views	Through the scenario view	--	Through step 2 of the guide (combine views)
Levels of abstraction associated with views	--	--	Informal (level of information)

Table 3.2. *A comparison between the three different approaches*

3.3.6. *Limitation of current approaches to software architecture*

Within software architecture, approaches working on the *view* concept have effectively contributed in the software development process. In fact, they have led to the reduction of the complexity of an AD by combining all the information and treatments related to specific concerns; it is the complexity caused by the multitude of concerns. However, some limitations may be noted. Among these limitations, we note:

– The persistence of complexity within views: in fact, if the views have solved the problem caused by the complexity owing to the multitude of concerns raised above, an AD must be able to provide some solutions for another form of complexity: the intraview complexity which is owing to the need to consider a hierarchical description at different levels. In fact, it is essential to take a hierarchical approach that reveals different levels of understanding in a view. In other words, the architect needs to decompose a view into several levels and needs to specify the links and types of links between these levels. Besides the fact that this description in multiple levels helps to reduce the complexity within a view, it assists us to better meet the requirements of stakeholders which, depending on the circumstance, need to study a detailed or semi-detailed overall description of a view and navigate between these levels of description.

– The proposal of a process of AD taking into account the two forms of complexity approaches: for instance, the Kruchten and Clements approaches proposed a guide for the selection of viewpoints and views, but none of them have formally integrated levels of hierarchies, in conjunction with views.

– The problem of inconsistency between the views: no approach has brought a formal solution to the problem of inconsistency between the portions of descriptions raised from different views which are inevitably complementary and dependent.

3.4. Definitions and basic concepts of multihierarchy/multiview software architectures

3.4.1. *Definitions*

3.4.1.1. *System*

The system concept can be given in several ways:

– a system can be compared to a combination of software elements connected to one another and forming one entity;

– a system can be described as a set of subsystems forming a unit that act and interact jointly to achieve a purpose;

– a system can be described recursively as a hierarchical organization of subsystems (principle of decomposability), which considered themselves as systems in their own right (principle of unitarity). The decomposition of a system is carried out in two forms: structural and behavioral.

These definitions are valid for any system, whether it is conceptual, concrete or abstract.

3.4.1.2. *Complex system*

In order to design "good" systems, it is essential to have models for structuring the complexity, often translated into technical, cognitive and social relationships of the said systems as well as in their interactions. The complexity is not, however, an objective characteristic of a system. In a system, the perception of complexity depends upon the chosen structure and method of resolution of the conceptual model to help it enhance understanding.

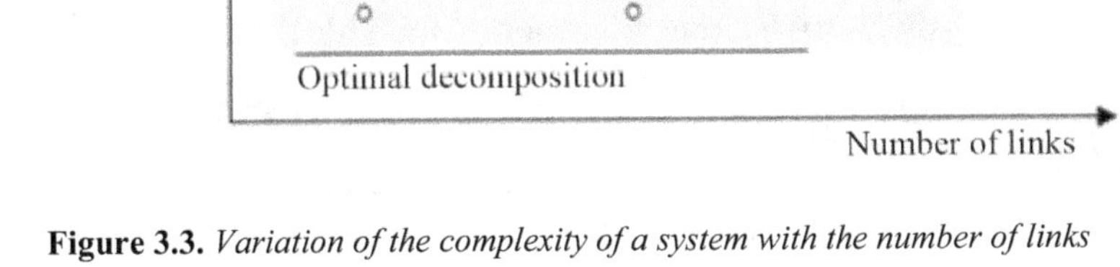

Figure 3.3. *Variation of the complexity of a system with the number of links*

3.4.1.3. *Software architecture*

A software architecture describes a system as a set of components that interact with one another through simple or complex links. The software architecture allows us to take into account high-level descriptions of systems and reason about their properties at a high level of abstraction (interaction protocol, compliance with other architectures, etc.). For instance, software architecture allows the explanation of the complexity of a software system in an understandable and modular manner.

Hereafter, we consider that software architecture is itself a system and therefore responds, in the same way as a system, to the set of concepts and modeling techniques that we introduce later in this chapter.

3.4.2. *Concepts and basics*

3.4.2.1. *Modeling*

Modeling is an act of identifying a system and then designing a model (or image) similar to this system. The similarity implies a one-to-one correspondence between the system and its image (model). This conceptualization of similarity can be translated by:

– An isomorphism: it is a bijective correspondence, such that every element of the model (co-domain) matches an element and only one element of the system (domain) and vice versa;

– A monomorphism: it is an injective correspondence such that any element in the system (domain) corresponds to at least one element of the model (co-domain), but not every element of the model has a correspondence with an element of the system;

– An epimorphism: it is a surjective correspondence, such that every element of the model (co-domain) matches at least one element of the system (domain), the opposite not being true.

It is clear that, to study a system, the ideal correspondence is isomorphism. However, on the one hand, it is often impossible to have this type of correspondence for feasibility reasons, and on the other hand, because a system generally requires several models to be represented (physical, thermal models, etc.). Also, we will give the following definition to modeling.

DEFINITION 3.1.– *Modeling is an epimorphism between a system and a model whose purpose is to provide a simplified and observable representation of the structure and behavior of the system.*

3.4.2.2. *Metamodeling*

The term "meta" is of Greek origin and means "succession, transformation, change". In scientific neologisms (metalanguage and metamathematical), meta means that which exceeds and includes (an object of thought, science) (Robert Dictionary). Nowadays this term is broken down endlessly: "a meta person says when he talks about what he or someone else said" [PIT 90]. In computing, the term metaknowledge refers to knowledge about knowledge, for instance a metamodel representing a model.

In our context, metamodeling is an act of modeling applied to a model. It is a question of developing a model by itself or of using a model to explain or develop another model. This act of modeling can also aim to document a model or to bear all or part of its lifecycle.

Metamodeling can also help a model to self-represent and therefore, in this case, it is called reflexive modeling.

3.4.2.3. *Model*

A model is a simplified and abstract representation of the structure and behavior of a system with a view to provide a line of reasoning related to the system considered.

A model plays the role of interface between a system and a user. No model should be separated from its modeler: it can provide a line of reasoning to the system considered and to the objectives of the modeler, but it cannot be used in another context. It is important to develop models describing their essential properties and ignoring properties that the modeler, based on expected results, judge minor. Any model must contain all the important aspects of the system studied while, at the same time, respecting the principle of simplicity. A model must be able to easily take into account the evolution of the system studied.

For instance, we may associate one or more models to software architecture, as a system, such as a conceptual model (or architecture) and a model of execution.

3.4.2.4. *Views and levels of hierarchy*

The key point of the modeling of a complex system, such as that of a software architecture, is structuring the pattern associated there with. Within a model, we also establish two types of structures:

– a vertical structure: paraphrasing the different views of the same model;

– a horizontal structure: corresponding to a hierarchy of levels of understanding (referred to hereafter as levels of hierarchy) in model views.

3.4.2.5. *Views*

On the basis of the fact that a system can be analyzed according to different views (from different angles), we can say that a model of a system generally consists of a distinct set of views reflecting different aspects during the successive stages of a given application. This approach can be compared to how a specialist within a certain discipline focuses on a specific problem. The most commonly used views, during the modeling phase, are the structural view and the behavioral view. However, this does not preclude other choices, such as taking into account the physical aspect or even the thermal aspect of a system. Thus, the list of views to be established is not fixed; quite the contrary, it develops and directly depends on the type of problem being studied as well as the scope of the application.

Models, seen from this angle, are called multiview models.

It is one of the views commonly used in the process of modeling a system:

– Behavioral views: a behavioral view specifies the behavior and characteristics of inputs/outputs of a "black box" system; knowledge of the physical realization of this element should not appear in this view type.

– Structural views: by structure we mean the topology of the model.

– Physical views: a physical view refers to the physical description of a particular model, i.e. the geometric aspects (geometric measurements) and components (materials, etc.).

The physical view can be described as lexical, with a structural view of the syntactic and the behavioral view of semantics.

If we take the example of the conceptual model of a component-based software architecture, we can define three views: a "component" view defining the different components of storage and computing software architecture, a "connector" view defining the various interactions between these components and a "configuration" view reflecting the topology of components and connectors.

3.4.2.6. *Levels of hierarchy*

Despite the opportunities that the multiview approach offers, it is common that the development of a given view of a model is too complex to be implemented directly. Also, and in order to control this complexity gradually, it is essential to take a hierarchical approach that reveals different levels of understanding in a view.

We identify four types of levels of hierarchy:

– levels of hierarchy of abstraction;

– levels of hierarchy of description;

– conceptual levels of hierarchy;

– levels of hierarchy of modeling.

3.4.2.6.1. Levels of hierarchy of abstraction

It is often necessary to describe a view of a model at a number of levels of abstraction. Human experts use this type of approach to address complex problems.

By defining an appropriate (suitable) level of abstraction for a given application phase, we limit the amount of semantic information being considered by relegating irrelevant details at a lower level of abstraction.

The level of abstraction of a view of a model includes:

– the structure of data of the model associated at that level;

– the tools whose use is specified by the domain expert to stipulate the types of reasoning attached to the model considered.

NOTE.– The number of levels of abstraction depends mainly upon the complexity of the views studied. The decomposition of a view of a model is not necessarily isomorphic to the decomposition of other views of the same model, although in certain types of design this isomorphism is imposed to facilitate verification problems.

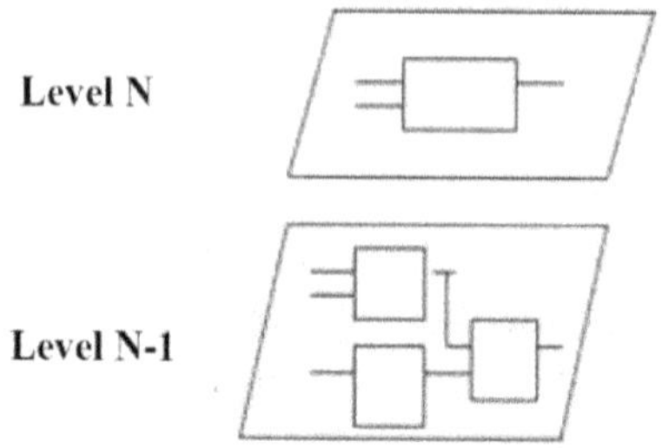

Figure 3.4. *Levels of hierarchy of abstraction*

3.4.2.6.2. Levels of hierarchy of description

This type of hierarchy is a "flat hierarchy", where it is possible to describe different representations of a given element, within the same level of abstraction, by providing more or less subtle descriptions while keeping the same types of inputs and outputs.

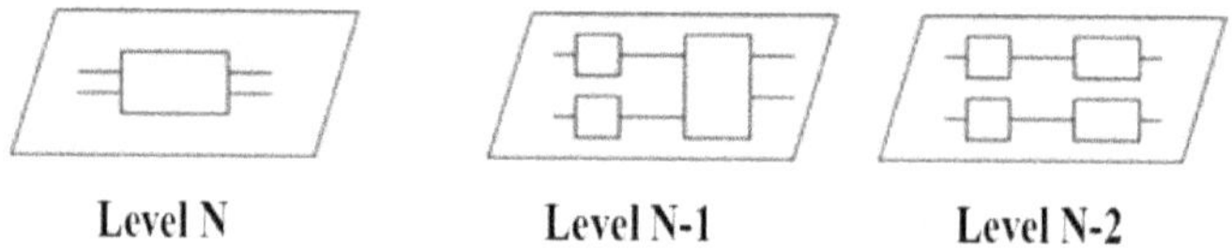

Figure 3.5. *Levels of hierarchy of description*

Figure 3.5 [AMI 10] shows how to break down function P_0 at the level of description L_n into a set of subfunctions $\{P_{01}, P_{02}, P_{03}\}$ at level L_{n-1}. Similarly each function of level L_{n-1} is broken down into a further series of subfunctions at level L_{n-2} and until level L_0. The last level of the hierarchy is a set of non-decomposable primitive functions representing the behavior described by elements that are available in the architect's library. The set of levels represents the hierarchy of description.

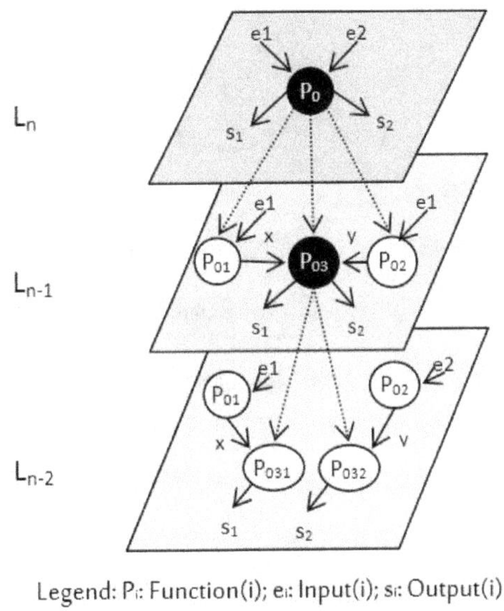

Figure 3.6. *Example of a function hierarchy description*

3.4.2.6.3. Conceptual level of hierarchy

Conceptual hierarchy, in a library, enables the organization of elements of levels of hierarchy of abstraction or of description by level of generality (generalization/specialization).

3.4.2.6.4. Level of hierarchy of modeling

This type of hierarchy allows us to establish the correspondence links between different levels of modeling (e.g. meta-metaarchitecture, metaarchitecture, architecture and architecture-instance), similar to the four levels of modeling of the pyramid models defined by the OMG [OMG 11].

Models incorporating these four types of hierarchy are called multihierarchy models.

3.4.2.6.5. Multihierarchy/multiview models

The complexity of a conceptual view of a model may, in its description, require a hierarchical approach, which emphasizes the different levels of hierarchy or range of resolution of the information to be represented.

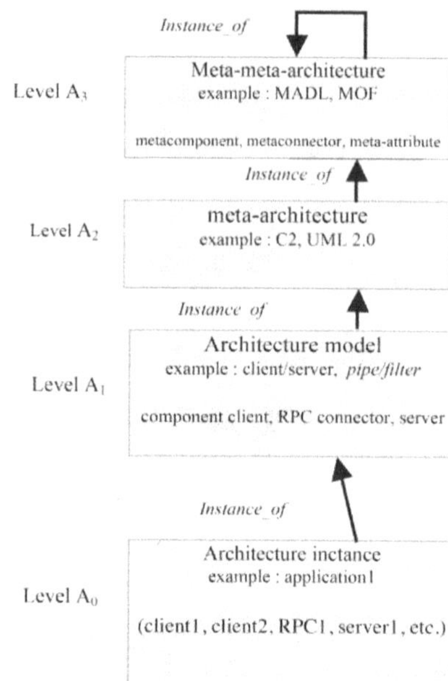

Figure 3.7. *Example of levels of hierarchy of modelization*

At a given level of hierarchy, only the essential information in relation to that level are represented, however the details of the same information are relegated to lower levels

Moreover, the different views of a given model are usually related. Two distinct views of the model considered can, in fact, express complementary aspects of this model or identical aspects with, however, the help of different concepts or distinct levels of hierarchies.

Consequently, manipulations of a view of a given model may have a knock-on effect on other views. Generating information in a view may require information, which comes from other views. This leads us to explicitly establish, on the one hand, existing links between levels of hierarchy of a view of a model and, on the other hand, between the conceptual views of the same model.

We have identified different types of links that are included in the definition of multihierarchy/multiview models:

– intralevel links: they generally refer to:

- existing connection links between two elements belonging to the same level of abstraction or description,

- existing inheritance links between two elements belonging to the same conceptual level.

– the interlevel links (also called intraview) among which we count:

- composition links: indicate existing links between an element belonging to a level of abstraction or description N and the elements corresponding to the more detailed description of the same element at lower abstraction or description level,

- aggregation links represent inverse semantics of composition links,

- expansion links allows us to process the input/output information of a level of abstraction to the adjacent lower level, which requires the use of a translator (a translator is used to define how the same data and protocols are represented in two different representations of data),

- compression links represent inverse semantics of expansion links,

- instantiation links existing between an element belonging to a level of modeling and its instance belonging to the lower level of modeling,

- inheritance links existing between an element of a level of abstraction or description and an element of a conceptual level,

- membership links existing between an element belonging to a level (of abstraction, description or conceptual) and a level modeling.

Hierarchy	Abstraction	Description	Design	Modeling
Abstraction	Connection Composition Expansion Aggregation Compression	Composition	Legacy	Membership
Description	Aggregation	Connection Composition Aggregation	Legacy	Membership
Design	-	-	Legacy	Membership
Modeling	Composition	Composition	Composition	Instantiation

Table 3.3. *Intra- and interlinks levels of hierarchy*

– *Inter-view* links: two cases are to be distinguished:

- The transition from one view to another is carried out between two representations of the same level of abstraction belonging to two different views. It is then generally algorithmic, for example the transition from an algebraic description of a Boolean function toward a representation in logic gates, this transition therefore relies on previous interlevel links.

- The transition is carried out between two different levels of abstraction of two views of a model. It is generally based on heuristics or model transformations, for example the case of a transition of a mask pattern (physical view) to the logical schema (structural view). In fact, in addition to the problem of changing concepts between the two views, one is faced with a problem of aggregation or decomposition.

– Users' links whose semantic is given by the different user categories (see section 3.4.2.7).

Figure 3.2 shows the existing relation(s) between line → column, for example a component of a level of abstraction is composed of one or more elements of the lower level of abstraction (via the composition link).

3.4.2.7. *Software architecture user categories*

The modeling that we propose allows an application developer, who is neither a domain expert nor a software architect, to effectively solve the problem via manipulation of multihierarchy/multiview models. The description of the models should be as simple as possible, in terms of both manipulated concepts and the amount of elements to describe. Therefore, we identified five user categories:

– To facilitate the task of the applications' end-user (UF) of a software architecture, we are led to distinguish between different categories of stakeholders.

– The librarian (BI) whose role is to build and manage libraries of reusable elements of each level of hierarchy of modeling (A3, A2, A1 and A0 in Figure 3.7), which helps to describe the more complex models. The librarian will thus prevent other users redescribing reusable elements.

– The applications architect (AA) holds knowledge about a given domain. He is the expert of the application domain. On the one hand, his role is to provide knowledge specific to a family of architectures and, on the other hand, to specify the tools and appropriate resolution strategies for a given architecture. The AA will allow the end user to only manipulate concepts known by the latter. The AA is concerned with the A1 level of hierarchy of modeling.

– The manufacturer of architectural language (CLA), better known by the name software architect, defines the architecture description language needed to describe and manipulate architectures. His role is to develop specific tools for experts (application architects and librarians) to release from software constraints. The CLA is concerned with the A2 modeling level.

– In addition to these four user categories (UF, BI, AA and CLA), there is the manufacturer of the architectural meta-language (CMLA), who defines the basic architectural concepts on which the CLA is based to define the AD language. The CMLA is concerned by the highest level of hierarchy of modeling, namely A3.

Each of these user categories may be associated with several points of view, but users belonging to the same category, for example in the automotive field, at the AA category, can be associated with mechanical, electrical and thermal points of view.

To summarize, at the A3 level (meta-metamodel), the CMLA builds standard basic building blocks to assist the CLA, at the A2 level (metamodel), to build a language for describing architectures. Due to this language, the AA at the A1 level (model) builds a class or family of architectures that will be used by the UF, at the A0 level, by instantiating this class of architectures and developing its application. In the meantime, however, the BI can intervene on all four levels of hierarchy of modeling to help each of thc other user categories to reuse, at their level, all information previously stored and filed and useful for building their different applications.

3.5. MoVAL: architecture based on models, views and levels of abstraction

3.5.1. *Introduction*

To illustrate all the concepts mentioned above, in this section, we present an approach, which we have developed and which we call *Model, View and*

Abstraction Level based software architecture (MoVAL) [KHE 13]. This approach aims to offer the software architect tools to facilitate his task of building a model that is documented through an associated AD, and that is understandable and easily manipulated by various stakeholders.

3.5.2. *MoVAL*

In the MoVAL approach, a model is conceptualized by a matrix (Figure 3.8), where the columns represent different views of said model and the rows represent the hierarchy of levels of abstraction associated with each view. Thus, the rows and columns, respectively, illustrate the two types of horizontal and vertical structures mentioned above in section 3.4.2.4.

In fact, this MoVAL structuring does not preclude the fact that in simple, trivial cases, the design matrix can be reduced to a single element; this is where the AA, for example, decides to associate with his/her model a single view having a single hierarchy level of abstraction.

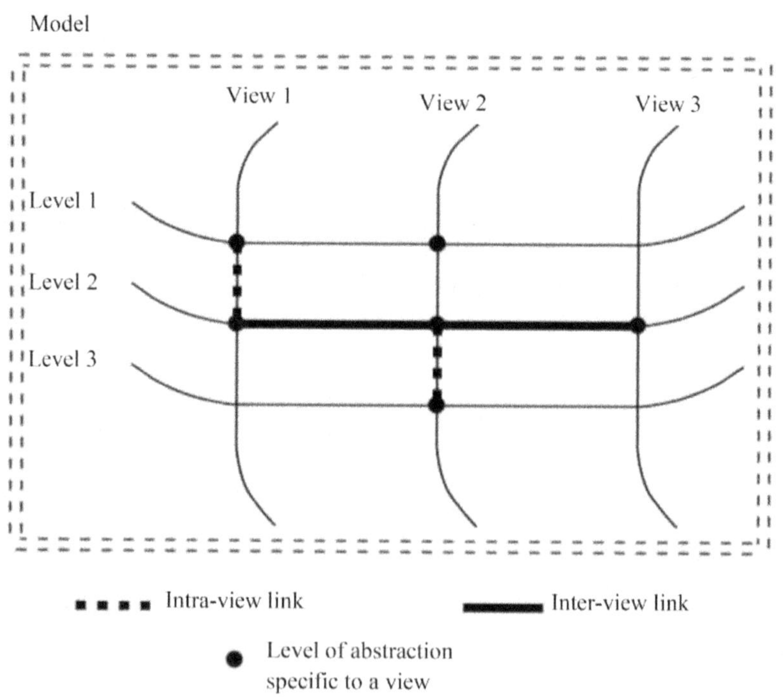

Figure 3.8. *Matrix representative of the MoVAL model*

3.5.2.1. *Views of a model*

Generally, a view from a MoVAL model can be seen as a representation of this model by considering some aspects of the development process and some problems associated with a specific category or a set of categories of stakeholders. In fact, these aspects and problems are grouped into viewpoints, which are themselves separate entities, also, grouping formalisms defining modeling languages and tools, combined with the disciplines covered by these viewpoints. Consequently, a view will always be associated with a specific viewpoint that can be predefined as the behavioral, structural and physical views (see section 3.4.2.5). Similarly, a view can be customized according to different fields of application, such as a mechanical viewpoint in a system of automotive construction.

3.5.2.2. *Levels of hierarchy of a view*

Each view of the MoVAL is described using a hierarchy of levels of abstraction and description.

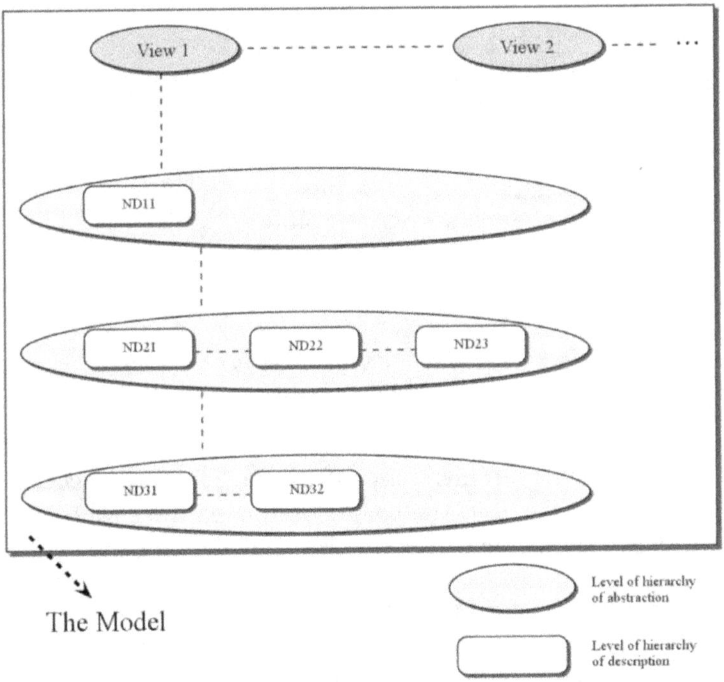

Figure 3.9. *View and levels of hierarchy*

3.5.2.2.1. Levels of hierarchy of abstraction

In the MoVAL, a level of hierarchy of abstraction represents a level of detail defined by the AA to implement certain details and relegate others considered irrelevant, to the lower levels of abstraction. The AA can model different views of the system by determining a collection of concepts that are common to certain points of view and grouped into levels of hierarchy of abstraction common (called common abstract bases), for example in Figure 3.10, V1, V2 and V3 views share the same common base at level of abstraction AL1, V1 and V2 views share the same common base at level of abstraction AL2 and finally views V1 and V3 share the same common base (different from the previous) at the level of abstraction AL2.

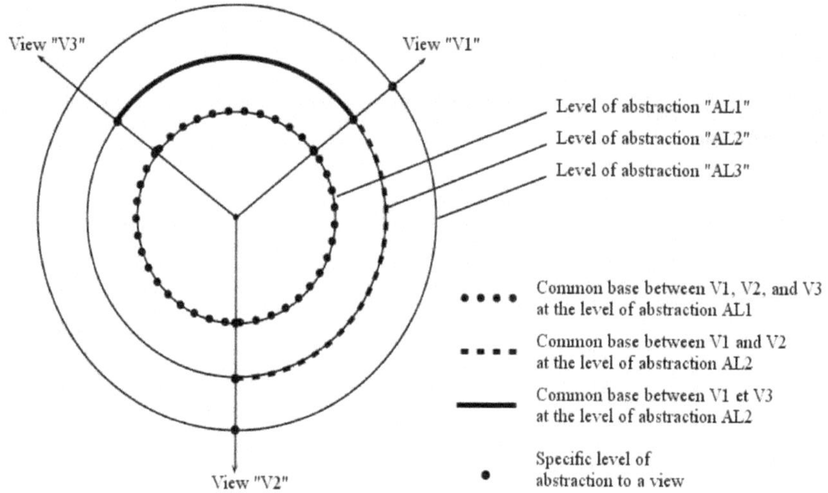

Figure 3.10. *Figure representing the common bases between the different views of a model*

In addition, a level of hierarchy of abstraction must accept specific formalisms that will be used in the definition of the different levels of hierarchy of description associated with this level of hierarchy of abstraction.

Note that the views of a MoVAL model are not necessarily isomorphic. In fact, a given level of hierarchy of abstraction can be defined in a view of the model but not necessarily in other views of this model. For example, as shown in Figure 3.8, level of abstraction 1 is only defined on view 1 and view 2 (expressed in the matrix by bold points).

3.5.2.2.2. Levels of hierarchy of description

The second level of hierarchy associated with a view is the level of hierarchy of description. In this level, the various structural elements of the level of hierarchy of abstraction will be described in a more or less subtle manner (see section 3.4.2.6.2) while respecting the formalism used in the level of hierarchy of abstraction involved.

3.5.2.3. *Links*

Links are structural elements defined in MoVAL to clarify and formalize the relationship between the different levels of hierarchy in a model. As already mentioned in section 3.4.2.6.5, these links are grouped in four categories, namely:

– inter-view links, which represent the relationship between two distinct levels of hierarchy belonging to two distinct views;

– interlevel links, representing similar relationships to those relations represented by the inter-view links, except that the two levels of hierarchy compared belong to the same view of the model;

– intralevel links, which represent the internal relationships between the elements of a same level of hierarchy;

– users links, which necessarily belong to one of the three categories above, and have attributes and structural or semantic properties defined *a priori* by the AA. In fact, this category of links provides modularity and the use and reuse of structural elements of a software architecture.

The links are defined in MoVAL through four main attributes:

– source: each link is defined by its origin which can be either a level of hierarchy of abstraction or a level of hierarchy of description of a view;

– destination: similarly, the destination of a link corresponds to either a level of hierarchy of abstraction or to a level of hierarchy of description of a view;

– semantic role: the semantic role of a link defines the nature of the relationship between the source and the destination, it is dependent on the associated categories of links and the type of source and destination elements. Thus, the semantics of a link can have one of these three roles:

- a simple connection that defines consistency rules between source and destination elements belonging to the same level of hierarchy. This type of link can only occur in the case of intralevel links,

- a composition, specifying the composition of the source elements in a lower level. This type of link concerns the interlevel links of abstraction or description,

- an expansion, specifying the transformations of input/output at the source abstraction level, to input/output at the destination (lower) abstraction level. Note that this type of relationship may only be valid in cases where the links are inter-view or interlevel and the source and destination elements are the levels of hierarchy of abstraction. Note that composition and expansion links are used in cases where the AA takes a top-down methodology of building architecture, however, in the case of taking a bottom-up methodology, other roles that have inverse semantics have been defined in MoVAL, which are respectively the roles of aggregation and compression.

– Semantic link: it includes a set of semantic attributes that embody the semantic role defined for this link. Among these attributes, we note:

- dependence: it specifies that the existence of the destination element depends on the source element,

- predominance: the semantics of the predominance is the opposite of that of dependence,

- consistency: it specifies the rules that must be followed by the destination element based on the parameters of the source element. These rules can be expressed through languages like OCL. These rules do not affect the existence of the destination element.

3.5.3. *MoVAL metamodel*

MoVAL metamodel is intended to be consistent with ISO/IEC/IEEE 42010. Thus, several factors have kept their definitions compared to those presented in the IEEE, for instance definitions of a system architecture, an AD, a stakeholder, a viewpoint or concerns. Other definitions have been introduced such as abstraction levels, description levels and semantic links.

As defined in IEEE, a system is a software entity regardless of its name, shape and size. Thus, a system can be an independent application, a subsystem or even a system of systems.

IEEE also defines stakeholders associated with a system as individuals, teams or organizations involved in one or more design, development and validation phase of the system (developers, architects, experts, users, etc.).

Simultaneously, a system has an architecture, which will be documented and described through an AD decomposed into several views. Each view is consistent with a particular viewpoint that encompasses a set of concerns, and is represented by a hierarchy of abstraction and description.

The description of a level of hierarchy, and thus a view, relies on a set of formalisms defining the lexical and syntactic elements of modeling specific to this level of hierarchy.

Figure 3.11 shows the MoVAL metamodel based on that of ISO/IEC/IEEE42010.

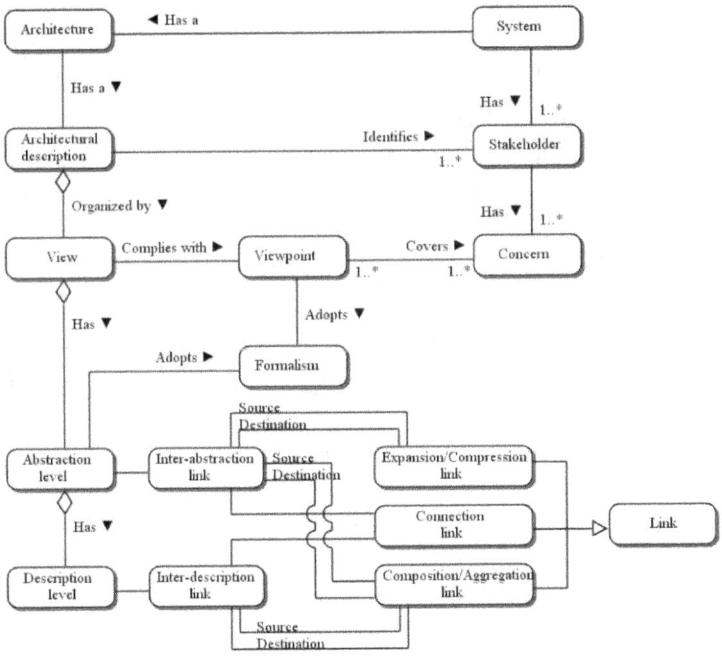

Figure 3.11. *MoVAL metamodel*

3.5.4. *Case study*

To clarify MoVAL concepts (described by the CA), a case study is presented in this section (described by AA). In what follows, let us consider an eCommerce web application, where stores are registered to exhibit their products for sale.

Consider the four following viewpoints (corresponding to four distinct UF):

– A physical viewpoint: referencing the resources used and the system hardware architecture under construction. This view is a predefined viewpoint, which is associated with a single formalism, namely the UML deployment diagram. The view associated with this viewpoint is represented by a single level of hierarchy of abstraction, which is itself represented by a single level of hierarchy of description as shown in Figures 3.12 and 3.13, respectively. Note that this view is associated with a stakeholder who is the system engineer;

– A database viewpoint: referencing the data structure (i.e. the database), and having formalisms such as ERD associated with it (i.e. the Entity Relationship Diagram) and the physical data diagram in 3NF. The stakeholder associated with this view is normally the database administrator;

– A site administrator viewpoint: representing the system from the viewpoint of the site administrator and illustrating the modeling of concerns associated with this stakeholder. Formalisms defined (by the AA) for this view are use case diagrams, sequence diagrams and UML class diagrams. The view associated with that view can be defined in two levels of hierarchy of abstraction illustrated in Figure 3.14;

– A store administrator viewpoint: representing the system from the point of view of the store administrators. This view, however, takes the same formalism of the viewpoint of the site administrator and is also represented by two levels of hierarchy of abstraction shown in Figure 3.15.

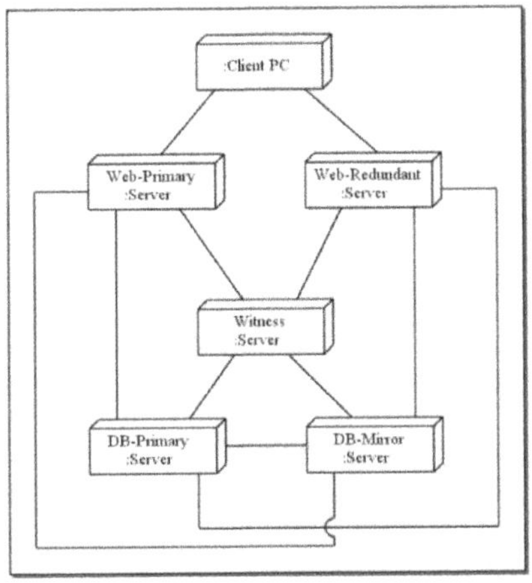

Figure 3.12. *The level of hierarchy of abstraction of the physical view*

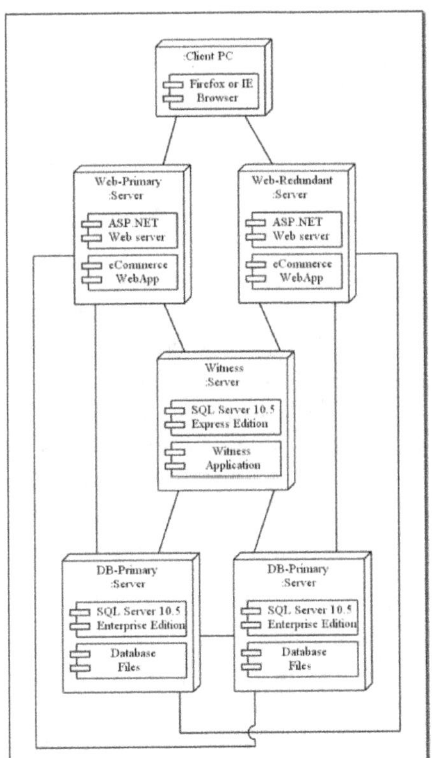

Figure 3.13. *The level of hierarchy of description of the physical view*

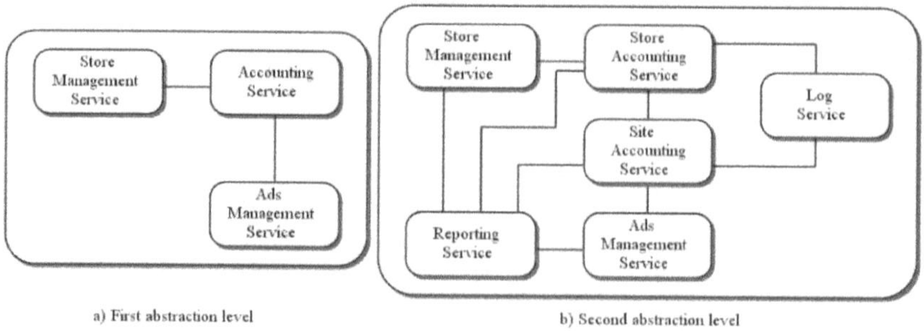

Figure 3.14. *The two levels of hierarchy of abstraction of the "site administrator"*

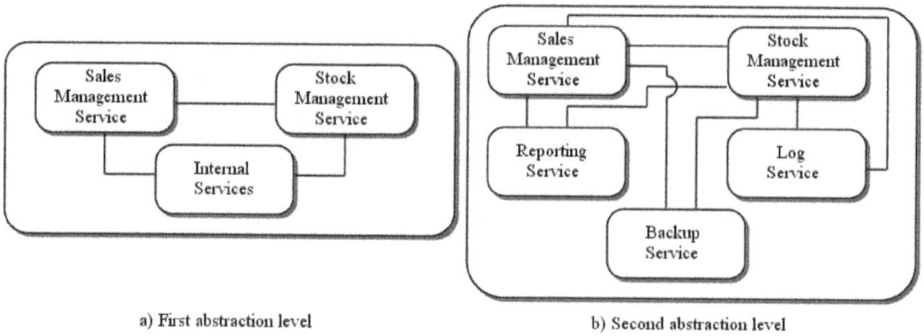

Figure 3.15. *The two levels of hierarchy of abstraction of the view "store administrator"*

The two levels of hierarchy of abstraction of the site administrator view can be associated with two levels of hierarchy of abstraction of the store administrator view, called the first and second functional level, respectively. Similarly, the level of hierarchy of abstraction of the physical view can be associated with the level of hierarchy of abstraction of the database view, called full level.

In addition, three links are established in this example:

– an interlevel link with the first functional level of the "site administrator" view as source and the second functional level of the same view as destination. This link is a composition link defining its semantic attribute of coherence of the composition of the "service accounts" by two other components in the level of hierarchy of destination, which are the "accounting department website" and the "store accounting service";

– an interlevel link with the first functional level of the "store administrator" view as source and the second functional level of the same view as destination. This link is an expansion link defining semantic attribute of coherence of the expansion of "internal services" into two other components in the level of hierarchy of destination, which are the "newspaper registration service" and "backup service";

– a user link, named "reuse", created by the AA represents an inter-view link between the views of the "site administrator" and "store administrator" and defining the reuse of the "customer service" in the second functional level of the "site administrator" view (source) and the same hierarchy level of the "store administrator" view (destination).

Figure 3.16 shows the matrix representing the ecommerce model achieved.

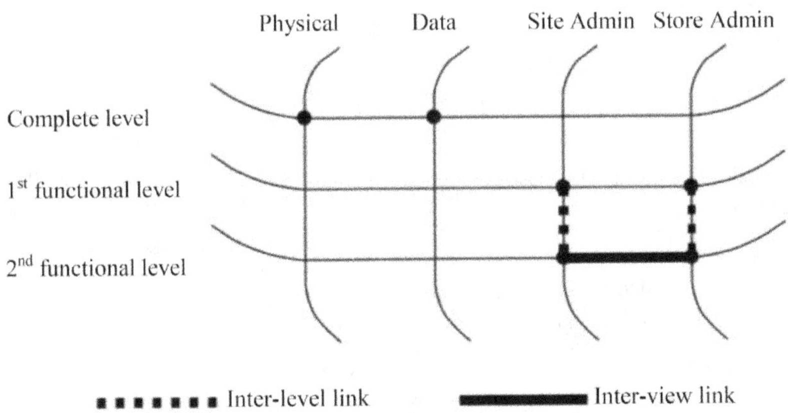

Figure 3.16. *The matrix representing the e-commerce model*

3.6. Conclusion

In this chapter, a literature review is made on the different approaches based on the viewpoints and the views arising from four fields related to software engineering, namely: requirements specifications, system modeling, system implementation and, finally, software architectures. In the field of software architecture, we identified the benefits and limitations of approaches, in which, in their proposals, the views, points of view and levels of abstractions have been incorporated.

Also, we have emphasized that the views and points of views are insufficient to develop the complex model of a software architecture and suggested the need for a hierarchical approach that reveals different levels of understanding in a view, thereby gradually controlling complexity.

Finally, we introduced our approach called MoVAL, which offers a description of a software architecture based on the concepts of views, points of views and levels of hierarchy. It helps to divide an AD into several views and levels associated with reducing the complexity of the models achieved and better meeting the expectations of various stakeholders, namely in the personalization of models, in their representations at gradual levels of complexities and thereafter, in a straightforward understanding of the models.

3.7. Bibliography

[AMI 10] AMIRAT A., Contribution à l'élaboration d'architectures logicielles à hiérarchies multiples, Doctoral Thesis, University of Nantes, 2010.

[ANW 10] ANWAR A., EBERSOLD S., COULETTE B., *et al.*, "A rule-driven approach for composing viewpoint-oriented models", *Journal of Object Technology*, vol. 9, no. 2, pp. 89–114, 2010.

[ANW 11] ANWAR A., DKAKI T., EBERSOLD S., *et al.*, "A formal approach to model composition applied to VUML", *16th IEEE International Conference on Engineering of Complex Computer Systems (ICECCS)*, Las Vegas, USA, April, 2011.

[BOB 77] BOBROW D.G., WINOGRAD T., "An overview of KRL, a knowledge representation language", *Cognitive Science*, vol. 1, pp. 3–46, 1977.

[BOB 83] BOBROW D.G., STEFIK M., *The Loops Manual: Preliminary Vision*, Intelligent Systems Laboratory, Xerox Corporation, 1983.

[BUS 96] BUSCHMANN F., MEUNIER R., ROHNERT H., *et al.*, *Pattern-Oriented Software Architecture, Volume 1: A System of Patterns*, Wiley, New York, 1996.

[CAR 90] CARRÉ B., DEKKER L., GEIB J.M., "Multiple and evolutive representation in the ROME language", *The 2nd International Conference on Technology of Object-Oriented Languages and Systems (TOOLS)*, Paris, France, 1990.

[CLE 02] CLEMENTS P.C., BACHMANN F., BASS L., *et al.*, *A Practical Method for Documenting Software Architectures*, Research Showcase, Carnegie Mellon University, 2002.

[DEL 90] DELUGACH H.S., "Using conceptual graphs to analyze multiple views of software requirements", *The 5th Annual Workshop on Conceptual Structures*, Linköping University, Boston & Stockholm, 1990.

[DIJ 08] DIJKMAN R.M., QUARTEL D.A.C., VAN SINDEREN M.J., "Consistency in multi-viewpoint design of enterprise information systems", *Information and Software Technology*, vol. 50, no. 7, pp. 737–752, 2008.

[FIN 89] FINKELSTEIN A., FUKS H., "Multiparty specification", *ACM SIGSOFT Software Engineering Notes*, vol. 14, pp. 185–195, 1989.

[ISO 11] ISO/IEC/IEEE, "Systems and software engineering – architecture description", ISO/IEC/IEEE 42010:2011(E) (Revision of ISO/IEC 42010:2007 and IEEE Std 1471-2000), 2011.

[KHE 13] KHEIR A., NAJA H., OUSSALAH M., *et al.*, "Overview of an approach describing multi-views/multi-abstraction levels software architecture", *8th International Conference on Evaluation of Novel Approaches to Software Engineering (ENASE 2013)*, France, July 2013.

[KRU 95] KRUCHTEN P., "The 4+ 1 view model of architecture", *IEEE Software*, vol. 12, no. 6, pp. 42–50, 1995.

[MCH 06] MCHEICK H., MILI H., SADOU S., *et al.*, *A Comparison of Aspect Oriented Software Development Techniques for Distributed Applications*, IADIS Press, 2006.

[MIL 99] MILI H., DARGHAM J., MILI A., *et al.*, "View programming for decentralized development of OO programs", *30th International Conference on Technology of Object-Oriented Languages and Systems (TOOLS)*, Santa Barbara, California, 1999..

[MIN 75] MINSKY M., "A Framework for Representing Knowledge", In P.H. WINSTON (Ed.), *The psychology of computer vision. New York: McGraw-Hill*, 1975.

[MUL 79] MULLERY G.P., "CORE-a method for controlled requirement specification", *The 4th International Conference on Software Engineering*, Munich, Allemagne, 1979.

[NAJ 98] NAJA H., "La Représentation Multiple d'Objets Pour l'Ingénierie", *Revue l'Objet: Logiciel, Bases de Données, Réseaux*, vol. 4, no. 2, pp. 173–191, 1998.

[NAS 03] NASSAR M., "VUML: a viewpoint oriented UML extension", *Proceedings of the 18th IEEE International Conference on Automated Software Engineering*, Montreal, Canada, 2003

[NAS 09] NASSAR M., ANWAR A., EBERSOLD S., *et al.*, "Code generation in VUML profile: a model driven approach", *International Conference on Computer Systems and Applications (AICCSA 2009) IEEE/ACS*, 2009.

[NUS 94] NUSEIBEH B., KRAMER J., FINKELSTEIN A., "A framework for expressing the relationships between multiple views in requirements specification", *IEEE Transactions on Software Engineering*, vol. 20, no. 10, pp. 760–773, 1994.

[OMG 11] OMG, "OMG unified modeling language (OMG UML), infrastructure", Object Management Group (OMG), August 2011.

[PAR 71] PARNAS D.L., "Information distribution aspects of design methodology", *Research showcase*, Carnegie Mellon University, 1971.

[PER 92] PERRY D., WOLF A., "Foundations for the study of software architecture", *ACM SIGSOFT Software Engineering Notes*, vol. 17, no. 4, pp. 40–52, 1992.

[PIT 90] PITRAT J., *Métaconnaissance: Futur de l'intelligence artificielle*, Hermès, Paris, 1990.

[ROB 90] ROBINSON W.N., "Negotiation behavior during requirement specification", *Proceedings of the 12th International Conference on Software Engineering*, Nice, France, 1990

[ROZ 11] ROZANSKI N., WOODS E., *Software systems architecture: working with stakeholders using viewpoints and perspectives*, Addison-Wesley Professional, 2011

[SOM 97] SOMMERVILLE I., SAWYER P., "Viewpoints: principles, problems and a practical approach to requirements engineering", *Annals of Software Engineering*, vol. 3, no. 1, pp. 101–130, 1997.

Chapter 4

Software Architecture and Tools: Distributed and Coordinated Dynamic Reconfiguration Management

Dynamic reconfiguration allows an application to be modified during runtime, depending on the constraint variation of its environment and the variation in the requirements of its users. Many works have proposed methods and mechanisms for adapting a centralized application. The case of distributed applications, however, has barely been addressed. In particular, the distribution of an adaptation system is very rarely contemplated. Moreover, when a decentralized and complex application runs in heterogeneous environments, distribution of reconfiguration management mechanisms is required to improve their quality parameters, especially efficiency, robustness and evolvability.

In this chapter, we propose an approach that aims to define a component-based software architecture allowing the distributed and coordinated management of dynamic reconfiguration. We define an architectural model of adaptation systems, which allow variability of system configurations and which include mechanisms capable of specialization to ensure coordination. We have chosen replicated data management to illustrate distributed and coordinated adaptation. We present the principles of

---

Chapter written by Mohamed ZOUARI, Maria-Teresa SEGARRA and Khalil DRIRA.

implementing a tool for the construction of distributed adaptation systems. Using this tool, we present the results of distributed adaptation experiments on a data replication system in the medical field for the care of a patient at home. The application developed by the tool is made context-sensitive and capable of dynamically reconfiguring itself to offer optimum quality service to users.

4.1. Introduction

Distributed systems are run very frequently in fluctuating environments, such as mobile environments, machine clusters and grid processors. They must continue to be run in all the conditions and to offer good-quality services. Reconfiguration tasks can often lead to procedures that are time-consuming and costly in term of human effort in order to accommodate changes. Therefore, it is necessary to facilitate these tasks and define solutions for automating them. In this context, the dynamic reconfiguration paradigm was introduced in several works in order to overcome the complexity of systems administration by automating tasks necessary for their management, to minimize human intervention [LEH 00]. In this paradigm, an information system is capable of making configuration changes depending on high-level rules, and of adapting itself to a change in the runtime context (e.g. availability of resources, the type of terminals used and user activity).

The state of the art on dynamic reconfiguration highlights a diversity of architectures and mechanisms in the context of different application fields, technologies and concerns. In this chapter, we deal with the concepts and mechanisms for distributed systems reconfiguration management and current work in this field. First, we present some aspects associated with reconfiguration management and analyze a set of works enabling distributed dynamic reconfiguration management. The dynamic reconfiguration paradigm was introduced in several works, in order to address the complexity of systems administration by automating tasks necessary for their management for the purpose of minimizing human intervention. Our first objective is to facilitate construction of the adaptation system for this type of application by offering tools to cover its lifecycle, from design to runtime. The second objective is to provide a dynamic reconfiguration management solution in a distributed and coordinated way. We are primarily focused on the architectural aspect of a distributed adaptation system, dividing it into elementary functions that identify and separate different concerns. Our main contribution is in defining mechanisms for distributing and coordinating dynamic reconfiguration management activities. We illustrate these using examples of data replication systems adaptation.

In the rest of this chapter, we introduce some basic reconfiguration concepts. We then analyze both centralized and distributed dynamic reconfiguration management approaches. In section 4.4, we focus on the specialization possibilities of adaptation infrastructures. Then, we present our method and tools for constructing a reconfiguration system in section 4.6. Section 4.7 details our software architecture model for a distributed and coordinated management of dynamic reconfiguration.

4.2. Context

In the field of information systems, reconfiguration means a change in the system to take into account a change in its runtime environment [LEH 00]. Indeed, the context upgrades constantly throughout the system execution. For example, the changes in execution environment (e.g. lack of resources, network partition, etc.) can lead to undesirable consequences for the application behavior like a decline in service quality or even a break in service continuity. Thus, dynamic reconfiguration presents a suitable solution for resolving problems that are likely to appear during the runtime of an application. Among the current definitions, [LAD 00] states that reconfigurable software evaluates its own behavior and changes it when the evaluation shows that it is not accomplishing what it is intended to do, or when a better functionality or performance is possible.

A number of summaries have been produced on reconfigurable systems, to sort and collect together current research efforts. A presentation of reconfigurable system architectures, their characteristics and the challenges in their implementation was given in [SAL 09]. An extensive study of the relations between reconfigurable architectures and communication protocols was conducted in [GAZ 10]. It identifies the techniques that make it possible to attenuate communication service failures. [TAY 09] compares reconfiguration techniques used with several architectural styles, such as service-oriented architectures and peer-to-peer architectures. This study shows the need to pursue the development of new architectural styles and reconfiguration techniques, in order to facilitate the development of reconfigurable systems. Moreover, there have been a large number of studies undertaken in the field of autonomic computer science [HUE 08, KLE 08]. This type of system is characterized by the properties of self-configuration, self-optimization, self-repair and self-protection to ensure that human intervention in the system is limited.

The phases to take place during a dynamic reconfiguration were presented by IBM, notably [FAR 06] with the Monitor Analyze Plan Execute-Knowledge (MAPE-K) model, defined to follow context changes and act consequently. A similar loop has been used in several works. The term "reconfiguration process" denotes the execution of all these phases: monitoring, analysis, planning and execution. We present the four phases that constitute the reconfiguration process below (Figure 4.1):

– The monitoring process collects data on the application and its environment and correlates them, provided that they can be analyzed. Data collection is done using the interfaces provided by sensors associated with the observable entities. These data can include information on resource use, application topology, component configuration, etc. Some data are static, whereas others change continually during the application runtime. The monitoring function correlates and filters information until it determines a symptom, which must be analyzed. Several platforms have been proposed for data collection and processing [CHE 03, DEY 01, GU 04, KOR 03, ROU 08].

– The analysis process reasons on the symptoms and history of the system and analyzes the situation in order to decide when a change must be made. For example, when the analysis process finds that the response time of a component no longer responds to demands, it can generate a demand for load distribution modification.

– The planning process determines what must be changed and the method of achieving the modification. It creates or selects a procedure, i.e. a set of actions, to make the desired modification. Its role is to order actions correctly, with some having to be done before others, e.g. instancing a component before establishing its links with other application components.

– The execution process applies the previously established plan of action. These actions are completed using interfaces provided by the effectors of elements to adapt. An effector finalizes the action and produces the expected effect.

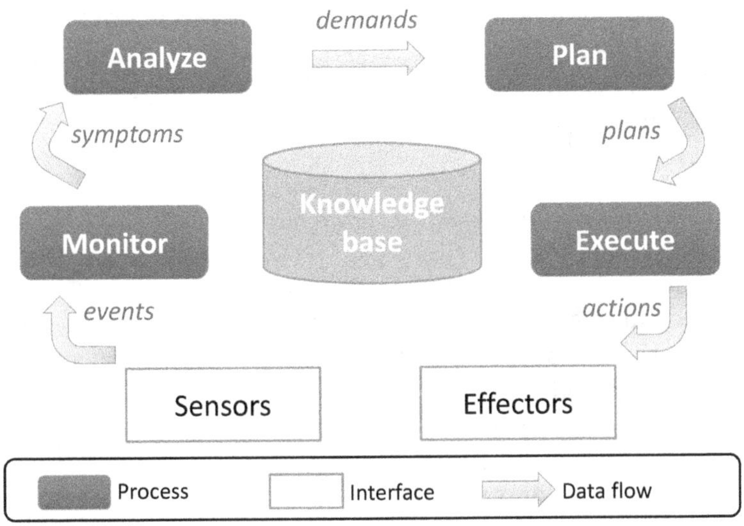

Figure 4.1. *Cooperating processes for dynamic reconfiguration*

A shared knowledge base contains the data set (history, measures, symptoms, etc.) necessary for the execution of processes. In this chapter, we have focused on the distribution and coordination of analysis and execution activities. Therefore, we chose the works discussed in the following sections, from among those that emphasize reconfiguration decision-making and the checking of adaptation actions execution.

4.3. Dynamic reconfiguration management mechanisms of distributed applications

Some research works have defined architectures and methods, which serve to provide a system of capacities for applying modifications to several entities that compose it, and on several network nodes. In this section, we are interested in this kind of reconfiguration. We present some current solutions for adapting multiple software entities during runtime and discuss their relevance for the reconfiguration of distributed applications. We call the software entity responsible for ensuring the stages of a reconfiguration process the "adaptation manager". Some approaches are based on one adaptation manager, which checks the reconfiguration of the whole application [BUI 07, FLO 06, GAR 04, ROS 06]. Other approaches allow reconfiguration management to be divided up between several adaptation managers [BRI 09, CHE 01, DOW 04]. We will examine the main characteristics of these two types of approaches and how well they fit with the distributed systems.

4.3.1. *Centralized dynamic reconfiguration management*

Reconfiguration management is centralized when it is carried out by only one adaptation manager, which applies the reconfiguration process. Then, we describe the principle of centralized reconfiguration management during the analysis, planning and execution phases. An example of current work is detailed for each of these phases.

4.3.1.1. *Centralized analysis process*

In several existing reconfiguration architectures, all the decision-making is carried out by one adaptation manager [BUI 07, DAV 03, FLO 06, GAR 04, ROS 06].

The analysis process uses a global view of the application and its environment. This global view enables the state of software entities and the characteristics of their environment to be evaluated, to determine suitable reconfiguration demands. The global view also makes it possible to take into account the dependencies between different entities, to keep the consistency of the application following a reconfiguration. For example, the choice of algorithm to implement with a reconfigurable entity requires knowledge of the algorithms, adopted by the entities that it depends on. This is essential for guaranteeing that the behaviors of all these entities are compatible with each other.

Several techniques have been used for decision-making, such as the evaluation of rules based on the event-condition-action (ECA) paradigm [DAV 03], the coupling of Bayesian and Markov decision models [PAU 98] or the use of utility functions [GAR 04].

Rainbow [GAR 04] represents a good example of an adaptation platform, simultaneously taking into account the global state of the application, and the characteristics of its runtime environment. Indeed, it relies on two types of models for making reconfiguration decisions: the architecture model and the environment model. The architecture model reflects system runtime states. It is in the form of a graph of interacting components. The curves of the graph are connectors displaying the interactions between components, which are generally realized by the middleware and distribution support. The environment model provides contextual information on the system, such as resources used and those available. For example, if additional servers are required for the execution of a service, the environment model indicates which servers are available. When a better connection is required, the environment model provides information on the bandwidth available on other communication routes. The analysis process is based on utility functions.

4.3.1.2. *Centralized planning process*

When reconfiguration management is centralized, one planner deals with providing the adaptation plan. A plan specifies the actions to apply to a set of application components, in order to achieve a new configuration. The planning process uses information concerning these components and their runtime environment, to determine the right plan. This information depends particularly on the new configuration to be achieved, and it generally includes connections between components, the state of runtime services and the availability of resources.

Some solutions have been defined to allow suitable adaptation actions to be selected [ZHA 04] or to use the effectors required during the execution of plans produced [YAR 99].

We detail the example of the approach of Zhang *et al.* [ZHA 04] because it takes into account the coexistence of several dependent software components. It is based on the analysis of dependencies to determine which software elements are affected by the reconfiguration of a component. A dependency relation specifies which components are coupled in their functioning, or the number of instances required for a component type. An adaptation graph (safe adaptation graph (SAG)) is constructed using this information to plan the reconfiguration. This graph displays a set of sequences of actions capable of producing the envisaged adaptation. It depicts the configurations as peaks and the adaptation actions as curves. Next, the Dijkstra's shortest route algorithm is applied on the graph to find a possible solution with a minimum load, where fixed costs (the length of time for reconfiguration, use of resources, etc.) are associated with adaptation actions.

4.3.1.3. *Centralized execution control process*

The execution control process implements the adaptation plan. In a centralized adaptation system, the execution of adaptation actions is controlled in a centralized way by an entity called "executor" [GAR 02, MOA 99, ORE 99, ROS 06, YAR 99, ZHA 04]. As many of the application entities are reconfigurable, a group of entities can be modified from the same adaptation plan. Adaptation actions are executed by the effectors associated with these entities. The execution of actions must be coordinated by the executor because several entities are involved. For example, if *A*, an adaptation action, for an entity cannot take place before having applied *E*, a set of actions, on other entities, then coordination consists of inserting a message into the plan to start up the action *A*, bound for its effector, after the reception of message operations indicating that *E* is finished. Coordination enables actions to execute correctly and thus ensures that the application achieves a consistent state at the end of the plan execution.

Several works have defined protocols for coordinating multiple adaptations and achieving a consistent application state. Thus, Appia [ROS 06] defines several stages and actions for reconfiguring a system. It is a framework for the composition and execution of communication protocols. Each communication channel is implemented by one or more protocol stacks on each node. In Appia, it is possible to modify protocol parameters (parametric reconfiguration), such as the message transmission expiry period. Furthermore, the adaptation manager tests three possible types of stack change (structural reconfiguration): replacing one of the protocols in one stack with another, adding/removing a single protocol in one stack and replacing one stack with an alternative stack. When a change in the protocol composition of one or more nodes is required, the adaptation manager tests the reconfiguration, due to the coordination with the effectors, called "reconfiguration agents", run on each node. To ensure reconfiguration, the agents carry out a set of tasks:

– making sure that each channel affected by the reconfiguration achieves a resting state before the reconfiguration;

– capturing the state that must be injected into the new configuration;

– deploying the new protocol stack;

– injecting the state taken from the previous configuration;

– coordinating with the agents on other nodes, via the adaptation manager, if necessary. Nonetheless, no specification of how this coordination is realized is given in Appia.

4.3.2. *Limitations of the centralized solution for distributed systems*

When reconfiguration management is centralized, the monitoring process offers knowledge concerning the global runtime context. This is ensured by periodically updating information concerning the state of the environment and the application. However, the description model of the application and environment becomes costly to produce and update, when the decentralized environment is very large and changeable. In such a case, the centralized approach leads to a network overload, to convey the information to a central server. Furthermore, access to all the nodes is not always possible in some environments, e.g. in the case of *ad hoc* mobile networks.

Moreover, controlling of the reconfiguration of several entities by one adaptation manager increases the complexity of analysis and planning processes. Indeed, the great number of reconfigurable entities and the fine grain of the reconfiguration increase the number of alternative configurations to consider in decision-making. Furthermore, the number of context parameters to analyze, to decide or plan reconfiguration, can be considerable. Consequently, the decision-making time risks are unsatisfactory. Finally, specialization of analysis and planning processes becomes a complex task.

For reconfiguration of a distributed system, the application of adaptation plans involves several geographically distant components. Then, execution control of these actions requires remote interactions between the executor and the different component effectors. These interactions increase the runtime period and network load.

In conclusion, approaches based on a centralized reconfiguration management do not always provide sufficiently suitable solutions for the distributed systems, especially when the environment is strongly changeable and large-sized.

4.3.3. *The stakes of distributed reconfiguration management*

In a distributed approach, the adaptation system is composed of a set of adaptation managers. Each manager is responsible for the reconfiguration of one or more software entities. This approach resolves some problems with the centralization of reconfiguration management. It is possible to operate the various remote resources and run several distributed reconfiguration processes in parallel, which may improve performance. The distribution leads to an approach operating the processing locality, and division of the global problem into subproblems. In the same circumstances, each adaptation manager oversees a subset of entities in a more reduced geographic space (e.g. the same machine). Hence, it has a partial view of the runtime context. This partial view is less costly to elaborate and update than a global view, in the case of the centralized solution. Furthermore, it is possible to place each manager close to the entities that it modifies, with the aim of reducing the cost of communication between the executor and effectors during the reconfiguration phase. Finally, reconfiguration distribution management offers flexibility in the specialization of reconfiguration processes. Indeed, the developer has the option of implementing each adaptation manager differently from the others. For example, the first group of managers can include an evaluator of specified rules following the ECA paradigm, whereas other managers can be based on learning mechanisms for decision-making.

However, dependencies between the software entities controlled by different adaptation managers will have to be taken into account. For this, mechanisms for the coordination of analysis, planning and execution activities of different managers must be introduced to prevent the occurrence of inconsistent configurations, or service malfunction, following a reconfiguration. For example, the adaptation policies used by different managers must be composable so that their application ensures the consistency of the overall system. Coordination mechanisms constitute an additional cost, as far as the reconfiguration process achievement time and resources consumed by the adaptation system are concerned. For example, a decision made collectively involves several managers late in converging on an ultimate solution, when it requires a high number of remote interactions between the managers involved. Furthermore, an additional development effort is required to implement the coordination mechanisms.

The choice of construction of an adaptation system composed of several cooperating adaptation managers thus results in a compromise, taking these different factors into account. Later on, we will give an overview of works that have followed a distributed approach to reconfiguration management, by focusing our attention on the coordination mechanisms that they define. This study aims to analyze the techniques used and determine their advantages and disadvantages in terms of flexibility and reusability in several fields of application.

4.3.4. *Existing coordination mechanisms*

In this section, we focus on the forms of coordination that are possible at the level of analysis, planning and execution processes in current works, and we show the limitations of the solutions offered.

4.3.4.1. *Coordination of distributed analysis processes*

We take distributed analysis to mean a set of actors cooperating, for decision-making, concerning the adaptation strategy requested. Hence, some works are focused on coordination as a technique allowing several participants to collaborate to choose the appropriate strategy.

Coordination allows organization of the participants in distributed decision-making, to determine the adaptation strategy. For example, the Ensemble system [REN 97] allows an analysis process to launch another on the layer above, in a layered application. This is realized when the initial process is found to be incapable of managing the symptom. In the K-component framework [DOW 04], an analyzer chooses to delegate decision-making to another on a neighboring node, when it estimates that a better solution could be found.

On the other hand, coordination also allows a form of cooperation for the resolution of conflicts between several adaptation policies. It allows a group of analyzers to be in agreement by avoiding inconsistencies and uncertainties over the adaptation strategies to apply. Indeed, a lack of coordination among the entities of a distributed system can lead to interference between the adaptive behaviors of different entities, or to conflicts over the use of shared resources, and thus to system under-achievement [EFS 02]. The application of an adaptation strategy to a software entity must suit all the different parts impacted by the reconfiguration. In some approaches, the analysis process is distributed between the clients using the services of a component and the middleware that adapts it. In this framework, the Carisma middleware [CAP 03] enables the resolution of conflicts using a method based on an auction protocol, where the middleware plays the role of the auctioneer, the clients are the bidders and the strategies (which the authors call policies) are the goods for auction.

In [CHE 01], the authors present quite a similar approach concerning the Cactus framework adaptation, where the necessity of an agreement process is highlighted, in which all adaptive components reach a consensus on the modification required. However, this framework does not implement mechanisms for achieving a consensus. These mechanisms must be defined and implemented by the developer.

4.3.4.2. *Coordination of distributed planning processes*

When the planning process is distributed, planning activities are divided up among a set of autonomic adaptation managers, each with its own planner. Coordination of a set of planning processes deals with situations in which a group of planners provide adaptation plans to apply, and there are dependencies between actions specified in different plans. Indeed, the adaptation plans may be in conflict because of incompatibilities from the system component states, runtime order of actions or use of resources. For example, an adaptation plan can specify actions to change the behavior of a component, while the latter must be removed in accordance with another plan, established in parallel. If this is the case, then the problem consists of detecting and resolving potential conflicts between these plans during the planning phase, so as to be able to run them consistently thereafter. Hence, it proves necessary to reason on the dependencies between adaptation plans and to foresee interactions between their executors to converge on a consistent configuration for the overall system.

Similar problems have been tackled in the context of multi-agent systems. Hence, we find several solutions to the problem of distributed multi-agent planning in this context. In the Georgeff approach, for example [GEO 83], each agent constructs a plan locally. Next, a coordinator agent gathers the plans and analyzes them to identify the conflicts arising from simultaneous access to shared resources. The coordinator agent resolves the conflicts by modifying different plans. The resolution is based on works relating to the problem of satisfying constraints, with the aim of preventing parts of conflicting plans from being run concurrently. Durfee and Lesser have suggested an approach called partial global planning (PGP) [DUR 87]. This approach does not aim to resolve conflicts between different agents' plans; its objective is to optimize the calculation time by reducing the inactivity of agents and eliminating the redundant tasks. The agents are hierarchically organized. They communicate their plans to the coordinator agent, higher in the hierarchy. The coordinator analyzes the different plans provided by the agents and identifies the differing aims of agents from their local plans. For the shared plans, it privileges those which execute actions concurrently, require the least resources, and approve or reject the pursuit of some other aims. Next, it eliminates the redundant plans and communicates to the agents final plans to run. Von Martial [MAR 92] suggested a plan coordination model reliant on the resolution of conflicts based on two types of negative and positive relations, capable of existing between these plans. Relations between the plans bring about a modification of the agents' plans. Negative (or conflicting) relations are those which hinder or prevent several actions from being accomplished simultaneously, and are in general due to incompatibility of aims, or conflicts over resources. For example, in an auction sale, two agents wish to acquire the same product. Positive (or synergetic) relations are those that enable actions to benefit each other. Hence, the execution of an action by an agent achieves in the same time an action which another agent should accomplish, or helps the achievement of an action by another agent. For example, *X*, *Y* and *Z* are in a room, the windows are closed and the shutters are down. *X* feels hot, and *Z* would like to have some light in the room. *Y* raises the shutters and opens a window.

However, the problems of distributed planning are not dealt with in works concerning distributed dynamic reconfiguration management. To the best of our knowledge, current adaptation systems do not provide forms of coordination between several planners. It is possible to adapt approaches defined for multi-agent systems to provide specific usable solutions in the context of distributed adaptation systems.

4.3.4.3. *Coordination of distributed execution control processes*

To implement the modifications in an application, each executor interacts with a set of effectors associated with software entities in order to apply the adaptation actions. It controls and coordinates these effectors to apply the actions specified in the adaptation plan correctly.

When several adaptation managers are associated with an application, the execution control can be divided among different executors. Several adaptation plans can act simultaneously on a distributed topology of software entities. If the planning process has taken into account the distribution of software entities to adapt and the distribution of executors, it is able to include the actions of synchronization and necessary information exchange between executors in the different plans. Thus, they only have to follow their plans. In the opposite case, different executors must themselves decide to interact, to exchange information and coordinate their activities of execution control of dependent plans.

Some works have proposed protocols that allow the coordinated execution of plans on several nodes. Chen *et al.* [CHE 01] define the *graceful adaptation protocol* in the Cactus framework. This protocol enables reconfigurations of component implementations to be applied during runtime, without stopping application proceedings. Changing an implementation is triggered at several stages. Coordination enables one stage of the reconfiguration to be achieved on all components involved in the reconfiguration before applying the following stage.

4.4. Specialization of reconfiguration infrastructures

The construction of reconfigurable systems poses several development challenges. Reusable software frameworks help to remove these challenges by using appropriate models and providing essential services for reconfigurable systems. Several frameworks, such as Dynaco [BUI 07], Madam [FLO 06] and Rainbow [GAR 04], were designed with this objective in mind. These are generic frameworks based on well-established standards and principles. These frameworks generally define the architecture capable of ensuring the reconfiguration phases. In this section, we are interested in the specialization possibilities of these frameworks, and study the facilities offered, in order to construct a concrete adaptation system.

4.4.1. *Specialization of behavior*

The dynamic reconfiguration framework specifies a set of component types, and the rules for interaction between them.

In some approaches, as in the case of the Cactus framework [CHE 01], the developer is responsible for writing the code to implement for each adaptation system component. In other solutions, the adaptation systems' framework implementations take charge of shared tasks in the development of such systems. As far as the analysis and planning processes are concerned, specialization can be achieved via external policies, which define the behavior expected. The most widely used form of policy is the policy of actions, which is presented in ECA [DAV 03, KEE 03] rule form. The platform offered in Rainbow provides a language of this type, called Stitch, but it is designed specially for displaying adaptation policies [GAR 04]. Other types of policies, such as the goal policy [BUI 07, LAP 05] (specification of a desirable state) and the utility function policy (expression of the value of each possible state) [CHE 01, FLO 06], are also used in the reconfigurable software. Rainbow [GAR 04] is also based on a utility function for calculating the best reconfiguration solution. K-component suggests the adaptation contract description (ACD) language [DOW 04]. The adaptation policy is described in the form of contracts using this language. These contracts stipulate the conditions associated with the events and the architectural reconfiguration operations that must be triggered by these same events.

As for execution control, the reconfiguration protocols are predefined and rigid, or to be implemented by the developer. Current approaches do not offer generic mechanisms, whose behavior can be personalized according to the application sought. They set the components involved, reconfiguration types (behavior, structure, distribution, etc.) and order of actions in advance.

4.4.2. *Specialization of the distribution of adaptation mechanisms*

When several application components are reconfigurable, a choice is necessary to associate these components with the adaptation managers that test their reconfiguration processes.

Some approaches associate an adaptation manager with each reconfigurable component. In the Accord framework [LIU 04], each autonomic component integrates a rules agent, which is tasked with managing its runtime. It oversees the component state and its context, and controls the behavior and interaction rules triggered. In [LAP 05], the authors envisage a hierarchy of autonomic elements. An autonomic manager is associated with each element. Due to this hierarchy of autonomic elements, it is possible to circulate high-level concerns from the root element to the elements at sheet level above so that the system achieves its objectives and responds to quality requirements. For Cactus [CHE 01], an adaptation manager controls each reconfigurable component. In particular, it initializes the reconfiguration when it notes that another alternative algorithm satisfies requirements better, in accordance with the environment state.

This totally distributed approach becomes complex when the number of components is increased. Indeed, as it manages each component in isolation, managing the dependencies between them is difficult. Each component must foresee interactions with other managers when the reconfiguration requires it.

Other works allow an adaptation manager to be instanced on each machine. In [MUK 05], an instance of the CASA (*CASA Runtime System* or CRS) framework is created on each node hosting reconfigurable applications. The CRS is tasked with overseeing changes in the runtime environment and adapting these applications. The policy adaptation of each application is defined in an application contract. It is not evoked by the cooperation mechanism between different nodes. Likewise in [DOW 04], an instance of K-component on each machine allows a subset of application components to be adapted on this node and their internal and external dependencies to be taken into account, using connectors. The Cholla framework [BRI 09] defines an adaptation controller on each node. This controller manages the reconfiguration of a set of components, organized in layers on the node hosting it, and communicates the state of its components to other nodes (and reciprocally). Finally, in [CAS 09], supervision and reconfiguration services are distributed depending on the resources (memory, power, processor speed, etc.) available on each device. For a non-constrained node, all services are used. In the case of a constrained node, a service may be limited or even absent.

This choice allows independent management of aspects of the context on each machine, and efficient modification of application components on the node, since there are not generally many. In these approaches, components situated on the same machine cannot be managed by different managers, e.g. to use different analysis algorithms. Conversely, components on several machines could be better managed by one manager. For example, it is simpler to specify one single policy that manages several components when the adaptation rules are the same, and there are strong dependencies between them. Finally, some nodes cannot get enough resources to run complex reconfiguration processes.

In conclusion, the method of dividing up reconfiguration management mechanisms in the context of distributed systems requires more in-depth study. Existing infrastructures lack the flexibility in the placement of adaptation managers, and in the criteria adopted for defining the scope of action for each one. These aspects can limit both the quality of the reconfiguration and adaptation system performance, either during the runtime period or in terms of resources consumed.

4.5. Summary of the limitations and challenges of dynamic reconfiguration of distributed systems

In practice, software architectures for managing dynamic reconfiguration in a distributed and coordinated way are still rudimentary. A limited number of works have addressed the problem of coordinating the reconfiguration process in the context of distributed systems. Most works in the setting of reconfiguration architectures use centralized analysis and planning processes. Relatively little research has aimed to provide a model allowing the activities of several distributed processes to be coordinated, to analyze symptoms and decide on the appropriate modification. Systems that have addressed the problem of distributed decision-making, using several actors who collaborate together, have not suggested facilities for detecting and resolving potential conflicts between them, as they stick to predefined cooperation operations statically guaranteeing consistency. This solution falls short in large-scale, very heterogeneous and very variable environments. As for execution control mechanisms for distributed adaptation actions, the growth in systems complexity has highlighted the limitations of centralized coordination models [MON 03]. Nevertheless, the distributed coordination mechanisms proposed are strongly specific to the applications that they adapt and to the type of reconfiguration. We therefore think that distributed coordination mechanisms have not addressed all the functions that a designer might be wished to reconfigure.

Moreover, current approaches for dividing up the adaptation system, are not flexible. Existing works are concerned primarily with specialization of the adaptation systems behavior, rather than with its structure and distribution.

There are no tools for personalizing the adaptation system structure and its distribution.

From our study, it appears that numerous improvements in the field of software architectures for coordinating the activities of several distributed adaptation managers are both desirable and identifiable. The effort required to specify coordination mechanisms currently remains too great to satisfy the growing need in adaptation systems for very dynamic and heterogeneous environments. Our contribution aims to simplify the development of distributed reconfigurable systems, by offering a generic distributed cooperation platform, responsible for coordinating several dynamic reconfiguration control modules, as well as means for implementing and using it.

4.6. An approach for the implementation of reconfiguration management mechanisms

In our approach, we follow the principle of separation between the reconfiguration and management aspects to ensure that the control mechanisms for application reconfiguration are externalized. If the application to reconfigure is designed modularly, its reconfiguration will be finer. Reconfiguration of non-modularly designed applications is possible, but they will be less specific.

For an application to be reconfigurable, one or more of its components must be adaptive. An adaptable component includes methods for its monitoring and for the modification of its behavior. It may involve base-level mechanisms provided by the component model used (e.g. creation/deletion of components), but it may also involve more advanced operations, based on these mechanisms. In both cases, the adaptable components show execution interfaces including these operations, interfaces that will be able to be used by a concrete adaptation system. By using these interfaces, an adaptation system enacts and oversees an application. We call the whole of an adaptation-application system, a self-adaptive application.

We design the adaptation system in a modular way in order to facilitate its specialization according to the target application to adapt (see Figure 4.2). We propose two tools to facilitate its construction. The first tool is an architectural model for reconfiguration management. It specifies the constraints to be respected by all the adaptation systems. An adaptation expert provides the architecture description for the adaptation system. In this description, the components that must constitute an adaptation system, the connections between them and connections with the application components, are specified.

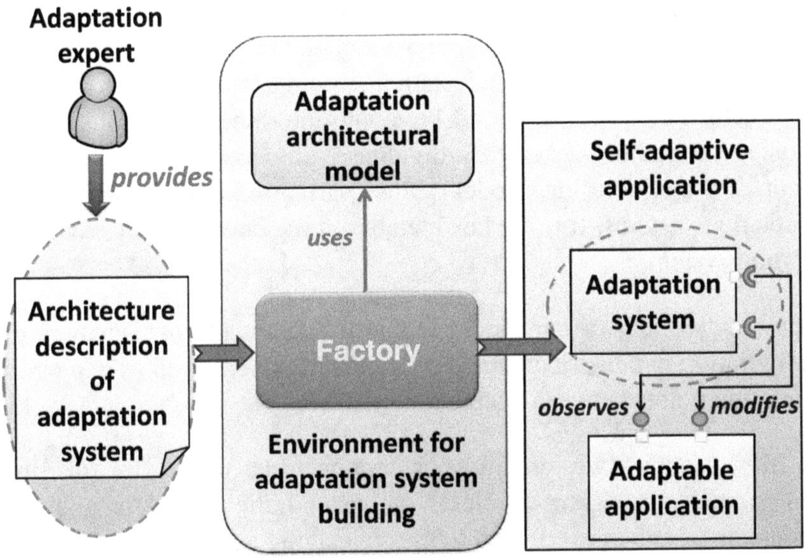

Figure 4.2. *Principles for the construction of an adaptation system*

The second tool is a factory, which, from the architecture description of the adaptation system to deploy:

– checks that the constraints of the architectural model are indeed adhered to by the architecture described;

– instantiates the adaptation system;

– looks for references to the adaptation control interfaces provided by the target application;

– connects the adaptation system with the application according to the connections specified.

4.7. Architectural model for distributed dynamic reconfiguration management

Distributed dynamic reconfiguration must be based on a model, methodology and tools enabling its design and implementation to be facilitated. For this, we have defined an architectural model for developing distributed adaptation systems. This model specifies the structure and semantics of a distributed adaptation architecture, and it imposes explicit constraints for constructing an adaptation system adhering to the architecture. This structuring is a means of breaking the inherent complexity of a distributed adaptation system, by dividing it into cooperating and reusable elements. Furthermore, the model defines variation points between a family of adaptation systems. It is the key element in the development process of an adaptation system.

The main benefit of our model is that it enables the management of the reconfiguration in a distributed and coordinated way, as well as expression of the variation points between adaptation systems.

In this section, we present our architectural model for distributing reconfiguration management. Next, we extend the model to support the coordination of software entity activities managing adaptation in a distributed way, and we specify techniques for coordinating decision-making and the modifications control of an application. Finally, we describe the negotiation protocol that we have defined in detail, with the aim of ensuring the coordination of adaptation decision-making generated by the analysis processes.

To define our model, we take into consideration the following set of constraints:

– independence with regard to current standards and components models;

– flexibility and extensibility of the model;

– modularity of the adaptation management mechanisms;

– the distributed nature of software to be adapted and the potential heterogeneity of their runtime environments.

4.7.1. *Component types for adaptation management*

The two main functions for making a distributed application reconfigurable are context management and adaptation management. They are ensured by two composite component types (see Figure 4.3): "ContextManager" (context manager) and "AdaptationManager" (adaptation manager). In Figure 8.3, the use of the "type" stereotype on components shows that it is a particular component type.

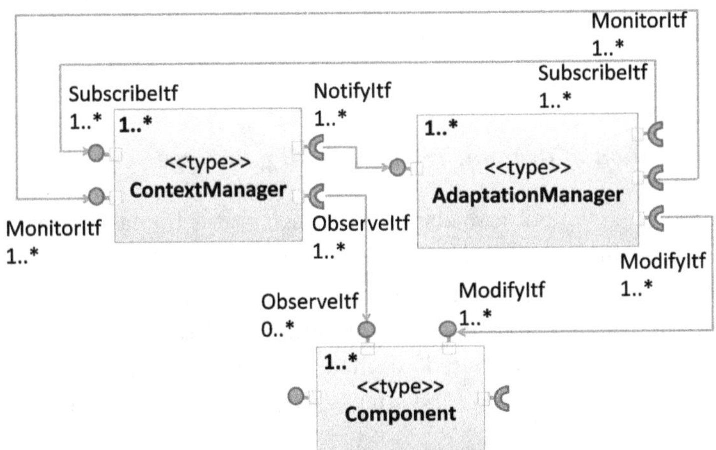

Figure 4.3. *Architectural model for a distributed management of reconfiguration*

A component can be observable and/or adaptable. Observation and adaptation are ensured by the sensors and effectors, which respectively show "ObserveItf", an observation interface, and "ModifyItf", a modification interface as depicted in Figure 4.3. For a component to be reconfigurable, it must be interconnected with an adaptation manager, and eventually a context manager.

The component type "ContextManager" ensures the monitoring process. It interacts with sensors associated with the runtime environment and the application in order to collect information needed to characterize the runtime context.

The component type "AdaptationManager" runs the analysis, planning and execution processes. It interacts with the effectors to control the execution in order to apply the adaptation of the behavior, structure and/or distribution of the software application.

An asynchronous interaction by a "publication-subscription" mechanism allows the adaptation manager to be notified via a "NotifyItf" interface of context changes that could require an adaptation. An adaptation manager subscribes to events near the context manager using a "SubscribeItf" interface. The detection of a significant context change triggers the notification of the subscriber. The adaptation manager can also ask the context manager, using the "MonitorItf" interface, to provide information useful for the adaptation in request/response mode.

4.7.2. *Distribution of dynamic reconfiguration management*

To distribute adaptation management, our approach enables an adaptation system architecture to be defined, composed of an arbitrary number of "ContextManager" components (multiplicity "1..*") and an arbitrary number of "AdaptationManager" components (multiplicity "1..*"). The control of the reconfiguration of a distributed application results from the activities of different managers included in the adaptation system (see Figure 4.3).

4.7.2.1. *Context and adaptation managers*

With each context manager, the range of activity is limited to a specific environment (WLAN, a group of neighboring nodes in an *ad hoc* network, etc.) or to a particular set of contextual aspects (e.g. a context manager for each layer: application, network and operating system). Several context managers can be used, especially when the runtime environment is strongly heterogeneous and a great volume of contextual information must be managed. Context management becomes more efficient because each context manager is dedicated to particular contextual aspects. In addition, the exchange of context information (collection of measurements and notification of changes) can be limited to network subdomains to reduce network traffic and latency.

Finally, a context manager is able to use an arbitrary number of physical or logic sensors. Thus, an "ObserveItf" client interface has "1..*" multiplicity.

Our approach also limits each adaptation manager range of activity to a subset of distributed application components. A subset is constituted of components that collaborate to ensure one or more specific services, and/or are placed geographically closely. The adaptation policy of a distributed application is divided into subpolicies each taking into account a limited part of the context information and is specialized to adapt a subset of the application components. Consequently, each manager has limited scope for action and the adaptation behavior results from the various local actions of different adaptation managers.

Each adaptation manager subscribes to events from one or more context managers, according to the components that it adapts, and the scope for action of these managers. Each context manager notifies the subscribed adaptation managers of events concerning it, and responds to requests for context consultation emerging from different adaptation managers. For this, the client and server interfaces "MonitorItf", "SubscribeItf" and "NotifyItf" have "1..*" multiplicity.

Finally, an adaptation manager reconfigures an arbitrary number of application components. The "ModifyItf" client interface has "1..*" multiplicity.

Figure 4.4 shows an example of an application and a set of instances (use of the "component" stereotype) of context and adaptation managers, associated with it to make it self-adaptive. The application is composed of five components distributed among three nodes; three of them are observable and modifiable. The adaptation system is constituted of two "ContextManager" components and three "AdaptationManager" components. The context manager *gc1* and the adaptation manager *ga1* are associated with the adaptable component *c1* only because it is placed geographically far from the other application components. The adaptable components *c2* and *c3* are placed on two close, but different, machines. The contextual aspects that interest us for these two components are similar. Hence, we instantiate only one context manager, *gc2*, to manage them. We apply different adaptation policies to the two components. Thus, each component is managed by a different adaptation manager (*ga2* and *ga3*) hosted on the same machine as the component that it adapts.

4.7.2.2. *Coordination*

The model mentioned enables the dynamic adaptation management to be distributed. However, some application components may be dependent.

Hence, some reconfiguration scenarios necessitate coordination of the adaptation managers' activities for collective decision-making and to reconfigure application components in a coordinated way. Coordination relates to interactions between a group of adaptation managers, to coordinate their modification analysis and execution control processes for different components. For this, the adaptation managers must integrate components suitable for coordination. Our proposal for managing the coordination aspect is presented in section 4.7.5.

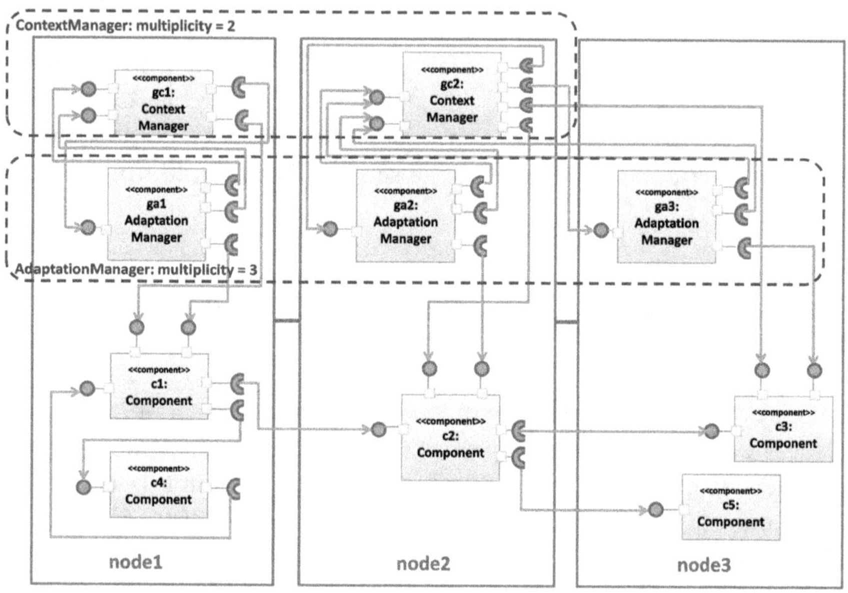

Figure 4.4. *An example of dynamic reconfiguration management distribution*

4.7.3. *Architectural model of the adaptation manager*

Figure 4.5 shows the basic architectural model of a component type "AdaptationManager". This model does not allow interaction between ("AdaptationManager") components of the same type, and will be extended to enable a distributed and coordinated reconfiguration management.

This model specifies three essential types of sub-components for adaptation management: "DecisionMaker" (analysis phase), "Planner" (planning phase) and "Executor" (execution phase). An adaptation manager is a composite, which contains a single instance of each type (multiplicity "1"). The three component types have a *node* attribute. Hence, we can specialize the node on which a component of each type is deployed. Furthermore, it is possible to specialize the behavior of "DecisionMaker" and "Planner" components by giving a value to the *algoParameters* attribute. This attribute serves to configure the algorithm that the component implements. The behavior specialization of an adaptation manager is detailed in the following section.

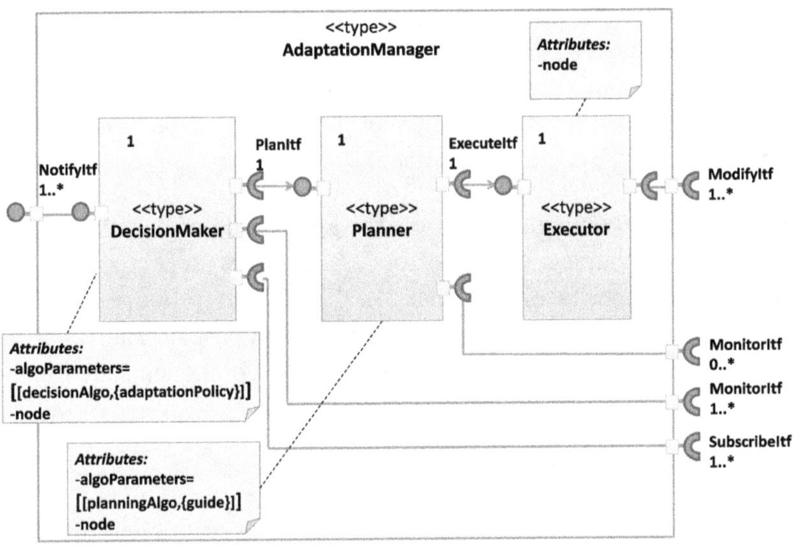

Figure 4.5. *Architectural model of an adaptation manager*

The "DecisionMaker" component deals with the analysis processes and provides an adaptation strategy to apply as output. It subscribes to events near one or more context managers using its "SubscribeItf" client interface with "1..*" multiplicity. It is thus notified of context changes by context managers via the "NotifyItf" interface server. Particular context measurements may also have to be undertaken, in addition to the information contained in the event. Therefore, the decision maker can be linked to one or more context managers through "MonitorItf", the client interface. The decision maker chooses the appropriate strategy, specifying the changes to bring to the current configuration (e.g. modifying the algorithm for replica placement). It informs the "Planner" component of this, using the "PlanItf" client interface.

The "Planner" component identifies a sequence of adaptation actions, in the form of a plan to implement the strategy chosen by the decision maker. For example, this may involve deactivating a component, replacing it with another and starting up the new component. A "Planner" component may need contextual information specifically regarding the application or environment. For this, it has a "MonitorItf client interface, with "1..*" multiplicity, to interact with an arbitrary number of context managers. Separating the decision-making and planning makes it possible to distinguish the objective to achieve (the strategy), from the manner of achieving it (the plan). Hence, the same strategy can be adopted by several components, but executed in different ways. The planner sends the adaptation plan to the executor using the "ExecuteItf" interface.

The "Executor" component controls the application of the adaptation plan that it receives. It interacts with effectors associated with components via the "ModifyItf" client interface, which has "1..*" multiplicity. It takes into account the runtime of the adaptable application, which is in progress, and coordinates the application of actions when several application components are involved.

4.7.4. *Specialization of reconfiguration mechanisms*

We adopt a policy-oriented approach where the reconfiguration logic is described in the form of external policies, dissociated from the implementation of services. This approach offers many advantages. First, policies facilitate the development of the reconfiguration system. By expressing the reconfiguration in a high-level language, the developer is not obliged to understand every detail of the reconfiguration service implementation during the definition, or reading, of a given policy. Second, it is easier to analyze the dependencies between different aspects of the reconfiguration and to detect the potential conflicts. Third, this approach offers the possibility to reuse the same reconfiguration services in different contexts by specializing them differently according to the application reconfiguration needs. Finally, with the level of uncoupling obtained, it is easier to enable the change in the reconfiguration logic during runtime, without having to recompile and redeploy the adaptation system.

In our approach, a policy is a set of rules in the ECA format. Each rule is composed of triggers that are set off when an event is received, by a condition which must be verified, and by an action to run. Indeed, one of the key demands of the reconfiguration mechanisms proposed is the ease of their specialization by a human stakeholder. The ECA rules are a well-known paradigm in the field of knowledge representation [BRA 04, SOW 00] and they offer a good readability of the representation of these rules. Furthermore, the use of these rules addresses one of the priority objectives during the design of a system, i.e. knowing the similarity to human thought and improvement of the ease of use [BEI 06]. Two types of components from one adaptation manager model use the policy concept: the decision maker and the planner. In both cases, the policy specializes the component behavior. Hence, the *algoParameters* attribute for these types includes a single parameter, corresponding to the policy to be used.

The decision maker interprets a policy that we call adaptation policy. This policy specifies the reasoning, making it possible to decide which modification is required. The decision maker uses the policy to choose a type of adaptation strategy and parameterize it. Hence, for example, Figure 4.6 shows the type available for defining adaptation strategies for a replica placement management component. In this type, the name of the placement algorithm, its configuration parameters and the node where the component must be deployed, can all be defined. An adaptation strategy for adopting a random placement algorithm with a degree of replication equal to 10 thus consists of initializing the *placementAlgorithmName* attribute with *"RandomPlacementStrategy"* and the *algoParams* attribute at the value "10". Another possible adaptation strategy is to migrate the component onto another machine. In this case, the name of the new node that will host the component must be specified, in the *hostName* variable. The number of attributes in this type of strategy is sufficient for applying two types of adaptation: behavior modification (algorithm and parameters) and distribution modification.

A planner interprets another type of policy, which we refer to as a guide, as in [BUI 07]. The guide enables the planner to choose a type of adaptation plan suitable for an adaptation strategy, and for configuring its variables, based on information shown in the strategy. For example, it can extract the name of the algorithm to use and the values of its configuration parameters from the adaptation strategy.

Figure 4.7 presents a plan that modifies the placement algorithm implemented by a component of a replication system. It contains *modifyPlacementAlgorithm*, a first adaptation action to modify the algorithm that the component implements and a second action, *configureParameters*, which configures its parameters (e.g. the attribute that specifies the number of replicas desired).

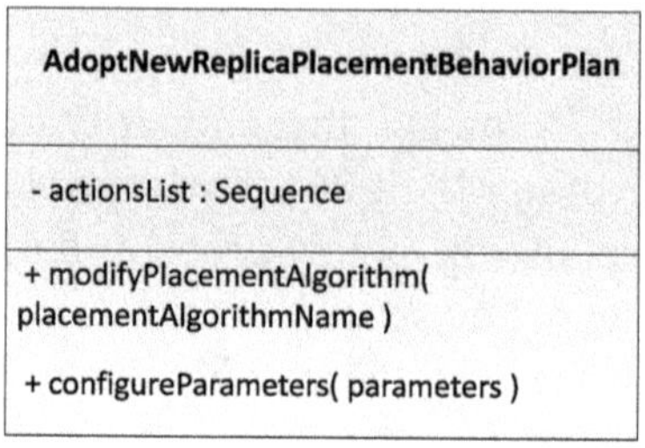

Figure 4.6. *UML class representing a type of adaptation strategy for a replica placement component*

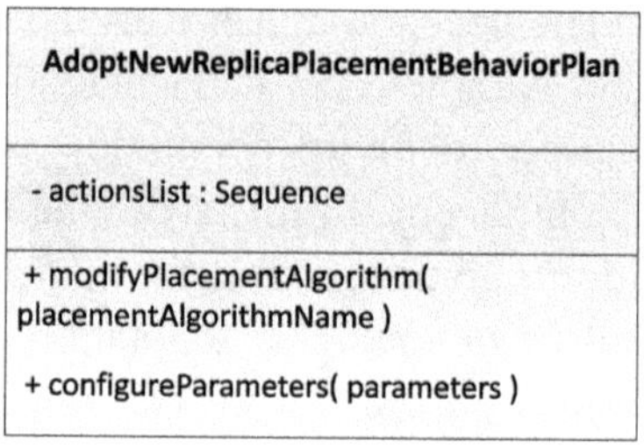

Figure 4.7. *UML class representing an adaptation plan of a replica placement strategy*

The parameterizing of strategies and generic adaptation plans makes it possible to reduce the effort needed to define the various possible strategies and plans for a particular application. For example, adding a new replica placement algorithm does not necessarily require the creation of a new type of plan.

As far as the executor is concerned, its behavior cannot be specialized by a policy. Indeed, it only runs the actions of the plan that it receives.

4.7.5. *Coordination of reconfiguration processes*

The reconfiguration management distribution results in an autonomy for each adaptation manager. These activities consist of making the adaptation decision, determining the adaptation plan and controlling the plan execution. However, they cannot be performed in isolation in all the adaptation scenarios. Some scenarios require coordination of the activities of a group of adaptation managers, when there are dependencies between their goals and the adaptation actions that they apply.

Indeed, each adaptation manager has a restricted view of the application and its runtime environment. It lacks knowledge concerning other components, the resources that they require, the preferences of users and of their services. Consequently, different adaptation managers can make conflicting decisions, if each undertakes its decision-making individually. For example, an adaptation manager must not apply adaptation actions increasing the rate of shared resource use by the entities that it adapts, by ignoring the resource needs of other entities associated with other adaptation managers. Furthermore, an adaptation manager may need to exploit the adaptation possibilities of other components, under the control of other managers. For example, the change in behavior of a component can considerably improve the service quality of an application, if another component also changes its behavior.

Moreover, the execution control processes of several plans modifying the application components in parallel can change the system to a non-consistent state. This arises from lack of control of the global application state, during and after adaptation, and also from lack of information on the runtime progress of different plans. Hence, coordinating the execution of several plans is indispensable when there are dependencies between the components that they modify.

For this, our approach defines mechanisms to:

– ensure the validity and efficiency of adaptation strategies chosen in parallel;

– provide plans that are applicable in parallel, and which include necessary processing to coordinate their runtimes;

– coordinate the simultaneous executions of several adaptation plans.

These mechanisms are described in the two sections that follow.

4.7.5.1. *Coordination of adaptation decision-making*

Coordination of decision-making aims to lead a group of adaptation managers in shared decision-making to ensure non-conflicting and complementary decisions. Collective decision-making results from the determining of a global strategy. We define a global strategy as the set of strategies chosen by the adaptation managers during a decision-making process. For example, a global strategy can be composed of two complementary strategies, one chosen by an adaptation manager associated with the placement service and another associated with the replica consistency management service. The former chooses to move to a new algorithm that enables the creation of some data replicas on mobile terminals. The latter decides to move to an optimistic consistency protocol for these data.

Decision-making must be relevant to the current overall situation and foresee the effect of adaptation strategies in order to avoid inconsistent situations. An adaptation manager cannot possess enough local information to allow it to choose a suitable adaptation strategy. It must choose strategies that allow its maximum number of objectives to be satisfied while adhering to the components constraints checked by other managers. The main concern of coordinating decision-making must thus be ensuring the compatibility of an adaptation strategy with the following constraints:

– maintaining a consistent composition of the application services;

– guaranteeing the concerns of other application entities in terms of resource and service sharing;

– ensuring good performances by the overall system.

For this, our approach is based on the principle of making several managers participate in the same decision-making process, and taking into account the non-local effects of adaptation strategies resulting from local decisions. Hence, the construction of a global strategy makes it possible to choose local adaptation strategies in such a way that the bad choices are avoided.

Coordinated decision-making is made possible in three stages. The first two stages are ensured at the level of a decision maker and consist of recovering the necessary context information (stage 1) and choosing an adaptation strategy (stage 2). At the end of stage 2, the coordination process (stage 3) is initiated. Here, we assume that one adaptation manager triggers this process. It is called the coordination initiator. Stage 3 involves the decision makers of other managers, called participants. During this stage, the decision makers may need to recover context information and do a reasoning to determine the definitive global strategy. The case of several decision makers simultaneously initiating coordination could be dealt with by abandoning the initiator role, except for one of them. The following sections detail the triggering of three stages of decision-making.

4.7.5.1.1. Component types for the coordination of decision-making

Our architectural model defines additional types of interfaces to the "DecisionMaker" component and a new type of component "Negotiator", in order to enable a decision maker to take part in a coordination process. Figure 4.8 presents the model specifying the two component types, "DecisionMaker" and "Negotiator", and the possible links between them to make a decision maker cooperative.

The optional "CoordinateItf" interface, with "0..*" multiplicity, enables a decision maker to communicate messages for an arbitrary number of decision makers. The policy defines when it is appropriate to start the interaction, the set of decision-makers involved, and the message content. An optional "Negotiator" component can be instanced and interconnected with the decision maker in order to allow the negotiation of a global strategy. In this case, a decision maker can start negotiations using the optional "NegotiateItf" interface, and a decision maker for a participating manager can be notified on the outcome of a successful negotiation due to the "NotifyItf" interface.

Moreover, the "Negotiator" components included in different adaptation managers are related to each other via "ProposeItf" interfaces. Each negotiator shows a server interface of this type and uses a client interface of the same type and "0..*" multiplicity. It has a "MonitorItf" client interface with "1..*" multiplicity for recovering contextual information. Hence, each "Negotiator" component has the option of communicating with an arbitrary number of negotiators and context managers.

The adaptation policy specifies situations requiring the triggering of negotiation by a "DecisionMaker" component. A negotiation policy specializes the behavior of the "Negotiator" component, by specifying the participants and control rules for the progress of each negotiation process. These policies are specified in the *algoParameters* attribute of "DecisionMaker" and "Negotiator" components, respectively. Another attribute of these components, the *node* attribute, enables their placement to be chosen.

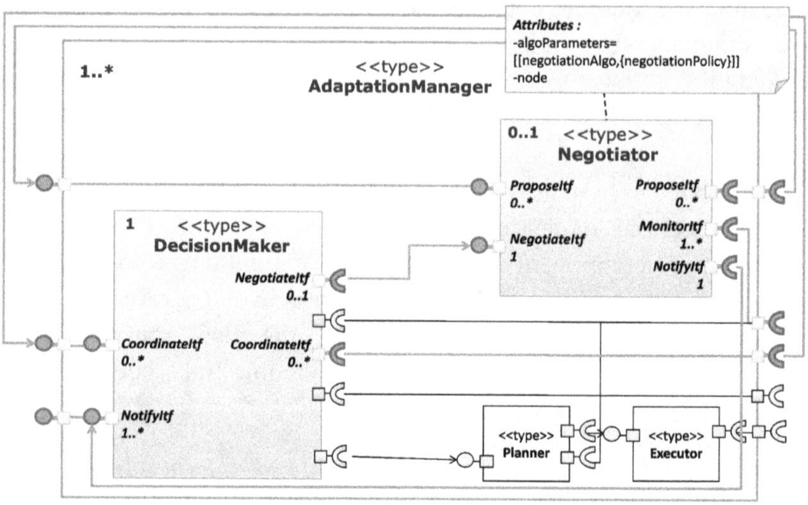

Figure 4.8. *Architectural model for coordinated analysis processes*

4.7.5.1.2. Decision-making coordination models

We have defined three decision-making coordination models between decision services: strategy choice by a master, strategy publication and strategy negotiation.

1) Strategy choice by a master

This model enables the coordination initiator to act as a master and treats the participants as slaves which follow its orders. The master chooses a global strategy individually. Next, it assigns the task of applying a specific strategy to each participant, using "CoordinateItf" interfaces. The message sent to each participant shows the strategy and what it must apply. Each participant starts a reconfiguration process to apply the assigned strategy by calling its planner.

This model is simple to specify and it limits the costs of communication between decision makers.

2) Strategy publication

This model enables the coordination initiator to notify the participants about the strategy chosen by it. Once a participant has been notified, it analyzes its context and chooses a suitable strategy, taking into account the decision made by the initiator. The strategy chosen must be consistent, and complement that of the initiator. As in the first model, the interaction between the initiator and participants via the "CoordinateItf" interfaces is unidirectional and a message sent to each participant shows the strategy adopted by the initiator. For example, a decision maker associated with a replica placement manager for a data group can choose a strategy consisting of increasing the number of replicas. Afterward, it announces this strategy to the decision maker associated with another replica placement manager, for a second data group. This second decision maker triggers an adaptation process by choosing a strategy for its data consisting of reducing the number of their replicas, as it finds the overall storage capacity to be weak.

This model can be used when each participant has options for ensuring a consistent global strategy and when it is easy to manage dependencies between the services provided by the components involved.

3) Strategy negotiation

This model enables the establishment of an agreement on the global strategy to apply, with a negotiation process between a group of adaptation managers. For example, the negotiation can take place between the adaptation managers associated with the components ensuring the update propagation service and running in environments having different characteristics. These managers negotiate the replica consistency protocol to apply, in order to improve the replication system performance by taking into account the characteristics of different environments, such as the availability of resources.

In this model, the negotiators exchange offers and counter-offers in order to reach an agreement. The initiator informs the others of the strategy that it wishes to adopt and/or requests that a specific strategy be adopted. Interaction between negotiators enables the offers to be accepted or refused, and the global strategy to be progressively modified until agreement is reached, or the negotiation is considered to have failed. In the negotiation process, the negotiators can have different interests regarding each application configuration and different intentions. The local context is used to make an offer or counter-offer in order to determine the final decision.

The major benefit of this model is that it makes it possible to modify the initial strategy chosen by the initiator, and construct the global strategy progressively, taking into account the different local contexts of the components involved. This guarantees better efficiency for the final strategy when the negotiation succeeds. However, it also increases the complexity of the decision process, particularly when there are a significant number of participants and reconfiguration alternatives. Indeed, managers risk delaying converging on a final decision and consume resources calculating and exchanging offers and counter-offers. We will return to this model in more detail in section 4.7.5.2.

Each decision-making coordination model is right for a particular adaptation process family. The choice of model depends essentially on the dependencies between the application components, the number of decision makers and the complexity of the coordination process. The use of policies makes our approach flexible. Indeed, each decision maker can support one or more models. For example, a decision maker can be a slave in an adaptation scenario and a negotiation initiator in another scenario. Furthermore, each decision maker can be specialized with the outcome that it chooses a model to use in an adaptation process depending on the context. For example, it behaves like a master when the network resources available are weak and it plays the role of a negotiation initiator when connectivity is high. The decision-making capacities of each adaptation manager are specified by either incorporating or not incorporating a negotiator and through the specification of its adaptation policy.

4.7.5.2. *Adaptation strategy negotiation protocol*

Negotiation is a cooperative process by which a group of adaptation managers reach an agreement on a global adaptation strategy. Our protocol which is different from other existing protocols thus focuses on determining adaptation strategies. Existing solutions provide approaches for negotiating for example, responsibilities between the software components [CHA 06] or the Quality of Service offered [CAV 02]. The negotiation must guarantee the independence of each of the adaptation managers in decision-making and ensure the global validity of a local decision. For this, the negotiators involved evaluate the situation according to the information that each one has, to find an acceptable compromise-based solution.

For example, a medical data replication system can initially use a replica placement algorithm based on predicting the placement of different healthcare professionals and an optimistic consistency protocol. Following an emergency situation, a collective adaptation is needed. A first adaptation manager may wish to change the system behavior to use an epidemic placement algorithm. Another adaptation manager desires a change in the consistency protocol, to ensure a strong consistency. However, there is a risk of the cost of update propagation rising in this case. A negotiation process ensures the coordination of decision-making. The result of it is, for example, to change the placement algorithm and to keep the same optimistic consistency protocol.

4.7.5.2.1. Negotiation process

When a decision maker requests the negotiation of a strategy, the negotiator creates an adaptation contract and initiates its negotiation with a set of participants. The contract is an object which specifies the initiator, participants and global strategy to negotiate. This is specified in the form of parameters, where each parameter specifies a local strategy, the manager tasked with applying them and the negotiators involved in its negotiation (see Figure 4.9).

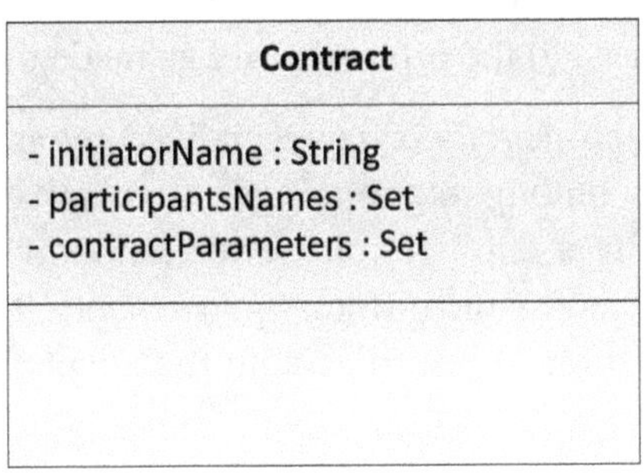

Figure 4.9. *UML class representing the attributes of a negotiated contract*

The participants in each negotiation process may be explicitly shown in the adaptation strategy. Another alternative is to make it so that the negotiation is triggered with all the negotiators that the initiator is connected to. Finally, our approach also enables automatic discovery of the list of participants in the negotiation. For this, a model of dependencies between the different adaptable components can be provided to the negotiators. For each component, the model specifies the types of its relations with other components:

– "uses" and "usedBy" to designate that the component uses, or is used by, another component;

– "affects" and "affectedBy" to designate that the component behavior influences the performance of another component or that its performance is influenced by the behavior of another component.

In this case, the adaptation strategy specifies the types of relations to take into account so that the negotiator automatically discovers the participants.

The negotiation process is divided into three phases:

1) The offer phase: this phase determines the contract to be offered to the participants by the initiator.

2) The conversation phase: during this phase the offers or modification requests are exchanged. The initiator collects the participants' responses. Each participant can either accept or reject the offer. It may also request or offer contract modifications. Following an offer or modification request from at least one participant, we find ourselves in a new offer phase.

3) The final decision phase: this phase ends either in the confirmation or in the cancellation of the contract. This decision is taken by the initiator according to participants' responses to the offers that it has made them.

The behavior of each negotiator is specialized by an external negotiation policy showing how, among other things, to resolve conflicts. The first possibility for resolving a conflict consists of randomly choosing a strategy from among those offered by the different participants. The second possibility is based on the association of priorities with the adaptation strategies offered by the participants.

Figure 4.10 describes the sequence of messages for negotiation of a contract between an initiator and participants. For clarity's sake, only one participant is considered.

The initiator decision maker chooses an adaptation strategy. Next, it uses its "NegotiateItf" interface and asks the negotiator to negotiate the strategy that it has chosen. This negotiator constructs the contract. The initiator uses the appropriate "ProposeItf" interfaces to offer each participant the contract concerning it, in parallel.

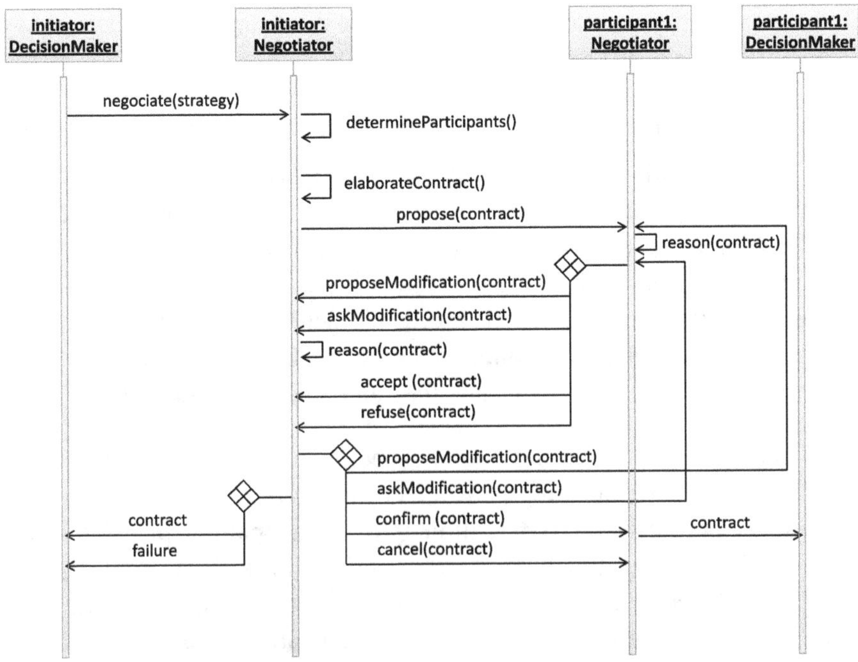

Figure 4.10. *Sequence diagram of the negotiation between two adaptation managers*

Each participant negotiator receives the contract and interprets its policy to reason on its applicability. It can then accept, refuse or offer/request a contract modification, and then it responds to the initiator. When the initiator receives all the responses, it reasons on the acceptance and/or applicability of the modifications requested or offered. When all participants accept the contract, the negotiation succeeds. In the opposite case, it detects and resolves the conflicts, and can then itself offer/request a contract modification. The negotiation process is stopped if a negotiator refuses a contract or if a stopping condition is verified. This condition can be in relation to the maximum negotiation time authorized, or the maximum number of negotiation cycles.

If the negotiation succeeds, the initiator negotiator returns the strategy resulting from the negotiation to the initiator decision maker and sends the final contract to each participant negotiator. Upon receiving this contract, the participant negotiator uses the "NotifyItf" interface to request the decision maker adopt the strategy resulting from the negotiation. In the opposite case, the initiator decision maker and the participants are informed of the failure of the negotiation and the adaptation is canceled.

4.7.5.3. *Coordination of parallel adaptation plans execution*

Coordinating the executions of plans addresses the issue of applying several adaptation plans in parallel with a group of adaptation managers when the plans contain dependent adaptation actions. In such a case, applying these plans must be coordinated, in the sense that a specific sequence of their actions execution must be taken in order to achieve a consistent application configuration. It may, for example, involve following a particular order to apply first an *a1* action of a *P1* plan, then an *a2* action of a *P2* plan.

In our approach, the coordination aspect of adaptation plan executions is considered since the planning phase. During this phase, we insert treatments needed to coordinate their execution into the adaptation plans, during the runtime phase. The treatments are specified in a plan in the form of coordination actions, in addition to adaptation actions. We call a plan including such coordination actions, which enable dependencies on other plans executed in parallel, a coordinated plan. Next, during the runtime phase, the interaction of adaptation managers enables coordination of the adaptation plans executions.

The determination of a coordinated plan is ensured by the "Planner" component. To run plans in a coordinated way, the adaptation manager must include an additional subcomponent type "Coordinator", and the "Executor" component is extended by new interface types, to communicate with its coordinator.

Then, we describe how to plan coordinated adaptation plans. Next, we specify how a group of coordinated plans are applied by cooperating executors. A replica consistency protocol adaptation example will illustrate our proposal.

4.7.5.3.1. Planning coordinated plans

Planning coordinated plans consists of determining adaptation plans to run simultaneously, using different executors. For this, the planner associated with each of these executors determines a plan, by considering dependencies between the adaptation actions specified in these plans. Each planner interprets its own adaptation guide, which allows it to choose and parameterize the right plan, including the coordination actions needed.

The coordination actions include two types of commands. The first type enables an executor to distribute local information necessary for the execution control of other plans. This information concerns its plan execution progress, or the states of the component application that it is controlling. The second command type enables the executor to delegate decision-making concerning the remaining plan execution proceedings to the coordinator, when it depends on other plans. In this case, the coordinator analyzes information provided by other executors, and shows this executor how to continue the plan execution. For example, it orders the next adaptation action to be started, or a set of actions to be ignored.

Information linked to execution progress is useful to ensure a specific execution order of certain adaptation actions, included in different plans. Indeed, adaptation actions are not identical in all the adaptation plans and the planners do not have information on the execution duration for each action. Consequently, the execution speed of each plan cannot be foreseen in advance and varies from one plan to another. However, some actions must be applied before others. Then, the execution control must be based on the shared information, so that this order is adhered to.

Moreover, the adaptation actions are not definitively defined during planning. During the plans executions, the coordination service makes decisions concerning the execution of certain adaptation actions. For example, some actions may be found to be useless, or a choice may need to be made between alternative actions. Indeed, a planner does not always have information about the states of entities controlled by other adaptation managers. Furthermore, adaptation actions do not all require the blocking of certain application services. Hence, blocking can take place during specific periods in the application of a plan, and not necessarily from the start of its runtime. During the plans executions, the coordination service will have necessary information on the progress of these executions, and on the current application state, to be able to decide the remaining adaptation action execution proceedings.

We consider the example of four adaptation managers (*am1..am4*), which control the consistency protocol adaptation together. This protocol is managed by two types of components: update propagation managers and access managers, an update propagation manager being connected to a set of access managers. We will describe an adaptation scenario for switching from an optimistic protocol to a primary copy pessimistic protocol [RAT 98]. Each planner for the four managers receives the strategy specifying the protocol name (*primary copy protocol*), the data group concerned (*group1*) and the list of adaptation managers participating in the adaptation (*am1..am4*).

Each planner chooses and parameterizes the appropriate plan, including coordination actions. Figure 4.11 shows the adaptation plan provided by each planner for our scenario. We display the plan in the form of an object associated with a UML class of which it is an instance. The first attribute, *actionsList*, is an ordered collection specifying the names of actions to apply and their order. The second attribute, *dataGroup*, is a sequence of characters representing the name of the data group concerned with the adaptation. The attribute *protocolName* sets the name of the protocol to apply. The last attribute, *participants*, is a collection specifying the names of the adaptation managers involved. Here, the four executors apply the same plan. Each executor is responsible for the adaptation of an update propagation manager, and the access managers connected to it. This plan contains four adaptation actions and will be applied simultaneously by the executors involved. First, the *freezeDataAccessService* action activates the interception of access requests to the *group1* data group and blocks their processing. Then, the *updateAllReplica* action forces the updating of all replicas of these data, since missing updates and potential conflicts between them cannot be managed by the new protocol after adaptation. The *modifyConsistencyProtocol* action changes the behavior of the update propagation manager and corresponding access managers, in order to change the protocol adopted for the *group1* data group. Finally, *restartDataAccessService* reactivates the data group access service and launches processing of the pending data access requests.

In this example, two coordination actions are required. The *checkEndReplicaUpdate* action tests the end of all the replica updates, as this requires the collaboration of update propagation managers, before changing their behavior. The *checkEndProtocolModification* action enables each executor to check that the behavior of all the update propagation and access managers has been adapted.

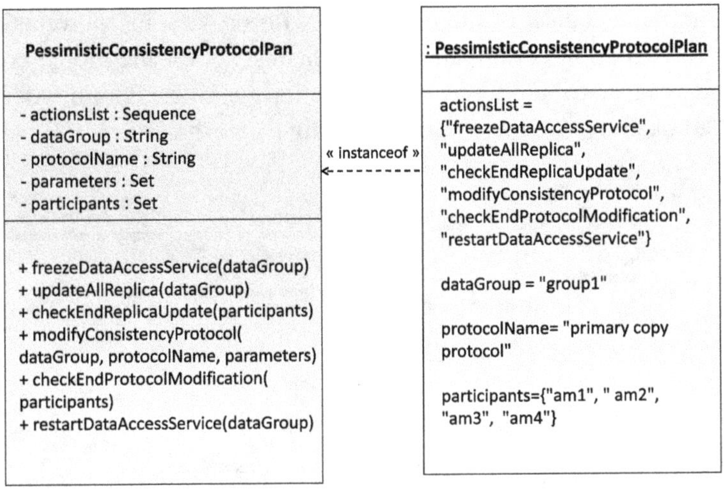

Figure 4.11. *UML class and the associated instance defining a collection of ordered actions of a coordinated adaptation plan*

4.7.5.3.2. Coordinated plans executions

Coordination of the activities of a group of executors consists of ensuring a global control of the execution of different plans. This control is performed by a coordination service, in addition to the local control ensured by each executor, by applying the adaptation actions defined in its own plan.

Our architectural model defines an optional "Coordinator" component, which is associated with an "Executor" component, giving it the ability to coordinate its activities with other adaptation managers (see Figure 4.12). A component type "Coordinator" is specialized by two attributes: *algoParameters* and *node*. The former must include a parameter corresponding to a coordination policy. The latter enables the component placement to be chosen. It may involve the same node that hosts the executor or another node.

Depending on the coordination actions presented in a plan, an executor communicates with the coordinator. This can exchange information with other coordinators, and produce orders to the executor by interpreting a coordination policy. This policy is a set of rules in event – condition – action form. The separation of the coordination concerns of executors and the execution control of a plan, as well as the use of external policies, enable an identical implementation of the executors, with or without coordination, and the reuse of execution coordination mechanisms. As for the global control, it is realized in a distributed and coordinated way, since it is divided up on different adaptation managers, each including a coordinator.

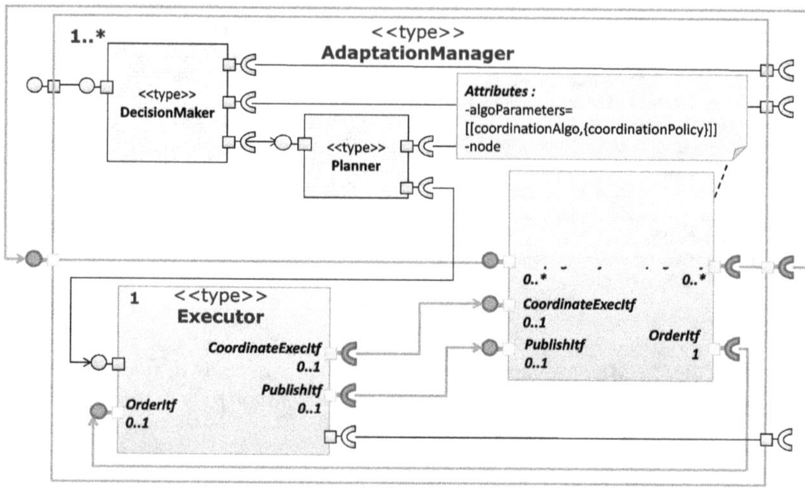

Figure 4.12. *Architectural model for coordinated execution processes*

During the runtime phase, the executors exchange information on the execution progress of adaptation plans using the coordinators. For example, an executor associated with an access manager must wait, before authorizing the processing of data access requests, so that other executors associated with update propagation managers can complete their behavior modification. Additionally, an executor can share information on the state of the components that it manages with others. This type of information may be essential for making adaptation action application progress consistently. For example, an executor needs to know if other update propagation managers that are not under its control are storing certain replica updates to be propagated. This knowledge is useful when deciding whether to change the behavior of the update propagation manager being adapted, or waiting until all updates have been propagated.

In our architectural model, a component type "Executor" has a "PublishItf" client interface to communicate information useful for the runtime progress of other plans. The component type "Coordinator" determines the group of coordinators that the information concerns, and uses the "PropagateItf" client interface to communicate with this group. This interface type has "0..*" multiplicity, in order to be able to interact with an arbitrary number of "Coordinator" components.

The "Executor" component can also use a "CoordinateExecItf" client interface to delegate decision-making regarding the remaining plan execution proceedings to the coordinator. The coordinator makes the decision based on information received from other coordinators. It informs the executor of this by sending an order via the "OrderItf" interface, an order such as "ignore the following adaptation action", or "apply the following action", or even "apply action X specified in the plan".

Reprising the consistency protocol adaptation example cited in the previous section, when an executor achieves the coordination action *checkEndProtocolModification* (see Figure 4.11), it uses the "Publish-Itf" interface to show that local modification of the protocol is complete (method "publish (subject = "endProtocolModificationConfirmation", content = "true")"), and then the "CoordinateExecItf" interface to show that it must wait for all executors to finish their local modifications to continue (method "command(subject = "endProtocolModificationCoordination", participants = ["am1", "am2", "am3", "am4"])"). This call is processed by the coordinator as an event, and the coordinator interprets its coordination policy. For this, the coordination policy specifies that the condition to verify is that all other participants have published a message, confirming the end of local protocol modification, before the expiry of a waiting period, as shown in the first rule in Figure 4.13.

The coordinator then launches a process that awaits reception of the publications expected concerning this subject, until the expiry of a waiting period. Some publications may already have been received upon launching the waiting process, according to the coordinator in question, and the speed of the plans executions. Let us assume that all the executors completed and published their local modifications. Each coordinator obtains the knowledge required before the period is up, and it is positive. Each coordinator then sends the order *applyNextAction* to the executor it is associated with, to run the next action in the adaptation plan. In the case of the waiting period expiring before all the publications are received, the second rule in Figure 4.13 is triggered, and the adaptation is canceled.

```
Rule1
When:
    commandReception (" endProtocolModificationCoordination ", " all ")

Condition:
    isAvailable (" endProtocolModicationConfirmation ", " all ")
    and hasValue (" endProtocolModicationConfirmation ", " true ", " all ")
    and not timeOut ( 10 )

Action:
    Order (" applyNextAction ")

Rule2
When:
    timeOut ()

Condition:
    hasSubject (" endProtocolModicationConfirmation ")

Action:
    order (" rollBack ")
```

Figure 4.13. *An example of coordination rules for plans execution*

4.8. Conclusion

In this chapter, we have presented the concept of dynamic reconfiguration, first in general and then by emphasizing the stakes of distributed reconfiguration management. We have examined the current works from a conceptual point of view, on the one hand, and the way in which they were implemented, on the other hand. At this level, we have in particular sought to identify the mechanisms for coordinating several distributed reconfiguration processes. Finally, we have studied the facilities proposed for using reconfiguration infrastructures.

We have presented the fundamental concepts linked to our approach for the reconfiguration of distributed component-based applications. Our contribution consists of defining an approach for constructing distributed adaptation systems. In particular, we focused on the definition of a flexible architectural model and generic mechanisms for ensuring the coordination of several adaptation managers' activities.

The flexibility of our model enables the behavior, structure and distribution of an adaptation system to be specialized. Our approach offers several ways of coordinating the decisions of adaptation managers. In particular, the negotiation of adaptation strategies enables distributed and parallel decision-making, the automatic resolution of conflicts between them, and the guarantee of their autonomy. Regarding the reconfiguration execution, our approach enables various plans for different types of modification to be parameterized and run, and a variety of actions to be included according to the strategy to be adopted. Furthermore, it makes it possible to coordinate the parallel and distributed executions of several adaptation plans. The definition of a factory and the policy-oriented approach facilitate the construction of adaptation systems. Nonetheless, the role of the adaptation expert is fundamental, especially for specializing the behavior of adaptation managers with policies ensuring harmonious functioning of the global system. The generic nature of our approach makes it applicable to several distributed software families.

Our contributions (sections 4.6 and 4.7) constitute a response to some problems identified in the first part of this chapter. However, several pathways are open to exploration, whether for broadening the use prospects of our approach or correcting its limitations. Automatic verification of the consistency of behaviors chosen for different adaptation managers would be interesting. Furthermore, other techniques may be foreseeable, such as automatic learning and distributed decision-making techniques inspired by voting systems or bidding systems, and adapting the choice of them to the context of adaptation systems at the time of their specialization. Another research pathway concerns the reliability of the adaptation system. Indeed, the probability of a partial malfunction of the adaptation system or interconnection network cannot be overlooked in some distributed environments. The objective is thus to ensure the continuity of services offered by the reconfiguration processes and to avoid inconsistencies in the application due to these failures.

4.9. Bibliography

[BEI 06] BEIERLE C., KERN-ISBERNER G., "Methods of knowledge-based systems", *Computational Intelligence*, vol. 2, pp. 42–59, 2006.

[BRA 04] BRACHMAN R., LEVESQUE H., *Knowledge Representation and Reasoning*, Morgan Kaufmann Publishers, San Francisco, CA, 2004.

[BRI 09] BRIDGES P.G., HILTUNEN M.A., SCHLICHTING R.D., "Cholla: a framework for composing and coordinating adaptations in networked systems", *IEEE Transactions on Computers*, vol. 58, no. 11, pp. 1456–1469, 2009.

[BUI 07] BUISSON J., ANDRÉ F., PAZAT J.-L., "Supporting adaptable applications in grid resource management systems", *GRID '07: Proceedings of the 8th IEEE/ACM International Conference on Grid Computing*, Washington, DC, IEEE Computer Society, pp. 58–65, 2007.

[CAP 03] CAPRA L., EMMERICH W., MASCOLO C., "CARISMA: context-aware reflective middleware system for mobile applications", *IEEE Transactions on Software Engineering*, vol. 29, pp. 929–945, 2003.

[CAS 09] CASSAGNES C., ROOSE P., DALMAU M., "KALIMUCHO – software architecture for limited mobile devices", *ACM SIGBED Review*, vol. 6, no. 3, pp. 1–6, 2009.

[CAV 02] CAVANAUGH C., WELCH L.R., SHIRAZI B., *et al.*, "Quality of service negotiation for distributed, dynamic real-time systems", *Proceedings of the 15 IPDPS 2000 Workshops on Parallel and Distributed Processing*, Springer-Verlag, London, UK, pp. 757–765, 2002.

[CHA 06] CHANG H., COLLET P., OZANNE A, *et al.*, "From components to autonomic elements using negotiable contracts", *ATC*, ofin *Lecture Notes in Computer Science*, Springer, 2006-12-06, vol. 4158, pp. 78–89, 2006.

[CHE 01] CHEN W., HILTUNEN M.A., SCHLICHTING R.D., "Constructing adaptive software in distributed systems", *ICDCS '01: Proceedings of the The 21st International Conference on Distributed Computing Systems*, Washington, DC, IEEE Computer Society, p. 635, 2001.

[CHE 03] CHEN H., FININ T., JOSHI A., "An intelligent broker for context-aware systems", *Adjunct Proceedings of UbiComp*, pp. 183–184, October 2003.

[DAV 03] DAVID P.C., LEDOUX T., "Towards a framework for self-adaptive component-based applications", *DAIS '03*, Springer Verlag, pp. 1–14, Paris, France, 2003.

[DEY 01] DEY A.K., ABOWD G.D., SALBER D., "A conceptual framework and a toolkit for supporting the rapid prototyping of context-aware applications", *Human-Computer Interaction*, vol. 16, pp. 97–166, 2001.

[DOW 04] DOWLING J., CAHILL V., "Self-managed decentralised systems using K-components and collaborative reinforcement learning", *WOSS '04: Proceedings of the 1st ACM SIGSOFT workshop on Self-managed systems*, New York, NY, ACM, pp. 39–43, 2004.

[DUR 87] DURFEE E.H., LESSER V.R., Using partial global plans to coordinate distributed problem solvers', *IJCAI 1987875883*, Report , Amherst, MA, pp. 875–883, 1987.

[EFS 02] EFSTRATIOU C., FRIDAY A., DAVIES N., *et al.*, "Utilising the event calculus for policy driven adaptation on mobile systems", *POLICY '02: Proceedings of 3rd International Workshop on Policies for Distributed Systems and Networks*, IEEE Computer Society, pp. 13–24, 2002.

[FAR 06] FARHA R., LEON-GARCIA A., "Blueprint for an autonomic service architecture", *ICAS '06: Proceedings of the International Conference on Autonomic and Autonomous Systems,* IEEE Computer Society, p. 16, 2006.

[FLO 06] FLOCH J., HALLSTEINSEN S., STAV E., *et al.*, "Using architecture models for runtime adaptability", *IEEE*, vol. 23, no. 2, pp. 62–70, 2006.

[GAR 02] GARLAN D., SCHMERL B., "Model-based adaptation for self-healing systems", *WOSS '02: Proceedings of the first workshop on Self-healing systems*, New York, NY, ACM, pp. 27–32, 2002.

[GAR 04] GARLAN D., CHENG S., HUANG A., , "Rainbow: architecture-based self-adaptation with reusable infrastructure", *Computer*, vol. 37, no. 10, pp. 46–54, 2004.

[GAZ 10] GAZIS V., PATOUNI E., ALONISTIOTI N., *et al.*, "A survey of dynamically adaptable protocol stacks", *Commun Surveys Tuts*, vol. 12, no. 1, pp. 3–23, January 2010.

[GEO 83] GEORGEFF M., "Communication and interaction in multi-agent planning", *Proceedings of 3rd National Conference on Artificial Intelligence (AAAI-83)*, pp. 125–129, August 1983.

[GU 04] GU T., PUNG H.K., ZHANG D.Q., "A middleware for building context-aware mobile services", *59th IEEE Vehicular Technology Conference (VTC Spring)* vol. 5, pp. 2656–2660, May 2004.

[HUE 08] HUEBSCHER M., MCCANN J., "A survey of autonomic computing degrees, models and applications", *ACM Computing Surveys*, vol. 40, no. 3, pp. 1–7:28, 2008.

[KEE 03] KEENEY J., CAHILL V., "Chisel: a policy-driven, context-aware, dynamic adaptation framework", *POLICY '03: Proceedings of the 4th IEEE International Workshop on Policies for Distributed Systems and Networks*, Washington, DC, IEEE Computer Society, p. 3, 2003.

[KLE 08] KLEIN C., SCHMID R., LEUXNE R.C., *et al.*, "A survey of context adaptation in autonomic computing", *Proceedings of the Fourth International Conference on Autonomic and Autonomous Systems (ICAS '08)*, Washington, DC, IEEE Computer Society, pp. 106–111, 2008.

[KOR 03] KORPIPAA P., MANTYJARVI J., KELA J., *et al.*, "Managing context information in mobile devices", *Pervasive Computing, IEEE*, vol. 2, pp. 42–51, 2003.

[LAD 00] LADDAGA R., "Active software", *Proceedings of the first International Workshop on Self-Adaptive Software* (IWSAS' 2000), Secaucus, NJ, Springer-Verlag, New York, pp. 11–26, 2000.

[LAP 05] LAPOUCHNIAN A., LIASKOS S., MYLOPOULOS J., *et al.*, "Towards requirements-driven autonomic systems design", *DEAS '05: Proceedings of the 2005 Workshop on Design and Evolution of Autonomic Application Software*, New York, NY, ACM, pp. 1–7, 2005.

[LEH 00] LEHMAN M.M., RAMIL J.F., "Towards a theory of software evolution and its practical impact", *Invited Talk, Proceedings of International Symposium on the Principles of Software Evolution (ISPSE 2000)*, Press, pp. 2–11, 2000.

[LIU 04] LIU H., "A component-based programming model for autonomic applications", *ICAC '04: Proceedings of the First International Conference on Autonomic Computing*, Washington, DC, IEEE Computer Society, pp. 10–17, 2004.

[MAR 92] MARTIAL F.V., *Coordinating Plans of Autonomous Agents*, Springer-Verlag, New York, Secaucus, NJ, 1992.

[MOA 99] MOAZAMI-GOUDARZI K., Consistency preserving dynamic reconfiguration of distributed systems, PhD Thesis, Imperial College, London, 1999.

[MON 03] MONTRESOR A., MELING H., BABAOGLU O., "Toward self-organizing, self-repairing and resilient distributed systems", in SCHIPER A., SHVARTSMAN A.A., WEATHERSPOON H., *et al.*, (eds.), *Future Directions in Distributed Computing, Research and Position Papers*, of *Lecture Notes in Computer Science*, Springer-Verlag, New York, vol. 2584, pp. 119-126, 2003.

[MUK 05] MUKHIJA A., GLINZ M., "Runtime adaptation of applications through dynamic recomposition of components", in BEIGL M., LUKOWICZ P. (eds.), *Systems Aspects in Organic and Pervasive Computing – ARCS 2005, 18th International Conference on Architecture of Computing Systems Proceedings*, of Lecture Notes in Computer Science, vol. 3432, Springer, pp. 124–138, 2005.

[ORE 99] OREIZY P., GORLICK M.M., TAYLOR R.N., *et al.*, "An architecture-based approach to self-adaptive software", *IEEE Intelligent Systems*, vol. 14, no. 3, pp. 54–62, 1999.

[PAU 98] PAUL D., YALAMANCHILI S., SCHWAN K., "Decision models for adaptive resource management in multiprocessor systems", *IEEE Real Time Technology and Applications Symposium*, Colorado, USA, November 1998.

[RAT 98] RATNER D.H., Roam: a scalable replication system for mobile and distributed computing, PhD Thesis, University of California, Los Angeles, CA, 1998.

[REN 97] RENESSE R., BIRMAN K., HAYDEN M., *et al.*, "Building adaptive systems using ensemble", Report , Cornell University, Ithaca, NY, 1997.

[ROS 06] ROSA L., LOPES A., RODRIGUES L., "Policy-driven adaptation of protocol stacks", *ICAS '06: Proceedings of the International Conference on Autonomic and Autonomous Systems*, Washington, DC, IEEE Computer Society, p. 5, 2006.

[ROU 08] ROUVOY R., CONAN D., SEINTURIER L., "Software architecture patterns for a context-processing middleware framework", *IEEE Distributed Systems Online*, vol. 9, no. 6, 2008.

[SAL 09] SALEHIE M., TAHVILDARI L., "Self-adaptive software: landscape and research challenges", *ACM Transactions on Autonomous and Adaptive Systems*, vol. 4, no. 2, pp. 14:1–14:42, May 2009.

[SOW 00] SOWA J.F., *Knowledge Representation: Logical, Philosophical and Computational Foundations*, Brooks Cole, Pacific Grove, CA, 2000.

[TAY 09] TAYLOR R., MEDVIDOVIC N., OREIZY P., "Architectural styles for runtime software adaptation", *Joint Working IEEE/IFIP Conference on Software Architecture and European Conference on Software Architecture (WICSA/ECSA* '09), Cambridge, UK, pp. 171–180, 2009.

[YAR 99] YARVIS M., REIHER P., POPEK G.J., "Conductor: a framework for distributed adaptation", *Workshop on Hot Topics in Operating Systems*, Rio Rico, Arizona, March 1999.

[ZHA 04] ZHANG J., YANG Z., CHENG B.H.C., *et al.*, "Adding safeness to dynamic adaptation techniques", *Proceedings of ICSE 2004 Workshop on Architecting Dependable Systems*, Edinburgh, UK, May, 2004.

Chapter 5

Software Architecture for Product Lines

Software product lines were designed from the product line tested out by H. Ford at the beginning of the 20th Century, which led to the success of his automotive production. For 15 years, these methods have been visible in several software application fields: telephony at Nokia, televisions at Philips, print software at HP and flight applications at Boeing, among others.

The concept of architecture is crucial for classic software applications, and this concept is even more important at the level of domain engineering in product lines. In a product line, the so-called reference architecture generically describes the architectures of all the products in the family. This chapter describes the technical means and methods for defining a reference architecture for a software product line. It will also present the methods for operating this architecture through, for example, techniques emerging from model and software component engineering, or aspect-oriented programming. These concepts and techniques will be illustrated using a case study.

5.1. Introduction to software product lines

Software systems are complex, and the time consumption and amount of labor that they require are considerable. We have managed to observe, fairly

---

Chapter written by Hugo ARBOLEDA, Rubby CASALLAS, Jaime CHAVARRIAGA and Jean-Claude ROYER.

easily, that many software applications constructed in the same context share more common than unique points. An often-used approach is to define a new application of a given scale through modification and enrichment of an already-existing application. The strategy of reusing existing components has thus been seen as a good method for improving the software productivity. Reusing existing components not only facilitates the production but also improves the overall quality of components and applications. Product line engineering is a paradigm that places component production and the reuse strategy at the center of the development process [BOS 00, CLE 02]. Of course, the first aim of such an approach is to improve productivity: that is to reduce production and time costs, and to improve the overall quality of products.

The basic principle of software product line engineering is to develop several applications, which share common aspects.

DEFINITION 5.1.– *A software product line is a set of software applications that share certain characteristics: market trends, functional requirements, an architecture, software components, etc., and rationally constructed and planned from a set of components.*

A characteristic is called a *feature* in product lines. A synonym of product line is the term "product family", which is more commonly used in Europe. However, the sometimes-used term "software factory" is more ambiguous, since it only concerns the final aspect of automating application production. The first major point of a software product line is that the development cycle must produce several products or applications, while in most traditional approaches, only one application is produced at a time. The second point is that the applications share certain features – they belong to the same domain. The characterization of this domain is, moreover, a vital activity in a software product line and makes up a part of domain engineering. Characteristics shared by domain applications are common characteristics, thereafter referred to as similarities. Variability expresses the difference between applications and their unique points.

The engineering technique for developing a product line is presented in two phases: domain engineering and application or product engineering [POH 05]. Domain engineering must identify domain applications, characterize their similarities and variations, and structure this information.

The domain engineering phase is also essential since it takes on the task of defining the production plan and producing reusable elements for the product line architecture (reference architecture). These reusable elements (or *core assets*) are of various types, since they may be involved at all stages of the software lifecycle. They may relate not only to market or functional requirements but also to more technical elements for the design and implementation of software: use cases, unified modeling language (UML) models, architectural elements, software components, code in a given programming language, tests, etc. The production plan describes how the realization of an application will be undertaken from application features and reusable components.

The second phase of a product line is the efficient production of preplanned applications from their features and the production plan defined in the domain engineering phase. The usual task is to automate this last phase as much as possible; model engineering [ARB 12, RAS 11, STA 06] is the proven technique in this context.

It is necessary in software development to distinguish the problem area (which concerns application specifications) and the solution area (i.e. application design and implementation). Figure 5.1 shows the two phases of a software product line and the links with a classic lifecycle. The problem and solution areas cover all the usual development stages: specification, design, maintenance, tests, documentation, etc. In Figure 5.1, the reusable elements, often called the core assets, represent a central store provided by domain engineering and operated by applications engineering.

Businesses adopting this type of engineering can face various difficulties, as discussed in [CLE 02, CLE 06, KRU 06]. An initial investment is needed to set it up, and the effort to be put into training, as well as managing processes, cannot be neglected. Such an adoption can take several quite different forms, depending on the business context. An important point in such cases is the return on investment guaranteed to the business. To benefit from component reuse, a sufficient set of applications which can reuse them must be constructed. The domain size, i.e. its number of applications, must not be too large or too small. If it is too small, reuse will be poor, and if it is too large, variability may be a critical factor, since it will introduce a large number of reusable element combinations. The profits from a product line largely depend on the relationship between the similarities and variability.

The case studies mention a return on investment between three and five applications. Calculating this return is actually more complex because classic cost models are not really adapted for this type of engineering, among other reasons. For a fairly precise approach for calculating this, we can consult [BOC 04] and there is a comparison of several models in [ALI 09].

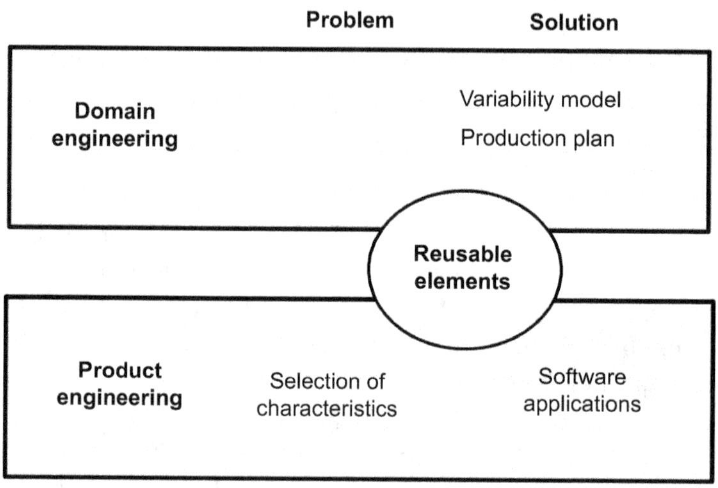

Figure 5.1. *Software product line engineering*

5.1.1. *Three development styles*

We differentiate between three implementation types: proactive, reactive or extractive (see [CLE 02, FRA 05, RAS 11]). The proactive approach sets the stages of a software product line in full motion: no application exists to begin with, and most of the reusable elements will have to be created from scratch. It thus requires a large investment to start the line, and will be beneficial in the case of a mature and stable domain. The reactive approach is more dynamic and iterative, seeking to extend or maintain an existing product line. The last approach, the extractive approach, assumes that there is an existing set of applications that the business wants to be migrated to a product line. In this case, the expertise of the business should facilitate the domain analysis and the presence of existing applications and components should reduce the costs of putting the line on the market.

5.1.2. *Variability management*

A recurring problem with reuse is that reusable artifacts (e.g. software components) are not always adapted to the exact requirements of the designer who wants to reuse them. To maximize the possibilities of reuse, domain engineering analyzes the domain, i.e. a circumscribed set of applications, for the definition of reusable domain components in great detail. We are in agreement with [SCH 04] that a domain may be:

– a management domain;

– a set of problems;

– a set of applications;

– a knowledge domain with a terminology.

The domain of a product line is defined as follows.

DEFINITION 5.2.– *The domain of a product line is the set of products or applications that will be constructed in the line. It defines the business domain, which is the target of the product line.*

There is no standard method for defining this set: it can be an enumeration completed using textual descriptions, or a constructive description using specific notations. These notations are of various types: features models [CZA 00, KAN 90], enriched UML diagrams [GOM 04], model engineering notations [ARB 12, CZA 05a] and variability languages such as common variability language (CVL) [HAU 12] and VML [LOU 08, RAS 11].

Variability management allows the domain to be formally defined by using the features model notations and product configuration.

DEFINITION 5.3.– *The variability of a set of software products is the set of differences and similarities of the features of products in the line described in a structured way.*

Several types of variability have been identified in product lines. For example, Pohl *et al.* looked at external (or essential) variability and internal (or technical) variability. The difference between the two is relative to the point of view of the client or designer, i.e. the point of view that we encounter, for example, in software quality models. External variability is concerned with the client since it is relative to user needs, i.e. it is visible to clients. Internal variability is only relevant to the designers as it relates to variations in the architecture, design language or development method.

DEFINITION 5.4.– *Variability management is the product line process which makes the variability of software artifacts explicit at an internal and external level, and which enables the configuration of different domain products.*

Pohl *et al.* [POH 05] define variability management as the set of activities defining and exploiting variability all throughout the lifecycle. Figure 5.2 shows the variability management process and its connections with other activities in a product line. This process covers the activity of variability analysis (identification, modeling and documentation) on the one hand and the resolution of variability and its realization in the product on the other hand. It is an essential process in a product line and creates an overlap between domain engineering and application engineering. In domain engineering, variability management is concerned with the analysis and modeling of external and internal variability and its documentation. In application engineering, variability management resolves external variation points in order to choose the functional configuration for products. The reference architecture, component library and production plan are then used to resolve internal variability and generate the final applications.

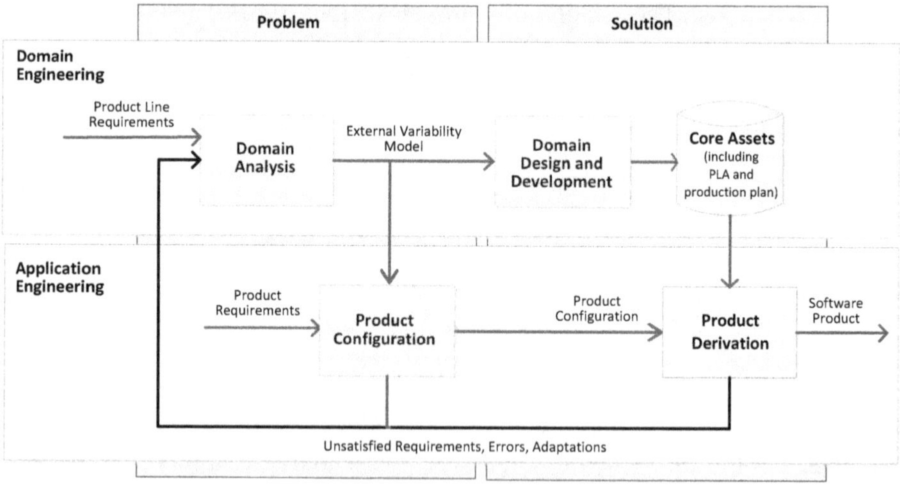

Figure 5.2. *The variability management process*

5.1.3. *The concept of architecture in product lines*

The concept of architecture is fundamental in the construction of modern software. Architecture provides a plan of work for the construction and assembly of the final product. Yet the architecture is also a documentation element that must be kept synchronized with the code, at the risk of deviation or degeneration. Architecture is not necessarily all in one piece, and we often have to use several points of view, as per Kruchten [KRU 95] or as in UML, for example. This is helpful with various static or dynamic analyses, e.g. checking the consistency of interfaces (typing), checking the flow of communication and *a priori* performance analysis. For a software product line, variability must be able to be managed using a suitable notation: a feature, meta- or decision model. However, this architecture can also integrate a more detailed design, and thus it does not need to be monostage. It can, for example, require several stages of configuration and resolution – it may be necessary to choose a particular network architecture, a programming language for certain components, design patterns, or even more configuration parameters for software components.

The architecture of products in a software product line is actually considered a reusable artifact and will be defined in the domain engineering phase. According to Clements *et al.* [CLE 02] and Bass *et al.* [BAS 12], the architecture of a product line is the original artifact of the reusable artifact kernel, and thus must be a main development objective.

DEFINITION 5.5.– *The architecture of a product line is an architecture specification shared by all the domain products. It is preplanned to support their common basis, variations and architectural requirements.*

The aim is to define an architecture that represents all the products in the family and thus integrates the common architecture and its variable elements. Using this concept allows the usual advantages to be added to those specific to product line engineering. However, the notations are more complex and using them to derive the product is more technical. A simple example is using a generic interface or pattern, which enables a family of types to be concisely described. However, a variable architecture often necessitates more complex, especially conditional, constructions for components and communications. For example, if the "modem" component is not present, the alarm is generated only at the main sound and light, but if it is present, then a telephonic alarm will be produced. Using an architecture for the product line enables the complexity to be better controlled, and thus production and maintenance costs to be reduced. In the methods for the product lines, reuse is set up with the creation of an architecture for the whole product rather than creating an architecture for each product. The concept of product line architecture (PLA), or reference architecture, is an artifact that captures this concept of shared architecture and is central in product line design methods. This "super" architecture defines the general design of the whole product from a set of reusable components, assembly rules and constraints. A concrete architecture for a domain product is actually an instance of this generic architecture or "meta-" architecture. The design of this PLA is thus essential, and assumes that there are notations and a method adapted for managing variability at the architectural level. There are some discussions in the literature about the differences between reference architecture and PLA. For most authors (and also for us), the two concepts are the same. For some authors, however, there is a difference in the abstraction level (see section 5.6 for further details). Some authors (e.g. Pohl *et al.*) and methods (such as domain-specific software architectures (DSSA) [TRA 93, TRA 95] and product line software engineering-DSSA (PuLSE-DSSA) [DEB 98]) rely on the definition of a reference architecture. In [DOB 08], the reference architecture represents the common architecture (that of the product's similarities) while variability is defined in the domain architecture.

DEFINITION 5.6.– *A reference architecture is a model (or PLA) or a set of architectural models, partially or fully instanced and aimed at making the reusable artifacts and their organization in all domain products of the product line more explicit.*

The aim of a reference architecture is to capture the essence of the architectural principles of a set of products from the same domain [CLO 10, GAL 11]. It thus not only involves reusable components, often obtained from existing projects, but also compositions, organization and architecture models that will give a structure to products in the line. This concept is thus similar to the principles of some standards or international bodies, which seek to promote application domains and formulate architecture standards. Some examples are the reference architectures for service-oriented systems, as defined by the OpenGroup[1] or at the OASIS initiative[2] or even AUTOSAR[3] for automotive systems. Such an architecture must provide assistance in the development of concrete architectures for products or new systems, in the evolution of products, or even in the improvement of product interoperability and standardization [GAL 11].

5.2. The music store example

As a case study for the application of previous concepts, we will consider a relatively limited-size example involving an online music store. The example, called "SongStock", was developed at the University of Los Andes in Colombia to provide ongoing support for the design and development of software product lines.

5.2.1. *The field*

Putting online music sales systems in place is a well-known phenomenon nowadays, which has tended to replace the traditional physical stores. According to the International Federation of the Phonographic Industry (IFPI)[4], in 2007 online music sales rose to 15% of the global music market, from 11% in 2006 and 0% in 2003. The 2012 revenues for the companies concerned were estimated to be at $5.6 billion, i.e. 9% more than that of 2011, and this represents a good third of digital industry revenues[5]. It is a global trend although the main market is North America; other countries such as India, Norway and Sweden also have their own digital music markets. The domain of music sales is thus in the process of migrating from a purely physical support-based domain to a digital format. There are different types of online stores that offer neighboring services, online radio stations (e.g. Pandora, Slacker and IHeartradio), personal playlist subscription services (e.g. Spotify, Deezer and Groveshark) and music stores (e.g. Apple's iTunes and the other services offered by Amazon, Google or Microsoft).

1 www.opengroup.org/standards/soa.

2 http://docs.oasis-open.org/soa-rm/soa-ra/v1.0/cs01/soa-ra-v1.0-cs01.html.

3 www.autosar.org.

4 IFPI Digital Music Report 2008, www.ifpi.org/content/section_resources/dmr2008.html.

5 *IFPI Digital Music Report* 2013, www.ifpi.org/content/library/dmr2013.pdf.

5.2.2. *The SongStock product line*

The reasons behind an online multimedia product line are variety of media, variety of consumer demand, considerable display variability and short waiting times for products to be put on the market. The principle of SongStock is to offer product software to companies wanting to set up a legal online music service. Normally, to set up such a business, companies acquire the rights to artists, albums or music editors. In our example, we will only consider products for song stores. A product in this family will be a *web* application, enabling information management for a virtual song store. The system must be able to show its catalog of albums and songs on sale. Each album has its name, genre and graphic display. Stores are specialized in the MP3 format and each song includes the following information: title, price, length, size and audio quality.

5.2.3. *Functional requirements*

Thereafter, we distinguish two stakeholders of the final products: the site administrator and the client. All SongStock applications must have the following functions:

– Catalog function: the system must offer a song catalog to the user (album or song name). The catalog is initially empty and the administrator can add albums, then songs, with the associated information.

– Client function: a user must be able to register with a name and password. This information allows the user to access the catalog and buy songs. The system must memorize the songs bought.

– The sales function: during shopping, the user has a shopping cart where the purchases that he or she wants to make are recorded. Individual songs can be added, as well as collections coming from albums. The user can remove songs from his or her cart, whether individual songs or a whole album. Once downloading has started, the system will send the invoice to the client in an electronic message. The system must gather statistics on the number of copies of the songs and albums sold.

Some SongStock applications may have the following characteristics:

– Audit: the application tracks carts and invoices generated by the system. This information is memorized in text form and will be of assistance in the event of an audit.

– Tax: this function enables the calculation of taxes to be paid by the shopper.

– Cloud access: a *cloud* memory function is offered to the client so that he/she can access his/her songs more freely.

– Cloud tax: this function is responsible for calculating added tax in the case of the cloud memory function being used.

Readers will have noticed the separation between the two types of functional requirements: those common to all the applications and those defining the variability of products in the line.

5.2.4. *The other main requirements*

SongStock applications must adhere to the following ergonomic, performance and architecture-related constraints:

– Usability:

- The purchase of a song or an album using the main cart must be relatively quick. The ergonomics and purchasing process must be clear and straightforward for the client. During shopping, completion must be achieved using less than three different points of view or shopping carts.

- The client interface must be uniform, intuitive and simple. The average time for a new user to learn how to use basic application functions (connection, searching, selection and purchase) must not exceed 45 min.

– Scaling up:

- The purchase of a song must not take more than 5 s, even in the case of multiple simultaneous purchases. The system must generate the invoice and memorize all useful information in less than 5 s.

- The system must be able to manage a large volume of contents (new songs, albums, artists and collections). The time required to update and upload a volume of new content must not exceed 10 min.

– Extensibility:

- The system must allow the introduction of new forms of interaction, such as a forum and chat. These additions must not change the existing functionalities, nor significantly damage the performance.

- The system must be able to accept new payment systems for the client. This must not affect the quality of the current system.

5.3. Domain engineering

Domain engineering is the process in which the similarities and variability of products in the line are defined [POH 05]. The development team starts with domain analysis to identify and model the common functions and product variables. This analysis, in fact, defines the domain, i.e. the set of products in the line. Furthermore, this process sets in motion a true lifecycle, allowing the reference architecture and product production plan to be defined. Finally, this process will lead to the creation or identification of reusable elements for the product.

DEFINITION 5.7.– *Domain engineering is the process which comprises domain analysis and design.*

5.3.1. *Domain analysis*

During domain analysis, the development team analyzes the functional requirements of products in the line to extract their similarities and variability.

DEFINITION 5.8.– *Domain analysis is the process that identifies, organizes and documents similarities and external variability from the functional requirements of products in the line.*

Due to the multiplicity and variability of products, requirements can be classified into several categories [CHE 98, KAN 90]:

– mandatory requirements, which must be realized in the whole product;

– optional requirements, which are present only in some products;

– alternatives that are choices exclusive to each other, which certain products must realize.

There are several approaches for realizing a domain analysis (e.g. [CHE 09, KHU 09]). Each of these methods proposes the capture of similarities and variability and some means of specifying these elements using the previous categories. The specification of external and internal variability is essential for the activity of designing an architecture for the product line. This specification can take two main forms:

– Integrated variability model: it involves extensions of classic notations in requirements analysis, such as the UML use case [GOM 04, HAL 03].

– Orthogonal variability model (OVM): this specification is seen as a new specification in addition to the usual development documents, using an original and adapted notation. Some examples include feature models [CZA 00, KAN 90] and the orthogonal variability model [POH 05].

5.3.2. *Use case with integrated variability*

The product line UML-based software engineering (PLUS) method is an example of domain analysis which specifies variability in functional requirements models [GOM 04]. This approach defines a set of UML stereotypes to designate the model elements that are mandatory, optional or alternative. These notations are first used in the use case to categorize the requirements, which is already mentioned.

In our SongStock example, it is possible to define a set of use cases for different products. Some of these will be present in all the domain products. This is the case with the functions relative to client management such as registering, updating information and changing the password, which will be included in the whole product. These cases will be marked by the `«kernel»` stereotype. Other cases, such as those that enable the calculation of taxes or memorization of transactions, are only present in some products. They will be identified using the `«optional»` stereotype .

Figure 5.3 shows part of the use cases for the SongStock product line. The figure includes requirements present in all the products such as `Update client information` and `Change password`. The figure also describes optional cases, e.g. `Cloud option` or `Cloud tax` which will only be available in products authorizing cloud use. Finally, there are two alternative use case types: payment with a `Credit card` and payment by `Bank transfer`. A product can include either of the two alternatives, but not both.

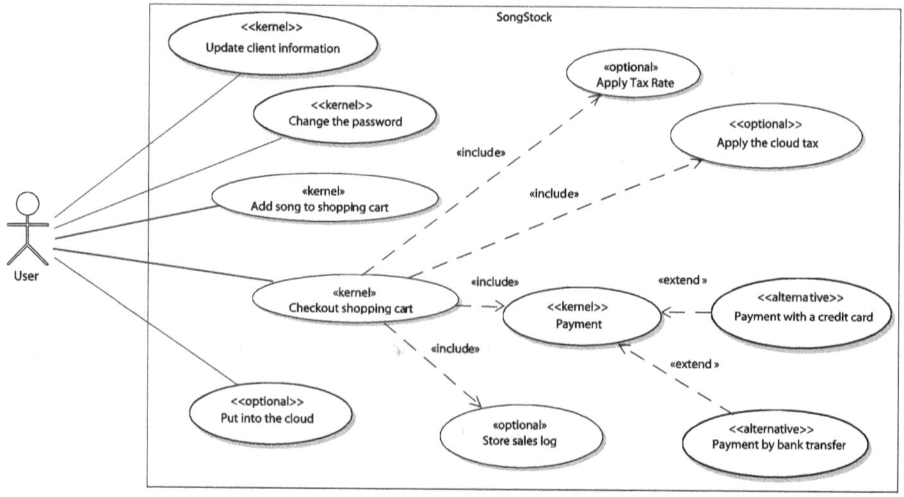

Figure 5.3. *Some use cases for SongStock products*

5.3.3. *The features model*

The features diagram is a classic way of displaying similarities and variability in a product line. It is common in product lines to have an OVM, which does not extend any classic notation in development software. The display is a tree of functional features with different knots to accompany the type: mandatory, optional or alternative. This description yields a point of view that is quite easy to read and browse when checking the functional composition of a product. Figure 5.4 shows part of the features model for SongStock, which refers back to the analysis done in Figure 5.3. In this figure, the black circles depict mandatory features, the white circles show the options and the black quadrants show alternatives.

Extensions of this basic notation have been introduced to increase the power of expression, e.g. cardinalities (as in UML), groups and attributes. One approach was suggested by Czarnecki *et al.* [CZA 04] with cardinalities and the concepts of solitary, grouped and group features. We suggest using this notation since it is relatively powerful. In particular, in Figure 5.4, a quadrant with the notation `[i .. j]` is a cardinality, i.e. the minimum and maximum number of choices in a product. For example, the payment method is defined as an alternative, since the cardinalities are `[1..1]`, i.e. by card or by transfer. As for the taxes, they may be absent, one of the two, or both, of the basic tax and that relative to the Cloud option. A final point in this figure is the arc denoted as `requires`, which indicates a dependency: the `Cloud tax` function is only present if the `Cloud option` is available (and thus has been chosen) in the application.

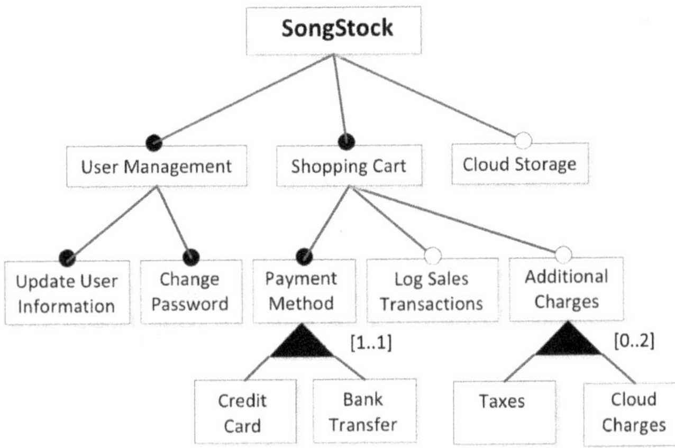

Figure 5.4. *Extract from the features model for the SongStock product line*

5.3.4. *Domain design*

Once the domain analysis is realized, a full design process for the product line is implemented. It involves defining a generic design for the products in the line, and thus we return to the usual stages of a development cycle. The design relies on a component-based approach favoring the reuse; thus, the design of reusable elements must be planned. This design must also take variability into account this will be the role of the reference architecture and the production plan.

DEFINITION 5.9.– *Domain design is the process concerned with the identification and design of reusable elements, definition of a reference architecture and a product production plan.*

Reusable elements are the artifacts used in the manufacture of products in the line. Their design in itself is classic and the methods used in the architecture or component-based programming are applied in [ATK 00, BAS 98, CZA 99, DAS 05, OMM 02]. These elements are varied and can be of any type whatsoever: requirements, UML class, Java class, test, documentation, script, etc. In this set, we will also find elements relating to savings (estimate of the cost and market requirements), performance (tests) or other non-functional aspects. One distinctive feature, however, is the reference architecture, which is a particular reusable artifact.

DEFINITION 5.10.– *The production plan is defined as a guide or a set of rules for the manufacture of products from a choice of functionalities, from the reference architecture and reusable components.*

This plan collects together a set of rules, which will be developed to manage the common and variable parts of the products. The principle is to have a part of the architecture which represents the part of functionalities common to the products and specific rules or mechanisms enabling variability management. Thus, a product will be assembled from components representing the common functionalities and other components realizing the variable part of the application.

5.3.5. *Designing the architecture of the line*

The reference architecture is an important artifact because it describes the assembly of reusable elements for defining the product while taking variability into account. This architecture is software architecture in the usual sense of the word, but enriched by mechanisms for realizing variability in the product. This mechanism uses the concept of variation points: the location of where a choice of functionality must be made. This point of choice is accompanied by possible variants. The resolution of variability is the mechanism that, given a choice of functionality, links it to a variant.

Variability is useful at each level of the development cycle and its realization uses variation mechanisms. For example, variation mechanisms at the component level are the inclusion or exclusion of a component, the selection of a version of a component from an interface, the conditional assembly of components, the conditional relation between components, etc. At the language level, heritage, aggregation, conditional compilation and the use of aspects are some known examples. A full taxonomy of these technical mechanisms is available in [SVA 05]. For our SongStock product line, we need to choose some variation mechanisms to realize the variability identified in the features model.

The first point to note is that common features are fairly classically implanted, since they are present in the whole product. In other words, there are no variation points. For example, for `Client management`, it is sufficient to include the component implementing this function in the whole product. This component must be defined in a reusable way, with good interfaces, but it is from more classic technology of the software component and architecture domain.

The variation points are relevant only for optional or alternative features. For example, some SongStock products provide tax calculation and also authorize payment following the two possible modes. In this case, the software architect must include two variation points to authorize the selection of tax calculation, and that of payment. These variation points and the corresponding variants can be specified by using an integrated variability model (e.g. annotations or UML stereotypes) or an OVM (often features models). For example, Pohl *et al.* [POH 05] have suggested the use of an OVM to specify the variation points and variants in a software artifact.

The rest of this section presents some examples of variation points and variants to illustrate this approach. The following examples are component diagrams where the variation points are implemented using an interface, and different components implement this same interface. In our example, the architecture must integrate the service interfaces for each variation point, thus one for the payment method and another for calculating charges. Figure 5.5 shows part of the SongStock architecture with two variation points (labeled `VP`) and variants (labeled `V`).

An architecture can combine different types of mechanisms for managing variations, since, in reality, situations can be a great deal more complex. For example, the SongStock line envisages an optional feature for memorizing transactions. This functionality can be implemented using an additional component, aspect programming or by conditional compilation. The following figures show two alternative designs for implementing the variation point corresponding to the memorization of transactions. Figure 5.6 describes a variant with a software component (`Sales memorization`), which checks a component responsible for the persistence of transactions. The variant in Figure 5.7 proposes a resolution based on the programming of an aspect for the same memorization functionality. The architecture of the SongStock line can integrate one or the other of these resolutions following adherence to certain quality criteria. It very often involves a compromise and evaluating the best compromise is not at all trivial. Readers will be able to consult Chapter 5 of [RAS 11] with interest, which describes a hybrid decision approach for rationalizing this type of choice.

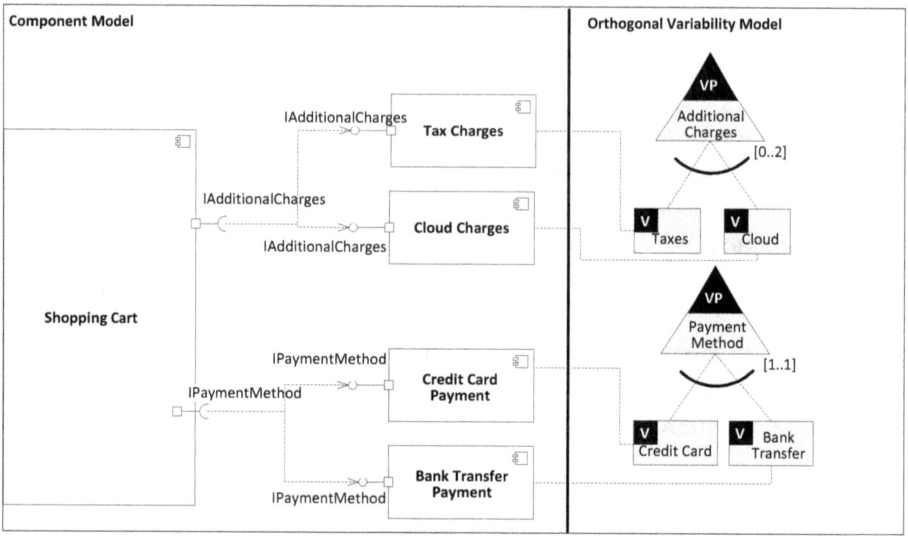

Figure 5.5. *Component-based architecture with two variation points*

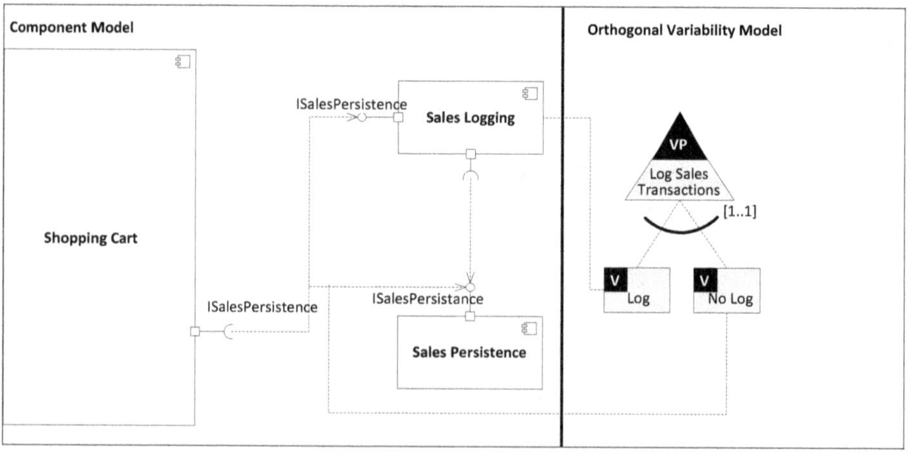

Figure 5.6. *Sales memorization architecture with a component*

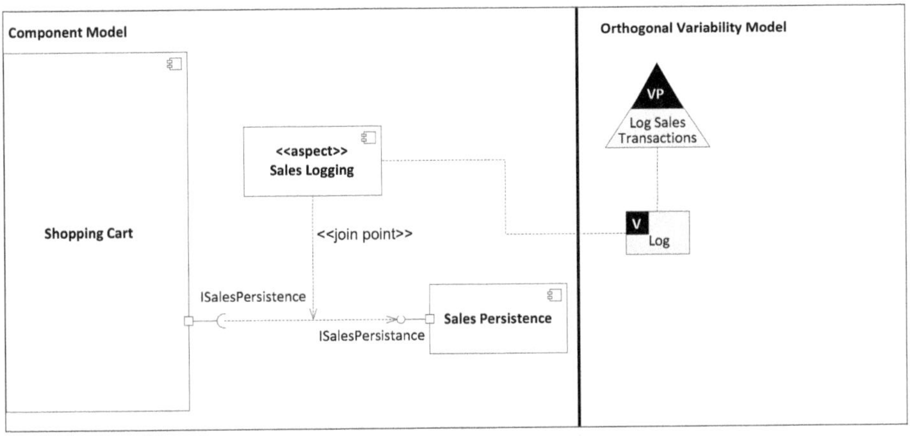

Figure 5.7. *Sales memorization architecture with an aspect*

Figure 5.8 shows a simplified, overall view of the PLA for SongStock with components satisfying the different functional requirements. Furthermore, this architecture includes a set of components and an aspect for implementing the options and alternatives identified in the features model in Figure 5.4. It thus defines a set of components that will be included in all products in the line (`Client management`), some optional components (`Sales tax`, `Cloud tax`, `Sales memorization` and `Cloud option`) and some exclusive components (`Credit card` and `Bank transfer`).

Generally, a feature is a complex functional requirement and will not be implemented by a single component, but by a portion of the architecture. For example, the feature `Shopping cart` will be implemented using various interconnected components: a user interface, sales memorization, transaction management, a connection to the payment service and a connection to the management of persistence. In practice, there is a gap between the variability at the functional (external) level and that at the design and implementation level (internal). The decision model concept [ATK 00, BAY 00, DHU 08, FOR 08] is a tool that allows the two variabilities to be linked. A decision model is an artifact that captures the variability of the line and establishes possible resolutions [BAY 00].

DEFINITION 5.11.– *A decision model captures external variability and defines the concrete resolution during the derivation of products.*

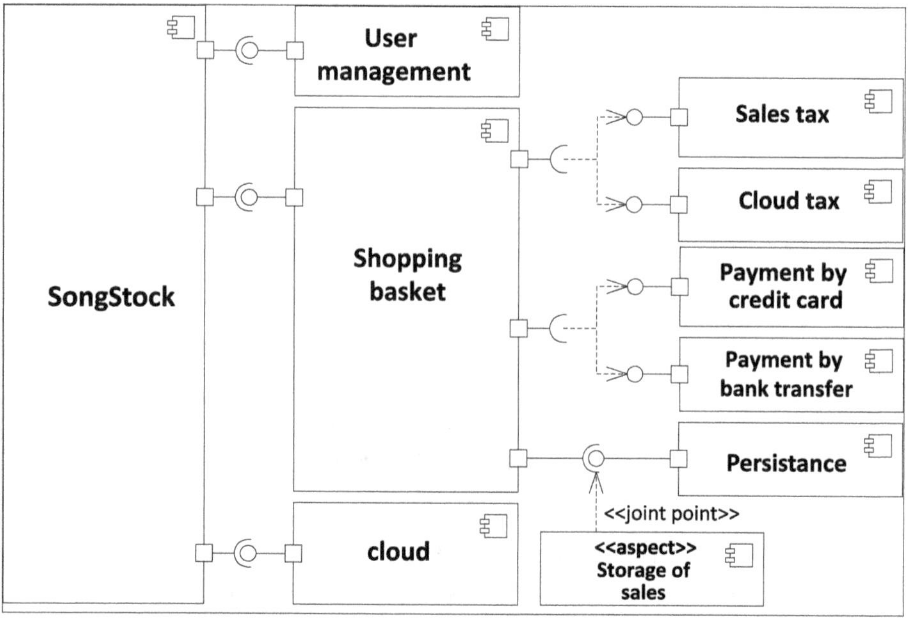

Figure 5.8. *An overview of the reference architecture for SongStock*

Each decision corresponds to a variation point associated with a set of possible resolutions that define how reusable elements can be adapted and assembled to relate the variability associated with this variation point.

There are several approaches for specifying the decision models in the product lines [SCH 11]. The KobrA approach [ATK 00, BAY 01] uses a textual table to describe how to solve a selection of features using reusable elements, architectural connections and the PLA. In our example, Table 5.1 shows such a model for the SongStock line.

5.4. Product engineering

Pohl *et al.* [POH 05] defined product engineering as the process in which member products in the line are constructed by composing reusable elements while taking variability into account.

DEFINITION 5.12.– *Product (or application) engineering is the process of producing products in the line that make up the reusable elements, while following the domain engineering production plan.*

Feature	Decision
Client management	to include the `Client Management` component
Shopping cart	to include the `Shopping Cart` component
Credit card	to include the `Credit card` component and the corresponding library in the product
Sales memorization	to incorporate the `Sales memorization` aspect, and include the library enabling «logs» in the product
Sales tax	includes the `Sales tax` component
Cloud tax	includes the `Cloud tax` component
Cloud option	includes the `Cloud option` component and i the Amazon library or Google libraries in the product

Table 5.1. *A decision model for SongStock*

During this process, the designer uses the identified variability and reusable elements created during domain engineering to ensure construction of the expected products. This process is divided into two stages: the individual configuration of the product from the features model and product creation by reuse. The first stage resolves functional variation points and the second stage will use the reference architecture and resolve the internal variation points. Following the type of engineering process, the creation of a new product can call for an interaction with the management process for the line, but we do not go into these aspects here.

5.4.1. *The configuration of a product*

In the activity of product configuration, the product designer is responsible for the selection of variants to be included in a product.

DEFINITION 5.13.– *The configuration of a product is the process of selecting a consistent and full set of variants to resolve the variation points of the features model.*

This configuration mandates that variability must be external or internal and several configuration stages are usually required in the course of producing a product. Configuration is a simple activity if we are only considering a feature-based model. This is, however, much more complex in real cases with cardinalities, groups and especially the complex dependencies between features. Some variations may be incompatible but others may involve multiple choice. The definition of a product thus demands validation of the combination of variants. The size of the information to manage is often a problem, and the main risk is of creating an inconsistent configuration, which does not correspond to any product. However, this validation can often be assisted by tools based on the satisfaction of constraints or verification of models, for example. Configuration assistants are the tools that aid in the creation of valid product configurations from a features model. Different tools have been proposed at different stages during the activity of production, for example [ANT 04, ASI 07, POH 06, WAG 05]. A well-known example based on a features model is the *FeaturePlugin* [ANT 04], a tool that integrates itself into the Eclipse platform which supports cardinalities, groups and attributes. There are industrial tools to help with the configuration of products such as "pure::variants" [PUR 10]. Yet there is still a great deal of work to be done in order to make academic results transferable to the field of business. The activity of resolving variability appearing in the product is often called variability realization time [BAC 03, BOS 02, POH 05]. Several authors have shown the advantages of deciding this resolution as late as possible, and thus, of having a variable realization time [ASI 07, CZA 05b, OMM 02]. The idea is, for example, to decide the choice of designs or techniques later on, which leaves the product more generic and open, likely to be dynamically adapted. In a general way, this uncouples internal variability from external variability, which adds flexibility for the designer and the user.

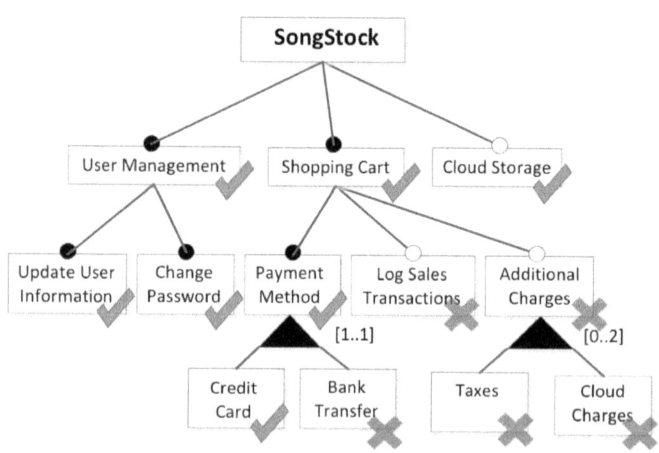

Figure 5.9. *An example of a configuration for a product in the SongStock line*

5.4.2. *Product derivation*

DEFINITION 5.14.– *Product derivation is the manual or automatic process that constructs the final product from a functional configuration and reusable elements in accordance with the production plan.*

The product functional requirements, which are captured in the configuration, are the main data for the product derivation. From there, the reusable elements must be adapted and assembled in accordance with the variants chosen in the variability model. The rules for constructing the product are defined in the production plan, and this makes use of the reference architecture. The production plan defines the general product assembly design.

DEFINITION 5.15.– *A resolution model is an instance of a decision model which links variability and defines the derivation of a product.*

In a resolution model, all decisions that were open in the decision model parent must be closed. A resolution model is intended for the creation of a particular product that will include a subset of variants, the subset of necessary reusable elements and the adaptations required for these elements.

A resolution model describes how to create a specific SongStock product in accordance with the features selected by the user. This model can also be presented in tabular format, including all the stages that the software engineer must follow to create the product. Table 5.2 shows the resolution of the product whose composition appears in Figure 5.9, adhering to the decision model in Table 5.1.

Feature	Resolution
Client management	include `Client management`
Shopping cart	include `Shopping cart`
Credit card	include `Credit card` and the corresponding library
Bank transfer	include `Bank transfer` and the corresponding library
Cloud option	include `Cloud option` and the Amazon library or Google libraries

Table 5.2. *An example of a resolution model for the configuration 5.9*

A business that needs to manage a large set of components and features for its products must use specialized software for the management of decisions and resolutions. Several authors [BAT 05, MEN 10, SCH 06] have proposed formalizations of these models to enable a configuration and the correct manufacture of products. Some formal tools based on these models, such as Clafer and eCos[6], are used in scenarios with billions of features, such as the Linux system or free software [BER 10]. Other approaches focus on the automation of product creation from decision and resolution models. Dhungana *et al.* suggested DOPLER, an approach entirely based on decision models, for deriving the products in a line [DHU 11]. The AMPLE project [RAS 11], with the TENTE approach, has proposed a quasi-automatic derivation of the line from the features model and a feature-oriented language. Finally, model-oriented approaches such as [ARB 09] and [WAG 08] consider methods for expressing the use of reusable elements in the realization of a selection of features.

5.5. The reference architecture design process

In the development process for a product line, the architect must satisfy a set of significant requirements [BAS 12]. This set comprises the functionalities expected, quality attributes and technological constraints that the architect must consider when designing the architecture. For example, in electronic business software, there are requirements relating to the functionalities which must be implemented in each business, which occur in commercial transactions. Some elements, such as the type of coding used, transaction protection (security) or even the protocol and technologies used, have an important impact on the architecture. In the SongStock line, the non-functional requirements listed in section 5.2.4 can give rise to architectural considerations, e.g. the modularity to favor scaling up and extensibility. To be effective, the architecture must take into account multiple considerations, including service quality, security or technological choice considerations. Normally, designing an architecture necessitates activities for specifying these requirements and constraints and also for evaluating the alternative architectures to choose the best compromise. The architecture design is strongly influenced by external and internal variability, but it is not the only aspect to consider.

6 http://gsd.uwaterloo.ca/clafer.

A reference architecture design process must take into account significant requirements for the products in the line, as well as the evaluation of the architecture of each product in relation to these requirements [DEB 98]. Hence, the software architect must, on the one hand, derive the concrete architecture of each domain product from the reference architecture and, on the other hand, evaluate this concrete architecture to determine whether it satisfies the significant requirements. If an evaluation is negative, the reference architecture must be reviewed since it is not right.

Approaches such as PuLSE-DSSA and the Software Engineering Institute (SEI) product line framework suggest the definition of an iterative process where the activities of variability management are integrated into a classic architectural design process [ETX 08]. For example, in their method, Clements *et al.* suggest the integration of the activity of variability management within their attribute-oriented method (ADD) for designing a software architecture based on quality scenarios for all the domain products [DEB 98]. Similarly, PuLSE-DSSA presents an iterative process where different types of scenarios are identified, then ordered and finally used to evaluate and refine the architecture.

Figure 5.10 shows an overview of the design process for an architecture by taking significant requirements into consideration. It is based on the plan proposed by PuLSE-DSSA in [DEB 98], but is adapted for the terms and concepts in this chapter. The figure shows a set of entries for the process, which include a model for external variability and a set of significant requirements for the architecture.

The model for external variability can be an orthogonal model such as a features model, or else it can be integrated into other models displaying the significant requirements for the architecture. From these entries, the software architect specifies a set of scenarios for evaluating the possible architectures. Then, he/she starts with an initial architecture which is iteratively evaluated, in comparison with a scenario; then, the evaluation results serve to refine the architecture and so forth. As highlighted above, these activities must be integrated into a current architecture design approach such as Attribute-Driven Design (ADD). At the end of the process, all the evaluations and refinements have been completed, and in principle, the architecture obtained integrates all the requirements necessary for the concrete product architectures. Figure 5.10 also shows the characteristic data produced by the process:

– a reference architecture for all the products in the line;

– an internal variability specification;

– a decision model relating external and internal variability [TAY 09].

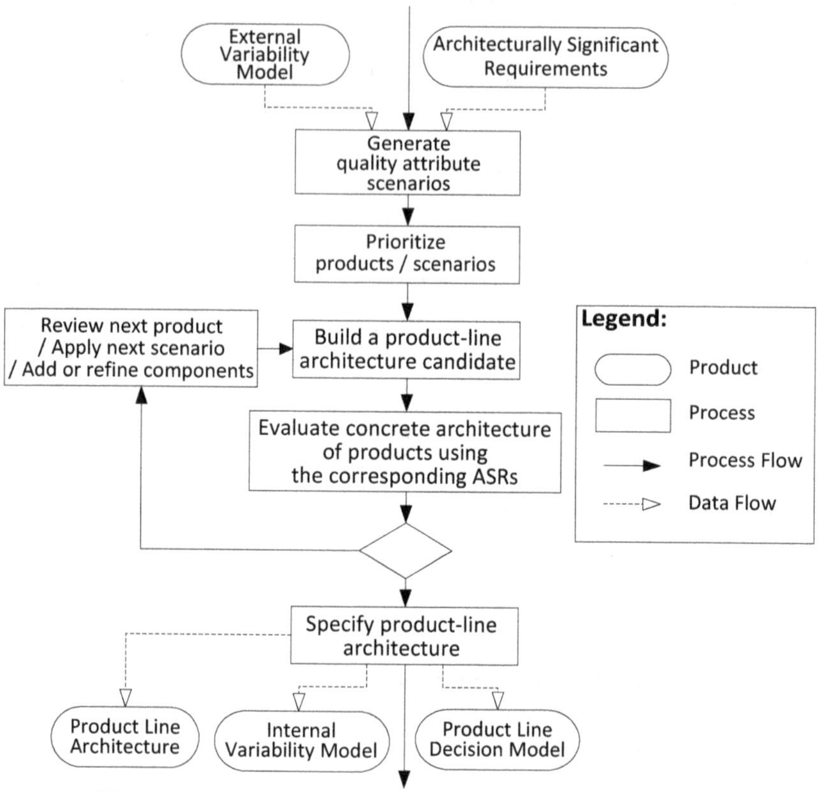

Figure 5.10. *Overview of a reference architecture design process*

Following the approach used, other data can be produced: reusable component specifications, software prototypes or reports on the evaluation of architectures [BAS 12, TRA 93].

Initiatives such as ConIPF Variability Modeling Framework (COVAMOF) [SIN 04], Quality-driven Architecture Design and Analysis Method (QADA) [MAT 02] and Quality Assessment of Software-Intensive System Architectures (QUASAR) [THI 02] extend traditional approaches to take into account quality attributes, significant architectural requirements and variability. An overview of these development methods, which take into account quality attributes, is presented in [ETX 08]. Finally, the approach suggested in Chapter 4 of Volume 2 is very close to that described here for the product lines. This approach concerns only software application families and is thus more general. The approach permits the creation of a domain architecture by integrating quality criteria. This can absolutely serve as the basis for defining a reference architecture for a software product line.

5.6. Further reading

In this section, we indicate and comment on some further reading, relating to the construction of software product line architectures. Currently, there are several books on product lines, especially [CLE 02, GOM 04, LIN 07]. The SEI site[7] is a mine of information on the subject. Moreover, the Software Product Line Conference[8] (SPLC) is the annual conference for this field. Readers seeking real examples of the success of product lines should consult the renowned *hall of fame* at http://splc.net/fame.html.

There are elements on the construction of PLA architectures, their evaluation, experiments on Model Driven Engineering (MDE) use and some concrete examples, but not from recent summaries. The summary in [HAR 01] is very much incomplete and outdated, given the great progress subsequently made into variability management, model engineering and generic architecture.

The construction of an architecture requires the use of adapted languages [MED 00] but a reference architecture must express variability and thus requires additional construction. On this subject, it is useful to consider the ISO/IEC/IEEE 42010 standard *Systems and software engineering – Architecture description*. In particular, the site contains the conceptual model description as well as a recent catalog of frames of reference[9].

A number of attempts have been made to express variability, for example Variability Modeling Language (VML) in the Aspect-Oriented Model Product Line Engineering (AMPLE) project [RAS 11] or even the CVL

7 sei.cmu.edu/productlines/

8 http://splc.net

9 iso-architecture.org/ieee-1471/afs/frameworks-table.html.

approach, which is an initiative on behalf of several manufacturers, with the aim of making a submission to the OMG[10]. There are three types of notations used for variability: the classic approach with features model notations, which exists in numerous variants, the model-oriented approaches in the sense of model engineering and decision models. More accurately, decision models are the software industry's pragmatic solution for the derivation of products. A recent, comparative summary of these notations can be found in [CZA 12]. These notations are important for the development of a product line and they occur at different levels: domain analysis, the creation of architectures or derivation of products.

5.6.1. *PLA and reference architecture*

The concept of a reference architecture is known in contexts other than product lines. They have been used to document common and reusable architectures in the manufacturing and technology fields. According to [ANG 12], reference architectures can be classified as standardization architectures, which are intended for several organizations, and help architectures, which are intended for only one organization. According to [ANG 12], a reference architecture for product lines is an example of help architecture, which is used to normalize the creation of products for the business.

The creation of a reference architecture (in addition to technical aspects, which are the objective of this chapter) necessitates management, organization and process aspects. A comparison of PLA design methods was published in ICSE in 2004 (see [MAT 04]). The aim was to compare five methods (COPA, FAST, FORM, KobrA and QADA) from the architectural design viewpoint. The paper describes a method evaluation framework based on the context, target user, content and validation. The stated objective was to give an overview of the state of the art in the design of architectures for product lines. The lessons obtained from this analysis are relatively abstract and they provide little clarity on useful architecture or variability practices for today's developers. An article by Niemela *et al.* [NIE 04] provides an introduction to basic elements for a product line architecture. The main contribution of the work is that it shows how to evaluate a product line

10 omgwiki.org/variability/doku.php.

architecture, in particular by taking into consideration different dimensions of the line. In [DOB 08], the authors suggest a consistent and integrated development strategy for embedded systems, which places the concept of architecture at the center of the process. The proposed method uses three points of view for the architecture: a reference architecture, a domain architecture and a product architecture. The reference architecture describes the architecture common to all the products, i.e. the common components and services. The domain architecture integrates the variability of products and the final view displays the concrete architecture of a product. This vision is based on practical testing, especially an example of software for the assessment of an X-ray spectrometer.

There is some controversy on the subject of differences between the concepts of reference architecture and PLA for a product line [NAK 11a]. In both cases, we dealt with an important artifact for the concrete architecture of the products in a line. Most authors do not find any real difference between the two; however, some authors see differences in the abstraction level, domain type, content or application of these two concepts [GAL 11]. Approaches such as DSSA [ALM 07] and AMPLE [RAS 11] favor the use of the term "reference architecture". Yet other authors consider a reference architecture to be different from a product line architecture [GAL 11, NAK 11a, TAY 09]. Nakagawa *et al.*, for example, have proposed a model and a method for specifying a reference architecture based on patterns and aspects [GUE 11, NAK 12], and a specific approach for specifying the architecture of the line [NAK 11b]. They posited that the reference architecture is centered around documenting patterns and examples for the design of a domain application and it must be a knowledge base for choosing patterns for product design, but it is not necessarily an architecture shared by the whole product. They also posited that the product line architecture can be designed by using one or more reference architectures. For example, the architecture for a software product line embedded in an automotive system uses architectural patterns and elements that we find in the reference architectures for Service Oriented Architecture (SOA) services and in AUTomotive Open System ARchitecture (AUTOSAR).

5.6.2. *Influential older works*

Product line engineering has its roots in the works of several authors. Parnas introduced the concept of a program family as a set of programs with major similarities, making it worthwhile to study common properties before moving on to the design of individual programs [PAR 76]. He also defined a set of techniques for the design of these program families based on the concepts of minimum subset and extension [PAR 79]. These techniques for program families have been used in several approaches for architectures and reusable components. For example, Tracz suggested the DSSA method to create reusable architectures and parametric programming languages [TRA 93]. Later on, Kang suggested the feature-oriented domain analysis (FODA) [KAN 98] approach which introduced the concept of the features model to identify similarities and variability in domain analysis.

In the 1990s, these ideas were incorporated into the process of engineering to create product families in AT&T [COP 98] and Nortel [DIK 97]. The family-oriented abstraction, specification, and translation (FAST) process, used by AT&T and Lucent Technologies, is described in [WEI 99]. This book includes an introduction to software product lines (described as families), a description of the activities of domain and product engineering and an application of the approach in two case studies.

At the end of the 1990s, several studies highlighted the importance of product line software: the CAFE, ESAPS and FAMILIES research projects[11] [LIN 02] and the book by Van der Linden *et al.* [LIN 07]. From these works, a catalog of methods and practices was established and validated in several industry projects in Europe.

In the United States, a similar project was developed by the SEI[12]. The book by Clements and Northrop presents a set of activities and practices that a business must put in place for the adoption of product line engineering [CLE 02]. The authors define a framework based on three essential activities:

– project management;

11 esi.es/Families/.

12 sei.cmu.edu/productlines/tools/framework/index.cfm.

– reusable element kernel development;

– application development.

They also describe 29 concrete practices, including architecture definition, component development, configuration management, market analysis and learning. They show how these practices can be combined by businesses following their organization and application domain. However, this is a set of good practices rather than a complete process or method.

The SEI suggested a set of methods relative to architecture design, which is summarized in Chapter 25 of [BAS 12]. In this book, the authors describe an approach for designing software architectures based on service quality scenarios (*quality-attribute scenarios*), i.e. a method for specifying requirements concerning quality attributes such as performance, security and availability. The scenarios, as well as the functional requirements and technical constraints, are used by software architects to select tactics and patterns enabling the architecture of an application to be developed. A new chapter in the new edition presents an overview of these ideas for defining architectures for product lines. It describes the quality attributes relating to variability and how to specify them in the case of product lines. It also shows some mechanisms for implementing variability in an architecture and how to evaluate the architecture of a line based on the previous scenarios.

Other books, sources of information on architecture design and software product lines, in particular, are [BOS 00] and [TAY 09]. In the first book, Bosch *et al.* present an approach for the design of software architectures for an application and a product family. Several chapters of the book relate to product lines, methods of implementing variability using components and objects and the evolution of reusable components in product line engineering. In the second book, Taylor *et al.* discuss the concept of a domain as the problem area and specific software architectures as the resolution area. This discussion ends with several examples, showing different approaches and architecture designs.

5.6.2.1. *Pohl, Böckle and Van der Linden*

An organization of useful practices into a set of processes for product line engineering is described by Pohl *et al.* in [POH 05]. The main advantage of this book is that it gives a general view of the engineering of a product line.

The concept of orthogonal models for variability was introduced in this book. Chapter 6 is mostly devoted to the concept of architecture, its use and the elements enabling it to be described. The coupling of an architecture with variability defines the reference architecture of the product line. Chapter 11 deals with the key mechanisms for integrating variability in the reference architecture. It also provides a precious indication of how to evaluate the qualities of an architecture – it must be flexible, evolvable and maintainable. Finally, Chapter 16 gives some indication of how to derive a concrete architecture for a product from the variability resolution in the reference architecture.

5.6.2.2. *The AMPLE project*

The collectively-produced work [RAS 11] is a summary of the results of the European AMPLE project[13], dedicated to advanced aspects of product lines. This book presents several chapters on variability analysis, evaluating a product line, traceability and two different approaches for implementing a product line. This book also presents some application examples and support tools. Chapter 5 provides a precise method for evaluating an architecture for product lines. The two approaches presented in this book (TENTE and Model and Aspect oriented Product Line Engineering (MAPLE)) use the model engineering and aspect programming techniques intensively. The TENTE approach privileges automatic derivation of products from the features model, but requires usage of an advanced programming language integrating a feature-oriented programming concept. Concerning MAPLE, it relies on more classic technologies in the modern business. Variability is managed at different levels with models and model transformations. With regard to variability management in architectures, a VML description is available in Chapter 4, accompanied by examples of architectures using VML4Arch. This language is dedicated to reference architecture modeling and enables architectural elements (components, interfaces and connectors) to be identified and the actions of compositions and transformations to be realized.

5.6.2.3. *Model engineering*

As has already been stated in several works, model engineering provides a complete relevant set of techniques in the framework of product lines. For a general introduction to model engineering, readers can consult the following

13 ample-project.net/

works: [CZA 05a, STA 06, VOE 07]. This form of engineering enables a uniform and flexible display of various information appearing in a product line. It also authorizes a display of the transformation process, while remaining within a homogeneous framework. Finally, it offers numerous tools for exploiting this information, which is indispensable for productivity and scaling up. The book by [ARB 12] is rightly centered on the use of model engineering for product lines. It proposes an approach for the fine-grained resolution of variability, which is sometimes necessary for describing and realizing applications. This approach is also equipped with support for Eclipse[14].

5.7. Conclusion

Product line engineering aims at rationalizing the development of a set of similar software applications by concentrating on the reuse of a component kernel. The ultimate aim of this form of engineering is to improve productivity, i.e. to reduce the cost of development and time taken to put on the market and to increase quality. The practical experiments done more than 15 years ago have shown that these benefits are on the cards as long as the development follows certain conditions.

An important component in this form of engineering is the reference architecture. It describes the encompassing architecture of all the domain products and associates variation points with mechanisms for adapting and assembling the components for generating the variable parts of products. To define a reference architecture, it is necessary to consider the external variability of products in the line, i.e. the similarities and the functional differences of applications. Very often, this variability is expressed through a features model, which is important for the architecture design and product configuration. The reference architecture must also integrate internal variability, i.e. that of the development choices or that emerge from non-functional requirements with an architectural impact. This variability can be displayed in various ways, using annotations, specific modeling languages or with the help of additional features models.

14 icesi.edu.co/i2t/driso/mdsplbook.php.

The process of developing a reference architecture is a complex process – the methods suggest evaluating the candidate architecture in an iterative process until the architecture can generate all the concrete architectures. The quality evaluation of a reference architecture is an important stage for the success of the derivation. This architecture must define the architectural platform common to all the products and enable the architecture of each product to be generated. The use of standards or norms such as UML can help with this evaluation, but the methods are still insufficient and the tools are hardly adapted.

The reference architecture plays a fundamental role in the derivation of products in the line. The concrete architecture of each product is created from the reference architecture by resolving the functional variation points and implementation corresponding to the full configuration of the product. This derivation takes a configuration, the reference architecture, the reusable component kernel and the production plan as input. The derivation can sometimes be fully automated by using model engineering techniques.

Variability management and the reference architecture are elements that are specific to the engineering of a product line. Particular attention must be given to them by any business that hopes to implement a software product line.

5.8. Bibliography

[ALI 09] ALI M.S., BABAR M.A., SCHMID K., "A comparative survey of economic models for software product lines", *EUROMICRO-SEAA*, IEEE Computer Society, pp. 275–278, 2009.

[ALM 07] ALMEIDA E.S., ALVARO R., GARCIA V.C., *et al.*, "A systematic approach to design domain-specific software architectures", *Journal of Software*, vol. 2, no. 2, pp. 38–51, August 2007.

[ANG 12] ANGELOV S., GREFEN P., GREEFHORST D., "A framework for analysis and design of software reference architectures", *Information and Software Technology*, vol. 54, no. 4, pp. 417–431, 2012.

[ANT 04] ANTKIEWICZ M., CZARNECKI K., "FeaturePlugin: feature modeling plug-in for Eclipse", *Proceedings of the Workshop on Eclipse Technology eXchange at OOPSLA '04*, pp. 67–72, 2004.

[ARB 09] ARBOLEDA H., ROMERO A., CASALLAS R., *et al.*, "Product derivation in a model-driven software product line using decision models", *Proceedings of the 12th Iberoamerican Conference on Requirements Engineering and Software Environments (IDEAS '09)*, Medellin, Colombia, pp. 59–72, April 2009.

[ARB 12] ARBOLEDA H., ROYER J.C., *Model-Driven and Software Product Line Engineering*, ISTE Ltd and John Wiley & Sons, London, 2012.

[ASI 07] ASIKAINEN T., MÄNNISTÖ T., SOININEN T., "Kumbang: a domain ontology for modelling variability in software product families", *Advanced Engineering Informatics*, vol. 21, no. 1, pp. 23–40, 2007.

[ATK 00] ATKINSON C., BAYER J., MUTHIG D., "Component-based product line development: the KobrA approach", in DONOHOE P., (ed.), *Proceedings of 1st Software Product Line Conference*, Norwell, Kluwer Academic Publishers, pp. 289–309, 2000.

[BAC 03] BACHMANN F., GOEDICKE M., DO PRADO LEITE J.C.S., *et al.*, "A meta-model for representing variability in product family development", *Proceedings of the 5th International Workshop on Software Product-Family Engineering*, Lecture Notes in Computer Science, Siena, Italy, Springer, vol. 3014, pp. 66–80, November 2003.

[BAS 98] BASS L., CLEMENTS P., KAZMAN R., *Software Architecture in Practice*, Addison-Wesley, Boston, MA, 1998.

[BAS 12] BASS L., CLEMENTS P., KAZMAN R., *Software Architecture in Practice*, 3rd edition, Addison-Wesley, Boston, MA, 2012.

[BAT 05] BATORY D., "Feature models, grammars, and propositional formulas", in OBBINK H. POHL K., (eds.), *Software Product Lines*, vol. 3714 of Lecture Notes in Computer Science, Springer, Berlin, Heidelberg, pp. 7–20, 2005.

[BAY 00] BAYER J., FLEGE O., GACEK C., "Creating product line architectures", *Proceedings of the International Workshop on Software Architectures for Product Families (IW-SAPF-3)*, Springer-Verlag, London, UK, pp. 210–216, 2000.

[BAY 01] BAYER J., MUTHIG D., GOPFERT B., The library system product line. A KobrA case study (IESE-Report, 024.01/E), Research report, Institute Fraunhofer IESE, 2001.

[BER 10] BERGER T., SHE S., LOTUFO R., *et al.*, "Variability modeling in the real: a perspective from the operating systems domain", *Proceedings of the IEEE/ACM International Conference on Automated Software Engineering (ASE '10)*, ACM, New York, NY, pp. 73–82, 2010.

[BOC 04] BOCKLE G., CLEMENTS P., MCGREGOR J.D., *et al.*, "Calculating ROI for software product lines", *IEEE Software*, vol. 21, no. 3, pp. 23–31, May /June 2004.

[BOS 00] BOSCH J., *Design and Use of Software Architectures: Adapting and Evolving a Product-Line Approach*, Addison-Wesley, Boston, MA, 2000.

[BOS 02] BOSCH J., FLORIJN G., GREEFHORST D., *et al.*, "Variability issues in software product lines", *Revised Papers from the 4th International Workshop on Software Product-Family Engineering (PFE '01)*, Springer-Verlag, London, UK, pp. 13–21, 2002.

[CHE 98] CHEONG Y.C., ANANDA A.L., JARZABEK S., "Handling variant requirements in software architectures for product families", in LINDEN F.V.D., (ed.), *Development and Evolution of Software Architectures for Product Families, Proceedings of 2nd International ESPRIT ARES Workshop*, Las Palmas de Gran Canaria, Spain, February 26–27, 1998, of Lecture Notes in Computer Science, Springer, vol. 1429, pp. 188–196, 1998.

[CHE 09] CHEN L., BABAR M.A., ALI N., "Variability management in software product lines: a systematic review", *Proceedings of the 13th International Software Product Line Conference*, San Francisco, CA, August 2009.

[CLE 02] CLEMENTS P., NORTHROP L., *Software Product Lines: Practices and Patterns*, Addison-Wesley, Boston, MA, August 2002.

[CLE 06] CLEMENTS P.C., JONES L.G., MCGREGOR J.D., *et al.*, "Getting there from here: a roadmap for software product line adoption", *Communications of the ACM*, vol. 49, no. 12, pp. 33–36, December 2006.

[CLO 10] CLOUTIER R., MULLER G., VERMA D., *et al.*, "The concept of reference architectures", *Systems Engineering*, vol. 13, no. 1, pp. 14–27, February 2010.

[COP 98] COPLIEN J., HOFFMAN D., WEISS D., "Commonality and variability in software engineering", *IEEE Software*, vol. 15, no. 6, pp. 37–45, 1998.

[CZA 99] CZARNECKI K., EISENECKER U.W., "Components and generative programming", *Proceedings of ESEC-FSE 1999*, pp. 2–19, 1999.

[CZA 00] CZARNECKI K., EISENECKER U.W., *Generative Programming: Methods, Tools, and Applications*, ACM Press/Addison-Wesley Publishing Co., New York, 2000.

[CZA 04] CZARNECKI K., HELSEN S., EISENECKER U.W., "Staged configuration using feature models", *Proceedings of the 3rd Software Product Line Conference 2004*, Lecture Notes in Computer Science, Springer, vol. 3154, pp. 266–282, 2004.

[CZA 05a] CZARNECKI K., ANTKIEWICZ M., KIM C.H.P., *et al.*, "Model-driven software product lines", *Companion to the 20th Annual ACM SIGPLAN Conference on Object-Oriented Programming, Systems, Languages, and Applications (OOPSLA '05)*, ACM, New York, NY, pp. 126–127, 2005.

[CZA 05b] CZARNECKI K., HELSEN S., EISENECKER U.W., "Staged configuration through specialization and multilevel configuration of feature models", *Software Process: Improvement and Practice*, vol. 10, no. 2, pp. 143–169, 2005.

[CZA 12] CZARNECKI K., GRÜNBACHER P., RABISER R., *et al.*, "Cool features and tough decisions: a comparison of variability modeling approaches", in EISENECKER U.W., APEL S. GNESI S., (ed.), *6th International Workshop on Variability Modelling of Software-Intensive Systems*, ACM, pp. 173–182, 2012.

[DAS 05] DASHOFY E.M., VAN DER HOEK A., TAYLOR R.N., "A comprehensive approach for the development of modular software architecture description languages", *ACM Transactions on Software Engineering and Methodology*, vol. 14, no. 2, pp. 199–245, 2005.

[DEB 98] DEBAUD J.-M., FLEGE O., KNAUBER P., "PuLSE-DSSA a method for the development of software reference architectures", *Proceedings of the 3rd International Workshop on Software Architecture (ISAW '98)*, ACM, pp. 25–28, 1998.

[DHU 08] DHUNGANA D., GRÜNBACHER P., RABISER R., "DecisionKing: a flexible and extensible tool for integrated variability modeling", *Proceedings of the 2nd International Workshop on Variability Modelling of Software-intensive Systems*, Essen, Germany, January 2008.

[DHU 11] DHUNGANA D., GRÜNBACHER P., RABISER R., "The DOPLER meta-tool for decision-oriented variability modeling: a multiple case study", *Automated Software Engineering*, vol. 18, no. 1, pp. 77–114, March 2011.

[DIK 97] DIKEL D., KANE D., ORNBURN S., *et al.*, "Applying software product-line architecture", *Computer*, vol. 30, no. 8, pp. 49–55, 1997.

[DOB 08] DOBRICA L., NIEMELÄ E., "An approach to reference architecture design for different domains of embedded systems", in ARABNIA H.R., REZA H., (eds.), *Proceedings of the 2008 International Conference on Software Engineering Research and Practice*, CSREA Press, pp. 287–293, 2008.

[ETX 08] ETXEBERRIA L., SAGARDUI G., BELATEGI L., "Quality aware software product line engineering", *Journal of the Brazilian Computing Society*, vol. 14, no. 1, pp. 57–69, 2008.

[FOR 08] FORSTER T., MUTHIG D., PECH D., "Understanding decision models. visualization and complexity reduction of software variability", *Proceedings of the 2nd International Workshop on Variability Modeling of Software-Intensive Systems*, Essen, Germany, January 2008.

[FRA 05] FRAKES W.B., KANG K., "Software reuse research: status and future", *IEEE TSE Transactions on Software Engineering*, vol. 31, no. 7, pp. 529–536, 2005.

[GAL 11] GALSTER M., AVGERIOU P., "Empirically-grounded reference architectures: a proposal", *Proceedings of the Joint ACM SIGSOFT Conference – QoSA and ACM SIGSOFT Symposium – ISARCS on Quality of Software Architectures – QoSA and Architecting Critical Systems – ISARCS, QoSA-ISARCS '11*, ACM, New York, NY, pp. 153–158, 2011.

[GOM 04] GOMAA H., *Designing Software Product Lines with UML: From Use Cases to Pattern-Based Software Architectures*, Addison Wesley Longman Publishing Co., Redwood City, CA, 2004.

[GUE 11] GUESSI M., DE OLIVEIRA L.B.R., NAKAGAWA E.Y., "Representation of reference architectures: a systematic review", *Proceedings of the 23rd International Conference on Software Engineering and Knowledge Engineering (SEKE '11)*, pp. 782–785, 2011.

[HAL 03] HALMANS G., POHL K., "Communicating the variability of a software-product family to customers", *Software and Systems Modeling*, vol. 2, no. 1, pp. 15–36, 2003.

[HAR 01] HARSU M., A survey of product-line architectures, Report, Software Systems Laboratory, Tampere University of Technology, October 2001.

[HAU 12] HAUGEN Ø., WASOWSKI A., CZARNECKI K., "CVL: common variability language", DE ALMEIDA E.S., SCHWANNINGER C., BENAVIDES D., Eds., *Software Product Line Conference*, ACM, pp. 266–267, 2012.

[KAN 90] KANG K., COHEN S., HESS J., *et al.*, Feature-oriented domain analysis (FODA) feasibility study, Report , Software Engineering Institute and Carnegie Mellon University, 1990.

[KAN 98] KANG K., KIM S., LEE J., *et al.*, "FORM: a feature-oriented reuse method with domain-specific reference architectures", *Annals of Software Engineering*, vol. 5, no. 1, pp. 143–168, 1998.

[KHU 09] KHURUM M., GORSCHEK T., "A systematic review of domain analysis solutions for product lines", *Journal of Systems and Software*, vol. 82, no. 12, pp. 1982–2003, 2009.

[KRU 95] KRUCHTEN P., "The 41 view model of architecture", *IEEE Software*, vol. 12, no. 6, pp. 42–50, 1995.

[KRU 06] KRUEGER C.W., "New methods in software product line practice", *Commununications of the ACM*, vol. 49, no. 12, pp. 37–40, December 2006.

[LIN 02] LINDEN F.V.D., "Software product families in Europe: the Esaps & Cafe projects", *IEEE Software*, vol. 19, no. 4, pp. 41–49, 2002.

[LIN 07] LINDEN F.V.D., SCHMID K., ROMMES E., *Software Product Lines in Actions: The Best Industrial Practices in Product Line Enginering*, Springer, New York, 2007.

[LOU 08] LOUGHRAN N., SANCHEZ P., GARCIA A., *et al.*, "Language support for managing variability in architectural models", *Proceeding of the 7th International Symposium on Software Composition*, of Lecture Notes in Computer Science, vol. 4954, Springer, Budapest, pp. 36–51, March 2008.

[MAT 02] MATINLASSI M., NIMIEÄ E., DOBRICA L., "Quality-driven architecture design and quality analysis method: a revolutionary initiation approach to a product line architecture", *Vtt-pubs-456*, VTT Electronics, 2002.

[MAT 04] MATINLASSI M., "Comparison of software product line architecture design methods: COPA, FAST, FORM, KobrA and QADA", in FINKELSTEIN A., ESTUBLIER J. ROSENBLUM D.S., (eds.), *26th International Conference on Software Engineering*, IEEE Computer Society, pp. 127–136, 2004.

[MED 00] MEDVIDOVIC N., TAYLOR R.N., "A classification and comparison framework for software architecture description languages", *IEEE Transactions on Software Engineering*, vol. 26, no. 1, pp. 70–93, 2000.

[MEN 10] MENDONÇA M., COWAN D.D., "Decision-making coordination and efficient reasoning techniques for feature-based configuration", *Science of Computer Programming*, vol. 75, no. 5, pp. 311–332, 2010.

[NAK 11a] NAKAGAWA E.Y., ANTONINO P.O., BECKER M., "Reference architecture and product line architecture: a subtle but critical difference", *Proceedings of the 5th European Conference on Software Architecture (ECSA '11)*, pp. 207–211, 2011.

[NAK 11b] NAKAGAWA E.Y., ANTONINO P.O., BECKER M., "Exploring the use of reference architectures in the development of product line artifacts", *Proceedings of the 15th International Software Product Line Conference*, ACM, vol. 2, pp. 28:1–28:8, 2011.

[NAK 12] NAKAGAWA E.Y., OQUENDO F., BECKER M., "RAModel: a reference model for reference architectures", *Proceedings of 2012 Joint Working IEEE/IFIP Conference on Software Architecture and European Conference on Software Architecture (WICSA/ECSA '12)*, pp. 297–301, 2012.

[NIE 04] NIEMELÄ E., MATINLASSI M., TAULAVUORI A., "Practical evaluation of software product family architectures", in NORD R.L., (ed.), *Proceedings of the 3rd International Software Product Line Conference*, Lecture Notes in Computer Science, Springer, vol. 3154, pp. 130–145, September 2004.

[OMM 02] OMMERING R.V., "Building product populations with software components", *Proceedings of the 24th International Conference on Software Engineering (ICSE '02)*, pp. 255–265, 2002.

[PAR 76] PARNAS D., "On the design and development of program families", *IEEE Transactions on Software Engineering*, vol. SE-2, no. 1, pp. 1–9, 1976.

[PAR 79] PARNAS D., "Designing software for ease of extension and contraction", *IEEE Transactions on Software Engineering*, vol. SE-5, no. 2, pp. 128–138, 1979.

[POH 05] POHL K., BÖCKLE G., VAN DER LINDEN F., *Software Product Line Engineering: Foundations, Principles, and Techniques*, Springer, Berlin, 2005.

[POH 06] POHL K., METZGER A., "Variability management in software product line engineering", *Proceedings of the 28th International Conference on Software Engineering (ICSE '06)*, ACM, New York, NY, pp. 1049–1050, 2006.

[PUR 10] PURE SYSTEMS, "Pure:Variants", 2010. Available at www.pure-systems.com/pure_variants.49.0.html.

[RAS 11] RASHID A., ROYER, J.C. RUMMLER A., (eds.), *Aspect-Oriented, Model-Driven Software Product Lines: The AMPLE Way*, Cambridge University Press, Cambridge, 2011.

[SCH 04] SCHMID K., JOHN I., "A customizable approach to full lifecycle variability management", *Science of Computer Programming*, vol. 53, no. 3, pp. 259–284, 2004.

[SCH 06] SCHOBBENS P.Y., HEYMANS P., TRIGAUX J.C., "Feature diagrams: a survey and a formal semantics", *14th IEEE International Conference on Requirements Engineering*, pp. 139–148, 2006.

[SCH 11] SCHMID K., RABISER R., GRÜNBACHER P., "A comparison of decision modeling approaches in product lines", *Proceedings of the 5th Workshop on Variability Modeling of Software-Intensive Systems (VaMoS '11)*, ACM, New York, pp. 119–126, 2011.

[SIN 04] SINNEMA M., DEELSTRA S., NIJHUIS J., *et al.*, "COVAMOF: a framework for modeling variability in software product families", in NORD R.L., (ed.), *Proceedings of the 3rd International Software Product Line Conference*, of Lecture Notes in Computer Science, Springer, vol. 3154, pp. 197–213, 2004.

[STA 06] STAHL T., VOELTER M., CZARNECKI K., *Model-Driven Software Development: Technology, Engineering, Management*, John Wiley & Sons, Chichester, 2006.

[SVA 05] SVAHNBERG M., GURP J.V., BOSCH J., "A taxonomy of variability realization techniques", *Software Practice and Experience*, vol. 35, no. 8, pp. 705–754, July 2005.

[TAY 09] TAYLOR R., MEDVIDOVIC N., DASHOFY E., *Software Architecture: Foundations, Theory and Practice*, John Wiley & Sons, 2009.

[THI 02] THIEL S., "On the definition of a framework for an architecting process supporting product family development", LINDEN F., (ed.), *Software Product-Family Engineering*, of Lecture Notes in Computer Science, Springer, vol. 2290, pp. 125–142, 2002.

[TRA 93] TRACZ W., COGLIANESE L., YOUNG P., "A domain-specific software architecture engineering process outline", *SIGSOFT Software Engineering Notes*, vol. 18, no. 2, pp. 40–49, April 1993.

[TRA 95] TRACZ W., “DSSA (domain-specific software architecture): pedagogical example”, *SIGSOFT Software Engineering Notes*, vol. 20, no. 3, pp. 49–62, July 1995.

[VOE 07] VOELTER M., GROHER I., “Product line implementation using aspect-oriented and model-driven software development”, *Proceedings of the 11th International Software Product Line Conference*, pp. 233–242, 2007.

[WAG 05] WAGELAAR D., “Context-driven model refinement”, *MDAFA*, of *Lecture Notes in Computer Science*, Springer, vol. 3599, pp. 189–203, 2005.

[WAG 08] WAGELAAR D., Platform ontologies for the model-driven architecture, PhD Thesis, Free University of Brussels, April 2008.

[WEI 99] WEISS D., LAI C.T.R., *Software Product-Line Engineering: A Family-Based Software Development Process*, Addison-Wesley Longman Publishing Co., Boston, MA, 1999.

Chapter 6

Software Architecture: Service Adaptation Techniques in the Context of Web Services Composition

A fundamental challenge in working with heterogeneous and autonomous Web services is the need to ensure their interoperability and compatibility. In the context of Web service interaction, significant research efforts focusing on the adaptation techniques have been made to tackle the services incompatibilities. In this chapter, we present an overview of proposed adaptation approaches dealing with service mismatches at the level of service functional specifications, i.e. service *interface* and *business protocol*. Service interface refers to the mismatches between service *signatures* whereas the business protocol concerns dependencies between message exchanges.

6.1. Introduction

With increasing use of platform-language independent software architectures in the paradigm of service-oriented architecture (SOA), Web service technology has been used to enable dynamic and flexible interoperation of distributed business processes within and across organizational boundaries. According to the World Wide Web Consortium (W3C), the definition of Web services is as follows: *A Web service is a*

Chapter written by Kamel BARKAOUI and Maryam ESLAMICHALANDAR.

software application identified by a URI, whose interfaces and binding are capable of being defined, described, and discovered by XML artifacts, and supports direct interactions with other software applications using XML-based messages via Internet-based protocols. Web services technologies allow the exchange of XML documents while they can be used to implement the interfaces and messages for SOA. To this end, SOA provides a general framework for Web service interaction that comprises *service provider*, *service broker* and *service customer*. The service provider implements his own Web service and publishes its information (i.e. description and functionality) to a public access *service repository*. A service broker manages the repository and allows the service customer to find an appropriate service (that has already been published) for binding to his own components. The service broker compares the actual Web service model published by the provider with an abstract Web service model submitted by the customer. Then, the service provider and the customer may bind their services and initiate interaction.

Web service technologies include (1) Extensible Markup Language (XML)[1] technologies like XML Schema, XSLT and XQUERY to support the data and document that is exchanged, e.g. transformation, process and manipulation; (2) Simple Object Access Protocol (SOAP) [BOX 00] which is the protocol for basic exchange of data and documents; (3) Web Services Description Language (WSDL) [CHR 01] to describe all details about services, messages and endpoints; and (4) Universal Description, Discovery and Integration (UDDI) [BEL 02] which is the infrastructure required to publish and discover services. There are two ways of binding Web services: *static* binding that is done at the design time where the service customer acquires required information about a service directly from the service provider (i.e. through a private channel like e-mail) and stores it in a local configuration file; and *dynamic* binding that occurs at runtime. When the client application runs, it dynamically locates the service using a UDDI registry and then dynamically binds it using WSDL and SOAP. This requires that the contents of the UDDI registry must be trusted. Currently, only private UDDI networks can provide such control over the contents.

The Web service description represents its *behavior*, *capability*, *quality* and *interface*. An instance of a given service corresponds to the execution of its activities. These activities are atomic units of work where the partial order

1 http://www.w3.org/XML.

of execution of the activities (modeled by a workflow) denotes the behavior of a service. The expected results and conceptual purpose of a service signify its capability. The Quality of Service (QoS) is realized by non-functional properties. A service interface represents its functionality. The interface describes service *signature* (i.e. comprising the operations, the inputs/outputs messages, message types and error parameters) facing an environment from an interactional standpoint. The interface of a service consists of a set of ports (i.e. connected by a channel) enabling the message exchange for a service using SOAP over the transport protocol such as HyperText Transfer Protocol (HTTP) or HTTPS. An XML-based language like WSDL defines the service interface.

Medjahed *et al.* [MED 03b] discuss the fact that Web services can potentially simplify the building of distributed applications and also describe the design of an impressive and useful system that realizes this promise. Felber *et al.* [FEL 03] introduce some algorithms to provide solutions for the problems associated with SOAP and related XML-based schemes that require further decoding to bind many kinds of requests. Papazoglou [PAP 03b] introduces the concept of software as a service, when he introduced an *extended service-oriented architecture* that includes separate tiers for service *composition* and *coordination*, for service *operations management* (i.e. to monitor the correctness and overall functionality of aggregated/orchestrated services in an open marketplace by using grid services).

The Business Process Execution Language for Web services (BPEL4WS or BPEL in short) [JOR 07] is an XML-based language to describe the behavior of business process based on Web services (in terms of WSDL). Originally, the BPEL has been released by Microsoft, IBM, Siebel Systems, BEA and SAP by merging the specification of Microsoft's XLANG [THA 01] and IBM's WSFL [LEY 01]. A BPEL business process interoperates with the Web services of its partners. The BPEL can be used to define two kinds of processes, namely *executable processes* and *abstract processes*. The abstract process is a protocol that specifies the message exchange between different partners without revealing their internal behavior. The executable process specifies the execution order of a number of activities. An activity can either be a *primitive* activity (e.g. *invoke*, *reply*, *receive*, *wait* and *assign*) or a *structured* activity. The structured activities are a combination of primary activities in order to enable the presentation of complex structures such as *sequence*, *switch*, *while* and *flow*.

To model, analyze and verify the behavior of service interoperability, various formalisms are applied to represent the BPEL activities, e.g. Petri nets [BON 08, OUY 07, LOH 08], finite state machines (FSMs) [BEN 06, FU 04] and process algebra [FER 04, MAT 07]. The authors of [VAN 09a, REI 07] apply the *open nets* [MAS 05] (e.g. open Petri nets/open WorkFlow net) to represent the service interactions where the Petri net is enriched by *interface places* for asynchronous communication with partners.

One of the challenges in working with heterogeneous Web services is the need to ensure their interoperability and compatibility. A variety of research efforts on Web services have fundamentally focused on adaptation techniques dealing with incompatibilities in service interaction. In this chapter, we abstract from non-functional requirements (e.g. time constraint and cost), data and information semantics. Hence, we focus only on the behavior and interface of Web services interacting with an environment.

The chapter proceeds as follows. In section 6.2, we discuss Web service composition and the crucial concepts on this area. Section 6.3 is devoted to review a number of service adaptation approaches from the viewpoints of their interfaces or business protocol mismatches.

6.2. Web service composition and verification

Service orientation allows for the creation of large distributed systems by composition of several heterogeneous, decentralized and autonomous Web services. Nowadays, the interoperability of Web services as the fundamental idea of SOA [BRO 06] for effective business-to-business collaboration [MED 03a] has received significant attention from both industry and academia, e.g. Extended Enterprise (Business-to-Business) pattern introduced by IBM[2]. Web service interoperability aims to provide seamless and automatic communication among independent services regardless of their location and platform. The ability of efficient composition of heterogeneous Web services increases the reusability and QoS, reduces costs and can satisfy a variety of business demands.

The process of service composition develops a composite service by taking a set of service components as input. A composite service is

2 IBM-WebSphere: Introduce Patterns for e-business.

recursively defined as an aggregation of elementary and composed services [DUS 05]. The composition of two or more services generates a new service providing both the original behavior of initial services and a new collaborative behavior to carry out a new composite task. This means that existing services are able to cooperate even though the cooperation was not designed in advance [BEN 04, NEZ 06]. There are two different service descriptions for a composition model: service *orchestration* and service *choreography* (also called *contract*) [PEI 03]. Although both are applied to model composite services in the SOA, service orchestration describes the service interaction from the viewpoint of a single participant service (orchestrator), while service choreography describes the interactions between a collection of participant services from a global perspective such that each party knows the business logic and messaging sequence. By choreography, we refer to the message exchanges that occur among partner services involved in a composite service. The languages such as BPEL4WS and BPMN[3] specify choreographies and orchestrations.

Benatallah *et al.* [BEN 05] describe the design and implementation of the *Self-Serv* system where Web services are declaratively composed using a model-driven approach, and the resulting composite services are executed in a decentralized way within a peer-to-peer and dynamic environment. Papazoglou [PAP 03] addresses the issues relating to the use of business transactions in Web service-based applications. The paper introduces a *business transaction framework* (based on collaborating Web services) that is necessary for building robust and extendible e-business applications. The author also introduces the standard Web service-based initiatives such as BPEL, WS-Transaction, WS-Coordination, the Business Transaction Protocol (BTP) and the ebXML Business Process Specification Schema (BPSS) that enable the description of the public interface of e-business processes. Dalal *et al.* [DAL 03] evaluate the application of BTP for practical cases that have been developed by OASIS to support the collaboration of commercial Web-based applications.

Alamri *et al.* [ALA 06] introduce the classification of dynamic Web service composition techniques as:

– *runtime reconfiguration*, using wrappers where one or more components are wrapped inside another component [TRU 01];

3 http://www.omg.org/spec/BPMN/1.1.

– *runtime service adaptation*, where the interface and behavior of services or components are changed at runtime, proposed for incompatible service composition;

– *composition language*, which provides a way to better describe component composition. A composition language is a combination of an Architectural Description Language (ADL), a scripting language, a glue language and a coordination language;

– *workflow-driven composition techniques*, which define an abstract process model to characterize the set of tasks and data dependencies of workflow in a composition;

– *ontology-driven service composition*, which facilitates the semantic dynamic composition of Web services;

– *declarative composition techniques* that use the composability rules to determine whether two services are composable [DUS 05].

Spanoudakis *et al.* [SPA 05] propose a framework to dynamically monitor composite services and dynamically identify the service which will substitute the malfunctioning services. The goal of the proposed approach is to detect and correct both functional and non-functional requirement violations. The framework can be applied on both service infrastructure and service composition layers. Skogsrud *et al.* [SKO 04] introduce a trust negotiation framework for Web services based on state machines, extended with security abstractions. This model-driven approach provides benefits for developers of composite Web services. Quintero *et al.* QUI 07] introduce a dynamic model for service composition which allows us to specify the structural and dynamic requirements of Web services compositions. In [CAS 00], Casati *et al.* developed eFlow, a system that supports dynamic composition and management of composite services. They illustrate how the eFlow enables the specification of processes that can automatically configure themselves at runtime according to the nature and type of services available on the Internet and the needs of each individual customer.

Barros *et al.* [BAR 05] propose a collection of patterns of service interactions which allow emerging Web services functionality, especially those associated with behavioral interface, choreography and orchestration. Each of the patterns captures the essence of a problem, collects references by means of synonyms, provides real examples of the problem and proposes solutions for implementation in terms of concrete technologies. They discuss the implementation of these patterns using BPEL. Van der Aalst *et al.* [VAN 09b] present a survey based on some foundational concepts of service interaction. The authors also provide a set of service interaction patterns to illustrate the relevant challenges. The paper focuses on the main challenges of service interaction comprising *exposing services*, *replacing and refining services* and *integrating services using adapters*. Hull *et al.* [HUL 05] provide a survey on the fundamental assumptions and concepts of service composition and related issues.

Nezhad *et al.* [NEZ 06] discuss the specifications of Web services interoperability based on *layers* concepts for better investigation of the relevant problems in different layers. The specifications in the lower layer are required properties in most applications while the higher layer specifications are not necessary:

– *Messaging layer*: in addition to the SOAP as a common protocol, in this level service providers may consider the desirable properties such as security or reliability as additional service specifications.

– Basic coordination (WS-transaction): these properties define the specifications associated with message exchanges among partner services (e.g. federate security management that is useful in many business processes developments).

– Business-level interfaces and protocols: this layer includes the functional properties of services (i.e. the service interface and service business protocol).

– *Policies and non-functional* aspects: the specifications of this layer comprise security policy, the QoS characteristics such as time-related properties and cost.

Although service providers prevent the publication of erroneous services and determine errors and weaknesses of their service before publication, nevertheless, for service customers it is crucial to verify whether a given Web service interacts properly with his components. Since such a composition is usually not foreseen at design time of single services, verification of composition of these services is inevitable. In the past decade, numerous research efforts have been focused on service composition verification by taking into consideration different aspects of Web service specification. A fundamental challenge arising from the distributed execution of heterogeneous Web services in flexible compositions is *compatibility*. Two services are compatible if any collaboration between them is accomplished successfully and if each of them can reach their expected results (final states). The authors in [BAC 04] provide a taxonomy of compatibility for Web service compositions:

– *Interface compatibility*: it is related to the syntax and types of messages between partner services.

– *Semantic compatibility*: this type of compatibility ensures that messages and their content are correctly interpreted.

– *Behavioral compatibility*: it means there are no deadlocks, livelocks and other unconventional situations in a composed model.

– *QoS compatibility*: it focuses on some quality parameters such as time-related properties or security standards.

The verification of the compatibility of collaborative business processes is crucial for the success of the interoperability between services [MAR 03, BOR 05, OAN 09]. In the case where a service composition is not compatible, Lohmann [LOH 08a] defines an algorithm to suggest changes of a service to achieve overall compatibility. Foster *et al.* [FOS 04] discuss a model-based approach to verify process interactions for coordinated Web service composition. The approach uses the FSM representations of Web service orchestrations. Lohmann *et al.* [LOH 08b] analyze the compatibility of BPEL services and compositions of BPEL services. They provide formal semantics for BPEL4Chor choreographies, which enables the application of existing formal methods to industrial service languages. This checking includes verification of compositions with respect to compatibility and the completion of partially specified service compositions. Martens [MAR 05] verifies and analyzes the compatibility of a composed system for Web service-based business processes by applying the Petri nets formalism.

At design time of single services, such a complete composition is usually not available; therefore, the notion of *controllability* [WOL 09] can be used for analyzing the correctness of a single service. A service is *controllable* iff at least one partner service exists such that their composition is compatible (well behaving). Controllability is an extension of compatibility to single services and can be seen as a fundamental soundness property for services in any possible composition. Lohmann and Weinberg [LOH 10] introduce the tool *Wendy*, which is a Petri net-based tool, to synthesize the partner services. Wendy analyzes controllability of an open net and synthesizes a partner if the net is controllable. Wu *et al.* [WU 09] propose an automatic method to check the behavioral compatibility in a service composition. The authors apply π-calculus to model service behaviors and interactions. In most research efforts, the authors apply the *model checking* [CLA 99] to automatically verify the compatibility of service interaction. Model checking treats the verification problem where undesired states are explored in a graph which models the system behavior.

In the next section, we argue the incompatibility of service interaction at interface and protocol levels, and also we discuss the proposed adaptation techniques dealing with these types of mismatches.

6.3. Web service incompatibility and adaptation

Despite tremendous efforts on the evaluation of the compatibility criteria among services [OUE 11, TAN 09, BAR 10], there is still significant attention required to verify the correctness of service collaboration. The typical approach for enabling incompatible services to interact is service *adaptation*. While standardization in Web services reduces the heterogeneity and makes their interoperability easier, adaptation still remains necessary. Adaptation functionality can be offered to enable integration inside and across enterprise boundaries. The need for adaptation in Web services comes from the following sources: *ensuring the interoperability*, *optimization*, *recovery* and *context change*. Primarily, the mediation concept was introduced for databases [WIE 97].

The authors in [NEZ 06, CHA 06, BAN 05] identify the needs for adaptation in Web services by addressing the heterogeneity at the levels of service *interface* and *business protocol*:

– The mismatches at service *interface* level include service *signature* incompatibilities (e.g. message and operation name, number, the type of input/output message parameters of operations and the parameter value constraint) with the following classifications:

- Syntactical: no equality exists between service's operations name and their input/output message names. The syntactical compatibility ensures that the interface provided by a service is equivalent with the required interfaces of the partner and vice versa.

- Structural: there are differences in the expected types or values of input/output messages.

- *Semantical*: there are differences in the interpretation of a data element's meaning or an operation's function.

- *Messages split/merge*: a single message of a service is matched with several messages in another service for the same functionality, or several message of a service have one matching message in another one.

– The mismatches at the *business protocol* (or service behavior) level are concerned with the message exchange dependencies among services (e.g. *deadlock,* where both partner services are mutually waiting to receive some message from the other, and *unspecified reception* in which one service sends a message while the partner is not expecting it):

- *Ordering constraint:* the constraint that services impose on message exchange sequences.

- *Extra/missing messages*: a service delivers a message that is not specified in another service partner and vice versa.

Numerous adaptation approaches have been proposed to tackle both service interface and business protocol mismatches between the provided and the required functionalities of services developed by different parties [ZHO 11, CAV 10, MAT 07, CAN 08, LI 10, KON 09, ESL 12]. The proposed approaches rely on one of the following two techniques: *service modification* or *synthesizing an adapter component.* The adaptation in terms of service modification requires applying some tuning actions to support the partner service's specifications. In service interaction where the adaptation is dealing with creating an adapter, a stand-alone component mediates the interactions between two services with potentially different interfaces and protocols such that the interoperability is achieved. In other words, the adapter compensates for the differences between their interfaces by data mappings (i.e. message transformation), and between their business protocols by rearranging the message exchanges or generating a missing message [YEL 97]. Many industrial tools have been developed for signature adaptation, such as Microsoft BizTalk Mapper[4], Stylus Studio XML Mapping Tools[5] and SAP XI Mapping Editor[6].

The aim of the mediator proposed in [GUE 08] is to generate the missing messages which are required to complete the Cartesian product. The accuracy of the mediator is also verified. Sheng *et al.* [SHE 02] develop a middleware for the composition of Web services by focusing on the dynamic and scalable aspects of Web services composition. Baresi *et al.* [BAR 03] define a modeling framework for adaptive information systems based on e-services. The authors propose adaptation rules enabling the composition and dynamically select e-service channels according to the constraints of available architectures and application-level requirements. Deng *et al.* [DEN 13] provide an evaluation of the *aggregation* problem for synthesized mediators of Web services (SWMs). The *aggregation* problem aims to optimize the realization of a given mediator. Li *et al.* [LI 10] propose an approach based on mediator patterns to generate executable mediators. The authors present several basic and advance mediator patterns to reconcile all possible protocol mismatches. They propose a heuristic technique based on message mappings to semi-automatically identify protocol mismatches between two partially compatible services. The technique selects appropriate basic mediator patterns according to the identified protocol mismatches. They also develop the corresponding BPEL templates of these patterns which can be used to generate the executable mediation code. Brogi *et al.* [BRO 04] present an approach to check whether two or more Web services involved in an interoperability are compatible or not. The authors also develop the algorithms to automatically generate the adapters. They apply the process algebra to represent Web service choreographies. Du *et al.* [DU 12] present an approach for mediation-aided composition of Web services. To analyze the compatibility, the authors propose automatic construction and analysis of the *modular reachability graph* (MRG) of composition where the problem of state space explosion is significantly alleviated. For the compatible composition, the BPEL code is automatically generated. Erradi *et al.* [ERR 06] present the policy-based middleware called Manageable and Adaptive Service Compositions (MASC) for dynamic monitoring and adaptation of Web services compositions. Ardissono *et al.*

4 http://msdn.microsoft.com/en-us/library/ms943073.aspx.
5 http://www.stylusstudio.com/.
6 http://www.wsw-software.de/en-sap_services-mapping_sap_xi.mapping-sapxi.html.

[ARD 10] present a mediation framework supporting the Web services interaction to resolve the protocol mismatches.

In the following, we review some of the service adaptation approaches (i.e. either generating an adapter or modifying services) where there are mismatches between their interfaces or business protocols.

6.4. Adaptation approaches

The issue of synthesizing adapters for incompatible services interaction has been studied in the area of SOA, as well as in the area of component-based software engineering. In the following, we review some of the approaches proposing adapter generation methods focusing on service interface or business protocol mismatches and/or both of them. Besides, numerous approaches presented techniques of adapter synthesis by taking the service behavior incompatibility into consideration in the interface matching. All adaptation approaches propose a common logic for an adapter: intercept a message sent by a partner service; store it if necessary; transform it to a required format supported by the other partner service and/or generates a new message and then send the message to the partner service that needs to receive it. In addition, we mention the approaches where the adaptation of Web services is performed by changing the participant services.

Yellin and Strom [YEL 97] present an approach to evaluate the existence of an adapter for *protocols-incompatible interfaces* by applying the *execution trace*. The authors discuss two *asynchronous* and *synchronous* protocol semantics of components collaboration, and propose an automated method of adapter generation based on *synchronous* semantics.

The adapter protocol is modeled using the FSM consisting of a set of states, a set of typed *memory cells* to store the messages received by the adapter and a set of *state transition rules*. The adapter's behavior is acquired by its transitions rules. Each rule describes a transition from one state to another in the adapter based on sending or receiving messages, along with a set of memory actions that store or retrieve messages in/from the cells. If the adapter is in a state with a send transition, the adapter may send a message to the appropriate component and enter the target state. If the adapter is in a state with a receive transition, the adapter may wait for a message to arrive and then enter the target state. A rule also constructs missing messages that have to be sent to partners. According to the synchronous semantic, when an adapter receives a message from a partner service, the adapter will not accept any message from this service until this message is forwarded by the adapter and a response is received for this message; afterward, the adapter will continue to receive other messages from this partner.

To synthesize the adapter specification for a pair of components, their interface mappings are required as the input (e.g. which messages should be mapped to which messages). The adapter synthesis process explores all possible interactions between the participant protocols and adds them to the adapter protocol. In cases where there are states leading to deadlocks or with unspecified reception, they are removed from the adapter protocol. The proposed adaptation approach defines *interface mapping rules* based on *parameters* rather than *message mapping*.

Taher *et al.* [TAH 11] present an adaptation approach based on the *complex event processing* (CEP) to automatically adapt both service interface and business protocol level mismatches. Therefore, they develop the operators for each of the transformation patterns associated with the mismatch types, e.g. *match-make, split, merge, aggregate and disaggregate.* These operators are modeled as *configurable automata* where transitions show both *observable* and *unobservable* actions. To generate a CEP adapter deployable in the CEP engine, each operator automata should be converted to a continuous query. For every message received by a CEP adapter, an input stream is created. Then an appropriate continuous query consumes the input stream and delivers the corresponding output stream for the target service. In a CEP adapter, all actions related to messages are molded as events. The CEP platform provides the conditions for running and analyzing the stream of data, and also the techniques to define the relationships between events.

Brogi *et al.* [BRO 06a] provide a methodology for the automated generation of adapters capable of solving protocol mismatches between the BPEL processes. Given two communicating BPEL processes whose interaction may not proceed, the adaptation process automatically synthesizes a full/partial BPEL adapter (if possible). The adaptation methodology consists of *service translation*, *adapter generation*, *adapter analysis* and *adapter development*. The proposed methodology applies the BPEL2YAWL translator [BRO 06b] for transforming the BPEL processes into YAWL, workflows that are used to model the service protocol. It also generates the YAWL workflow of the adapter, which can be used to check the properties (e.g. deadlock-freedom, reachability and liveness) of the interaction with the adapted services. The adapter generation phase generates the Service Execution Trees (SETs) of two partner services and an adapter mediating the interaction between them. The SET of a BPEL process is a tree describing all the possible scenarios of executing the basic activities. In this phase also the YAWL workflow of the adapter A from SET(A) is generated if the adapter has at least one successful trace.

Kongdenfha *et al.* [KON 06] present an adaptation approach in terms of service modification by proposing an *aspect-oriented* paradigm.

The main contribution of this approach is to apply the aspect-oriented programming paradigm to specify the adaptation template of each mismatch pattern in the form of an *aspect template*. Each aspect template includes a set of (*query*, *advice*) pairs that can provide a collection of *adaptation aspects*. These adaptation aspects can be merged with the *run-time instances* of an adapted service. The pair (*query*, *advice*) determines where and based on what logic the adaptation has to be applied. An *advice* defines the adaptation logic by comprising the procedures with one or more actions to resolve an associated mismatch. A *query* language is described as a *join-point* that specifies at what point a set of activities associated with the advice should be executed. The aspect template for interface mismatch can be initiated by providing the *query input parameters* and XQuery/XSLT transformation function as *advice input parameters*. In the case of a business protocol mismatch, if a service needs to receive an *ack* message, while the partner does not supply it, the adapter can provide such a message by evaluating the list of older message exchanges.

Moreover, the authors argue their motivation to exploit the aspect-oriented methodology for dynamic plugging and unplugging the adaptation logics to partner services at *runtime*. They also try to provide conditions for deciding where each of two methods, services modification (respecting aspect-oriented methods) and generating a stand-alone adapter, is preferable. In addition, they implement a tool that assists the developers in semi-automatic generation of their adapter logic.

Although the authors in [KON 09] present an approach by focusing on both adaptation methods (i.e. *developing stand-alone adapter* and *service modification*), they introduce *mismatch patterns* for service interface and business protocol mismatches. The proposed mismatch patterns include *adaptation logic templates* that can be initiated by developers to generate adapters for resolving the associated mismatches.

Benatallah *et al.* [BAN 05] present a methodology for developing adapters based on *mismatch patterns*, which are used to reconcile the possible differences between collaborative services. The proposed approach provides the *adapter template*s specified in BPEL code for each mismatch pattern scenario. Indeed, they characterize different kinds of adapter templates as a solution to resolve the associated mismatch that is identified among partner services. The reuse of these adapter templates help the developers to synthesize their stand-alone adapters.

Hung *et al.* [LIN 11] present an adaptation approach for *synchronous* service interaction. This approach only analyzes the mismatches at business protocol levels assuming that the service interface mismatches are resolved. The proposed framework represents Web services in the form of Interface Automata for Web Services (IA4WS) which is a customized model from Interface Automata [ALF 01]. The approach applies the idea of *one-session service* to avoid the *unwanted traces* by dealing with *unbounded messages* (i.e. which may modify the required functionality of services). The proposed adaptation approach includes (1) evaluating the interface level compatibility of services, (2) applying the model-checking tool SPIN to analyze the business protocol compatibility, (3) analyzing the need for adapter generation and (4) applying a *pushdown* model-checking for verification of adapter in terms of two specifications: *fairness property of looped transition* (unbounded messages) and *fairness property of branching transitions*.

A pushdown automaton, namely interface pushdown system (IPS), represents the adapter model. Within the IPS adapter, there are three kinds of transitions: *push transition* for messages reception, *pop transition* for message delivery and *internal transition* that is not related to message exchanges. The adapter model never creates a message by itself. Also, applying the model-checking technique for the verification of an adapter during its generation saves more time and money compared with the cases where service adaptation and verification are performed separately.

Tan *et al.* [TAN 09] present an automatic approach to service composition, formally checking the compatibility of two collaborative services respecting the *asynchronous* semantics. They also propose an adapter generation algorithm, if two services are partially compatible. The partial compatibility implies that two services are functionally compatible, but due to incompatibility in their interfaces or business protocols, direct composition is not possible.

The proposed adaptation approach applies a *state-space* method where the concept of *communication reachability graph* (CRG) arises, which concurrently constructs the *reachability graph* of two collaborative services using *data mapping*. The CRG is then verified to evaluate whether the adapter generation is necessary. The CRGs are used as a reduced state-space of the composite service. The authors discuss the incompatibility in the level of service interfaces. If the direct composition between interfaces is not possible, a request for data mapping is delivered to build the CRG to verify the adapter generation. The data mapping defines the rules as <*src*, *target*, *trans-flag*> to relate (syntactically and semantically equivalent) elements of two messages that are from two interfaces belonging to different services. For a direct map from *src* to *target*, the *trans_flag* Boolean variable is set to be *false* and otherwise is set to be *true* for additional transformation. In this approach, BPEL services are transformed into colored Petri nets.

Mateescu *et al.* [MAT 08] propose an adaptation technique which reduces the computational complexity of adapter generation using *on-the-fly exploration* and *reduction technique* (i.e. avoids full state-space generation of adapter structure). The adaptation method covers both interface and behavioral mismatches of services. In this approach, the service interface is modeled by the WSDL and its protocol is represented by means of *symbolic transition systems* (STS).

The proposed approach takes the parameters coming with a message into consideration in the interface matching. The adaptation approach first constructs the *adaptation contracts* which describe how mismatches can be resolved. The service interfaces and their adaptation contracts (interaction constraints specifications) are then encoded. Accordingly, the LOTOS code is generated. The LOTOS encoding allows the automatic generation of adaptor protocols. Moreover, LOTOS encoding enables the adapter verification using model-checking tools.

In this framework, applying on-the-fly algorithms increases the efficiency of the adapter generation. The reduction of the adapter is performed by removing all actions that are not related to the service business protocol (e.g. the internal transitions and all interactions with store activity). The authors also apply a model-checking tool to verify the generated adapter. The verification tool implements two operations: (1) *deletes the states eventually leading to deadlocks* and (2) *keeps only the states leading to the transitions labeled by a given action (here, Final)*. The adaptation contracts are built by a designer, hence additional adapter verification is required to implement several static evaluations for verifying that the adaptation contract is correct. The adapter behavior is also modeled in STS.

Dumas *et al.* [DUM 06] discuss the service adaptation at service *interface* level, and propose an approach to reconcile mismatches between *protocols-incompatible* interfaces. The authors present a *declarative* approach for an *adapter execution engine* rather than using programming language in order to reduce development and maintenance cost.

In this approach, service interface adaptation is accomplished via mapping operators such as *flaw*, *scatter*, *collapse*, *burst* and *hide* based on common mismatch patterns. Therefore, they propose a *visual notation* for mapping the interfaces using *algebraic* expression of transformation operators by focusing on *behavioral* aspects of interfaces. The behavioral interfaces are defined in terms of *communication action schema* using the UML activity diagram where actions are named according to the type of messages sent or received.

The *deadlock* situation (i.e. message ordering constraint in interface) is verified by defining the condition on interface mapping expression, i.e.: *it is not possible to send or receive the information that is dependent on other information that we have not yet sent or received.* The service *mediation engine* also supports the *visual notation*. The mediation engine is modeled by the FSM for an abstract representation of behavioral interfaces. The interface mappings are implemented in the mediation engine based on the logic of transformation operators. The mediation engine comprises an *administrative console* to monitor the histories of all actions carried out by the engine. Besides, the mediation engine can store an *unbounded* number of messages.

Nezhad *et al.* [NEZ 10] propose a semi-automatic adaptation approach for service interface matching by taking the protocol specifications into consideration. In terms of interface matching, the authors introduce a method to identify a type of split/merge message mismatch, where some elements of a message $m \in I_s$ (I_c) are matched with elements of $m' \in I_c$ (I_s) and some other elements of m are matched with some elements in $m'' \in I_c$ (I_s). The authors also present the protocol-based interface matching algorithms (i.e. *depth-based interface matching* and *iterative reference-based interface matching*). In a depth-based interface matching approach, messages with the same or similar depths in two protocols may have a higher chance of matching, and also the infinite loops are avoided. Iterative reference-based interface matching approach comprises the knowledge of previous matching (i.e. a pair of messages is selected as the best candidate match in each iteration and this pair is referred to as a reference pair for the next iteration. Potential deadlocks can be avoided by penalizing the conflicting match pair).

Seguel *et al.* [SEG 09] illustrate an automated approach of adapter generation to resolve protocol mismatches not for all interactions, but only for a minimal set of messages exchanged that need adaptation. The authors analyze service collaboration from a *synchronous* semantic standpoint.

The BPEL representation of a service protocol is modeled by a *protocol tree*. The leaves of this tree correspond to the basic activities and the internal nodes represent the structured activities. The proposed approach exploits the *behavioral relation* (*Seq*, *XOR AND*) of the protocol syntax (i.e. structure of the protocol tree) to identify the mismatches and recognizes the set of messages exchanged that have to be adapted. To this end, an interaction analysis matrix (IAM) is built over the pairs of interaction for comparing and assessing the behavioral relation of their nodes. Accordingly, they demonstrate an algorithm that can address the minimal set of interactions needing adaptation. Indeed, an IAM is able to evaluate which parts of a collaboration have to be adapted and which parts cannot be resolved. Therefore, the adapter generated through this approach has lower complexity and improved performance characteristic at run-time.

Shan *et al.* [SHA 10] present a technique for a flexible, on-the-fly adapter generation based on *message* and *control flow* adaptation. This approach can also combine control flow constraints into message adaptation. The main idea of their framework is to provide *message transformation patterns* which can be extended for a user's future requirements. Therefore, they first characterize the types of message mismatches, and then propose a set of patterns for resolving them. These patterns are defined as *message data generation*, *message data casting*, *message fragmentation and aggregation* and *message reconstruction*. The proposed approach also exploits a set of standard patterns for control flow adaptation (e.g. *sequence, parallel, choice* and *loop*). In addition, a *compatibility matrix* based on these patterns is represented as a guideline for incorporating processes. The authors also illustrate an adapter generation algorithm.

Mooij and Voorhoeve [MOO 09] present an automated approach for adapter generation. The authors develop a proof technique for partial adapters based on the open Petri net [KIN 97] formalism. They apply this technique to the adapter generation approach from [GIE 08] where behavioral adapters are proposed to adjust the communication between two services such that certain behavioral properties (e.g. deadlock-freedom and weak termination) are preserved in the composite service. The authors particularly address concepts like *operating guidelines*, *controllability*, *accordance* and *partial adapters*. Their proposed approach relies on the point that the adapters are regarded as controllers for the disjoint composition of two partner services.

As it has been pointed out, the authors in [GIE 08] present an automated adaptation approach (using Petri net formalism) that synthesizes the behavioral adapters. They propose a specification of elementary activities (SEA) consisting of a set of transformation rules on message types. Therefore, the adapter specification includes the given partners services and the SEA. In addition, their generated adapters do not need to be verified, since the synthesis of the adapter guarantees the adapter's correctness by construction.

Nezhad *et al.* [NEZ 07] present an approach to semi-automatically identify the split/merge type of interface mismatches and automatically recognize the protocol mismatches by generating a *mismatch tree*. Besides, they propose an *adapter simulation algorithm* which explores all possible message exchanges between two service interfaces to evaluate the respective protocol mismatches. The algorithm results in an *adapter protocol*, and a *message tree* that represents all deadlock situations between two service protocols. The interface matching is done by finding the match between *data elements* of the XML *schemas* associated to service interfaces. To increase the matching accuracy, they suggest the inclusion of message name and message type in an operation definition.

Furthermore, the authors discuss some *evidences* that can be used to identify (create) messages in common deadlocks:

– evaluating the relation between the data structure of message *m* (which is engaged in deadlock and needs to be identified) and all of the messages of the same interface that have been received before the deadlock point in the adapter. Indeed, if the elements of message *m* could be matched with the elements of any of these messages, there is the possibility of creating the message *m*;

– applying the previous interactions' logs;

– providing *the adapter developer's input* to identify the missing message in a deadlock and the input parameters of the transformation function.

In this work, the service business protocols are modeled in the form of FSM. They also argue that for a given interface mapping, it is necessary to take the service protocol incompatibility into account.

Wang *et al.* [WAN 08] characterize a *runtime adaptation* approach for service *behavioral interface* incompatibilities. To this end, they introduce a *service adaptation machine* that includes a repository of *mapping rules* where each rule is associated with an *adaptation scenario*. When a directed single mapping rule cannot be applied, the adaptation machine exploits *backward-chaining* algorithms for firing the rules to detect the behavioral mismatches, i.e. *deadlock* and *information loss* (*unspecified message*).

The adaptation idea of this paper has been implemented as a tool named *Service Mediation Engine* (Megine). The Megine manages a number of adapters associated with specific pairs of service instances by using the *identifiers* and *references* of the received messages. In addition, the Megine, through an *administrative console*, is able to implement an adaptation scenario where, before forwarding a message by adapter to a partner service, it is possible to check whether the target service is in a given state to consume that message. In this approach, both the partner service interface and adapter protocol are modeled using the FSM specifications.

Wohlstadter *et al.* [WHO 06] present the policy-based programming model, architecture and details of their proposed middleware project called *Cumulus*. They also discuss new challenges like distribution of middleware services that arise from such a context. The *Cumulus* middleware can be dynamically customized to support diverse Web services interoperability protocols that the applications need to engage in. The authors aim to find an appropriate programming model to *describe*, *discover* and *compose* middleware as separate services (MW services). Besides, the technical details of the *Cumulus4BPEL* prototype are provided, which developed specifically to support run-time interoperability in dynamic SOAs.

Becker *et al.* [BEC 06] present an engineering approach for component adaptation which is based on the introduction of a taxonomy of component mismatches and identification of a number of adaptation patterns to be used as generic and systematic solutions for eliminating them. The provided taxonomy summarizes the different types of component mismatches into categories and classifies them according to a hierarchy of *interface models*. Each of the distinguished interface models determines a set of properties that belongs to a component interface as follows:

– the *syntax-based interface model*, which focuses on *signatures* as constituent elements of component interfaces, supports the identification and elimination of signature mismatches;

– the *behavioral interface model* that contains assertions (i.e. pre- and postconditions) for the operations, which have been declared in the required and provided interfaces. By making use of an interaction-based interface model, which focuses on describing the interaction that takes place between connected components in the form of message calls, developers are able to diagnose and eliminate *protocol mismatches* (i.e. ordering and extra/missing of messages);

– the *quality-based interface model*, which focuses on the description of QoS (i.e. which is being provided by each of the interface operations by describing a set of quality attributes). By making use of an interface model that is based on the ISO 9126 quality model, it is possible to detect and eliminate the quality attribute mismatches such as *security*, *persistency*, *transactions*, *reliability* and *efficiency*;

– a *conceptual* interface model, which describes the conceptual semantics of component interfaces as an ontology, supports the identification and elimination of so-called *concept mismatches*.

The presented approach demonstrates both functional and non-functional adaptation patterns.

Bucchiarone *et al.* [BUC 10] propose an extension of a basic iterative service-based applications (SBA) lifecycle along with the elements to deal with the adaptation-specific needs. From the viewpoint of the authors, adaptation works properly only in the case where the application is designed to be adaptable; so they focus on the design phase and suggest a number of design principles and suitable guidelines to enable adaptation. For the same SBA, several adaptation strategies can be adopted and the selection of the most suitable one can be a complex issue, hence multiple criteria have to be considered. Therefore, they provide the guidelines to support this selection. The authors also discuss the effectiveness of the proposed methodology by means of the real-world scenarios over various types of SBAs. The paper aims at overcoming the fragmentation in current approaches for SBA adaptation.

Ardagna *et al.* [ARD 07] developed a general framework for flexible and adaptive execution of managed service-based processes. The framework, Processes with Adaptive Web Services (PAWS), coherently supports both process design and execution. The PAWS provides methods and a toolset to support design-time specification of all information required for automatic run-time adaptation of processes according to dynamically changing user preferences and context. The authors focus on how PAWS selects and adapts candidate services for a composed process.

In PAWS, both service discovery and service selection are driven by functional and non-functional aspects. From a functional perspective, PAWS includes a *mediator configurator* to support setup of the related runtime module – the *mediator engine* (i.e. to translate between the two service-interface signatures). If it is not possible to automatically derive message transformations, the designer defines them during process execution by providing additional information about parameter and service mappings. Their proposed mediation engine supports service invocation, the dynamic binding of a generic candidate service without requiring stub compilation at design time, and the management of service substitution that might involve services that are described by different signatures but have the same choreography.

Whenever the BPEL engine invokes a task, the mediator selects the first service from the optimizer's ranked candidate-services list. If the candidate service's interface differs from the interface that the task definition requires, the mediator retrieves the proper mapping document produced by the mediator configurator, and then invokes the candidate service by sending transformed messages. The mediator manages candidate-service invocation through sessions.

Cavallaro *et al.* [CAV 08] identify a number of possible interfaces or protocol level mismatches between the interacting partners in a dynamic service composition. The authors address basic mapping functions for solving the simple mismatches. In addition, they propose to combine such mapping functions in a *script* (defined in a domain specific language) to solve complex mismatches. Both simple functions and scripts are executed by a *mediator* to perform the required adaptations.

The script language is composed of the *rules* structured into two parts: the *mismatch definition part* that specifies the type of mismatch to be solved by the rule, and the *mapping function part* that contains the name of the function to be used to solve the mismatch. The rules can characterize the solutions for protocol or interface mismatches.

Denaro *et al.* [DEN 06] present an approach to design self-adaptive service-oriented architectures. The authors propose a self-adaptive solution that enables the client applications to easily and automatically adapt their behavior to the alternative Web services providing compatible functionality through different business protocols. The proposed framework automatically synthesizes the models which approximate the interaction protocols by tracing the successful interactions of Web services. It then dynamically handles the adaptations of the client. On this concern, the approach adds an Interaction Protocol Service Extension (IPSE) to the SOA such that each Web service is associated with an IPSE that serves as a proxy for the Web service. Before forwarding the requests to the Web service, the IPSE monitors the interaction sequences between the client and the Web service. The IPSE uses this information to incrementally synthesize a model that infers the interaction protocol of the Web service. The main limitation is the manual testing by the developers to analyze the candidates.

Jiang *et al.* [JIA 11] propose an approach for the adaptation of two or more services. The authors introduce a new model, called *protocol structure*, to characterize the service business protocol using message and message dependencies. They also provide formal definitions for mismatches. The proposed approach covers various forms of service interactions such as *one-to-zero*, *one-to-one*, *one-to-many*, *zero-to-one* and *many-to-one* exchange of messages, and *message broadcast*. In addition, the approach can automatically detect multiple mismatches at a time and automatically resolve them. The authors present a simple visual tool for the automatic adaptation of services and the generation of BPEL adapters. The process of developing an adapter includes:

– the *initial adaptation set* (*initial* message dependency relation of adapter) is semi-automatically generated based on *interface mapping* among services;

– the creation of protocol structure of adapted composition of two services using the initial adaptation set;

– the *final* and *correct* adaptation set among services is obtained through automatic detection and resolution of the message ordering mismatches in the protocol structure (i.e. using an algorithm to compute dead configuration):

- extra messages are received and stored in the buffers by the adapter;

- new messages are provided for missing messages (deadlock);

- automatic generation of the BPEL adapter based on the final adaptation set.

6.5. Conclusion

Numerous adaptation approaches have been proposed to cope with incompatibilities of Web service composition. In this chapter, we made an overview of those approaches which focus on service interface and behavioral mismatches. A body of research studies, in this sense, can enforce the flexibility and efficiency of such techniques generating the adapter at run-time.

6.6. Bibliography

[ALA 06] ALAMRI A., EID M., EL SADDIK A., "Classification of the state-of-the-art dynamic web services composition techniques", *International Journal of Web and Grid Services*, vol. 2, no. 2, pp. 148–166, 2006.

[ALF 01] DE ALFARO L., HENZINGER T.A., "Interface automata", *ACM Sigsoft Softw. Eng. Notes*, vol. 26, no. 5, pp. 109–120, 2001.

[ARD 07] ARDAGNA D., COMUZZI M., MUSSI E., *et al.*, "Paws: a framework for executing adaptive web-service processes", *IEEE Softw.*, vol. 24, no. 6, p. 39–47, 2007.

[ARD 10] ARDISSONO L., FURNARI R., PETRONE G., *et al.*, "Interaction protocol mediation in web service composition", *Int. J. Web Eng. Technol.*, vol. 6, no. 1, pp. 4–32, 2010.

[BAC 04] DE BACKER M., "On the verification of web services compatibility: a Petri net approach", *On the Move to Meaningful Internet Systems 2004: OTM 2004 Workshops*, vol. 3292, pp. 810–821, 2004.

[BAN 05] BENATALLAH B., CASATI F., GRIGORI D., *et al.*, "Developing adapters for web services integration", *Advanced Information Systems Engineering*, Springer, pp. 415–429, 2005.

[BAR 03] BARESI L., BIANCHINI D., DE ANTONELLIS V., *et al.*, "Context-aware composition of e-services", *Technologies for E-Services*, Springer, pp. 28–41, 2003.

[BAR 05] BARROS A., DUMAS M., TER HOFSTEDE A.H., "Service interaction patterns", *Business Process Management*, Springer, pp. 302–318, 2005.

[BAR 10] BARKAOUI K., ESLAMICHALANDAR M., KAABACHI M., "A structural verification of web services composition compatibility", *6th International Workshop on Enterprise and Organizational Modeling and Simulation* (*EOMAS 2010*), CEUR-WS, pp. 30–41, 2010.

[BEC 06] BECKER S., BROGI A., GORTON I., *et al.*, *Towards an Engineering Approach to Component Adaptation*, Springer, 2006.

[BEL 02] BELLWOOD T., CLEMENT L., EHNEBUSKE D., *et al.*, Universal description, discovery and integration specification (UDDI) 3.0, 2002.

[BEN 04] BENATALLAH B., CASATI F., TOUMANI F., "Web service conversation modeling: a cornerstone for e-business automation", *Internet Comput. IEEE*, vol. 8, no. 1, pp. 46–54, 2004.

[BEN 05] BENATALLAH B., DUMAS M., SHENG Q.Z., "Facilitating the rapid development and scalable orchestration of composite web services", *Distributed And Parallel Databases*, vol. 17, no. 1, pp. 5–37, 2005.

[BEN 06] BENATALLAH B., CASATI F., TOUMANI F., "Representing, analysing and managing web service protocols", *Data Knowl. Eng.*, vol. 58, no. 3, pp. 327–357, 2006.

[BON 08] BONCHI F., BROGI A., CORFINI S., *et al.*, "Compositional specification of web services via behavioural equivalence of nets: a case study", *Applications and Theory of Petri Nets*, Springer, pp. 52–71, 2008.

[BOR 05] BORDEAUX L., SALAÜN G., BERARDI D., *et al.*, "When are two web services compatible?", *Technologies for E-Services*, Springer, pp. 15–28, 2005.

[BOX 00] BOX D., EHNEBUSKE D., KAKIVAYA G., *et al.*, Simple object access protocol (SOAP) 1.1, 2000.

[BRO 04] BROGI A., CANAL C., PIMENTEL E., *et al.*, "Formalizing web service choreographies", *Electronic Notes in Theoretical Computer Science*, vol. 105, pp. 73–94, 2004.

[BRO 06] BROWN P.F., METZ R., HAMILTON B.A., Reference model for service oriented architecture 1.0, Technical report, 2006. Available at http://docs. oasis-open. org/soa-rm/v1. 0/soa-rm.

[BRO 06a] BROGI A., POPESCU R., "Automated generation of BPEL adapters", *Proceedings of International Conference on Service-Oriented Computing* (*SOC '06*), pp. 27–39, 2006.

[BRO 06b] BROGI A., POPESCU R., "From BPEL processes to YAWL workflows", *Web Services and Formal Methods*, Springer, pp. 107–122, 2006.

[BUC 10] BUCCHIARONE A., CAPPIELLO C., DI NITTO E., *et al.*, "Design for adaptation of service-based applications: main issues and requirements", *Service-Oriented Computing. ICSOC/ServiceWave Workshops*, pp. 467–476, 2010.

[CAN 08] CANAL C., POIZAT P., SALAUN G., "Model-based adaptation of behavioral mismatching components", *IEEE Transactions on Software Engineering*, vol. 34, no. 4, pp. 546–563, 2008.

[CAS 00] CASATI F., ILNICKI S., JIN L., *et al.*, "Adaptive and dynamic service composition in eFlow", *Advanced Information Systems Engineering*, Springer, pp. 13–31, 2000.

[CAV 08] CAVALLARO L., DI NITTO E., "An approach to adapt service requests to actual service interfaces", *Proceedings of the International Workshop on Software Engineering for Adaptive and Self-managing Systems*, pp. 129–136, 2008.

[CAV 10] CAVALLARO L., DI NITTO E., PELLICCIONE P., *et al.*, "Synthesizing adapters for conversational web-services from their WSDL interface", *Proceedings of the 2010 ICSE Workshop on Software Engineering for Adaptive and Self-Managing Systems*, pp. 104–113, 2010.

[CHA 06] CHAFLE G., DASGUPTA K., KUMAR A., *et al.*, "Adaptation in web service composition and execution", *International Conference on Web Services (ICWS '06)*, pp. 549–557, 2006.

[CHR 01] CHRISTENSEN E., CURBERA F., MEREDITH G., *et al.*, Web services description language (WSDL) 1.1, 2001.

[CLA 99] CLARKE E.M., GRUMBERG O., PELED D., *Model Checking*, MIT Press, 1999.

[DAL 03] DALAL S., TEMEL S., LITTLE M., *et al.*, "Coordinating business transactions on the web", *IEEE Internet Computing*, vol. 7, no. 1, pp. 30–39, 2003.

[DEN 06] DENARO G., PEZZE M., TOSI D., *et al.*, "Towards self-adaptive service-oriented architectures", *Proceedings of the Workshop on Testing, Analysis, and Verification of Web Services and Applications (TAV-WEB '06)*, pp. 10–16, 2006.

[DEN 13] DENG T., FAN W., LIBKIN L., *et al.*, "On the aggregation problem for synthesized web services", *J. Comput. Syst. Sci.*, vol. 79, pp. 873–891, 2013.

[DU 12] DU Y., LI X., XIONG P., "A Petri net approach to mediation-aided composition of web services", *IEEE Transactions on Automation Science and Engineering*, vol. 9, no. 2, pp. 429–435, 2012.

[DUM 06] DUMAS M., SPORK M., WANG K., "Adapt or perish: algebra and visual notation for service interface adaptation", *Business Process Management*, vol. 4702, pp. 65–80, 2006.

[DUS 05] DUSTDAR S., SCHREINER W., "A survey on web services composition", *International Journal of Web and Grid Services*, vol. 1, no. 1, pp. 1–30, 2005.

[ERR 06] ERRADI A., MAHESHWARI P., TOSIC V., "Policy-driven middleware for self-adaptation of web services compositions", *Proceedings of the ACM/IFIP/USENIX 2006 International Conference on Middleware*, pp. 62–80, 2006.

[ESL 12] ESLAMICHALANDAR M., BARKAOUI K., NEZHAD H.R.M., "Service composition adaptation: an overview", *2nd International Workshop on Advanced Information Systems for Enterprises (IWAISE '12)*, pp. 20–27, 2012.

[FEL 03] FELBER P., CHAN C.-Y., GAROFALAKIS M., *et al.*, "Scalable filtering of XML data for web services", *IEEE Internet Computing*, vol. 7, no. 1, pp. 49–57, 2003.

[FER 04] FERRARA A., "Web services: a process algebra approach", *Proceedings of the 2nd International Conference on Service Oriented Computing*, pp. 242–251, 2004.

[FOS 04] FOSTER H., UCHITEL S., MAGEE J., *et al.*, "Compatibility verification for web service choreography", *Proceedings of the IEEE International Conference on Web Services*, 2004, pp. 738–741.

[FU 04] FU X., BULTAN T., SU J., "Analysis of interacting BPEL web services", *Proceedings of the 13th International Conference on World Wide Web*, pp. 621–630, 2004.

[GIE 08] GIERDS C., MOOIJ A.J., WOLF K., Specifying and generating behavioral service adapters based on transformation rules, Preprints CS-02-08, Institute of Computer Science, University of Rostock, 2008.

[GUE 08] GUERMOUCHE N., PERRIN O., RINGEISSEN C., "A mediator based approach for services composition", *6th International Conference on Software Engineering Research, Management and Applications (SERA '08)*, pp. 273–280, 2008.

[HUL 05] HULL R., SU J., "Tools for composite web services: a short overview", *ACM Sigmod Rec.*, vol. 34, no. 2, pp. 86–95, 2005.

[JIA 11] JIANG J.-M., ZHANG S., GONG P., *et al.*, "Message dependency-based adaptation of services", *IEEE Asia-Pacific Services Computing Conference (APSCC)*, pp. 442–449, 2011.

[JOR 07] JORDAN D., EVDEMON J., ALVES A., *et al.*, *Web services business process execution language version 2.0*, Oasis Standard, vol. 11, 2007.

[KIN 97] KINDLER E., "A compositional partial order semantics for Petri net components", *Application and Theory of Petri Nets 1997*, Springer, pp. 235–252, 1997.

[KON 06] KONGDENFHA W., SAINT-PAUL R., BENATALLAH B., *et al.*, "An aspect-oriented framework for service adaptation", *Proceedings of International Confernce on Service-Oriented Computing (SOC '06)*, Springer, pp. 15–26, 2006.

[KON 09] KONGDENFHA W., NEZHAD H.R.M, BENATALLAH B., *et al.*, "Mismatch patterns and adaptation aspects: a foundation for rapid development of web service adapters", *IEEE Transactions on Services Computing*, vol. 2, pp. 94–107, 2009.

[LEY 01] LEYMANN F., Web services flow language, Technical report, IBM, 2001.

[LI 10] LI X., FAN Y., MADNICK S., *et al.*, "A pattern-based approach to protocol mediation for web services composition", *Inf. Softw. Technol.*, vol. 52, no. 3, pp. 304–323, 2010.

[LIN 11] LIN H.H., AOKI T., KATAYAMA T., "Automated adaptor generation for services based on pushdown model checking", *18th IEEE International Conference and Workshops on Engineering of Computer Based Systems (ECBS '11)*, pp. 130–139, 2011.

[LOH 08a] LOHMANN N., "Correcting deadlocking service choreographies using a simulation-based graph edit distance", *Business Process Management*, Springer, pp. 132–147, 2008.

[LOH 08b] LOHMANN N., KOPP O., LEYMANN F., *et al.*, "Analyzing BPEL4Chor: verification and participant synthesis", *Web Services and Formal Methods*, Springer, pp. 46–60, 2008.

[LOH 08c] LOHMANN N., MASSUTHE P., STAHL C., *et al.*, "Analyzing interacting WS-BPEL processes using flexible model generation", *Data & Knowledge Engineering*, vol. 64, no. 1, pp. 38–54, 2008.

[LOH 10] LOHMANN N., WEINBERG D., "Wendy: a tool to synthesize partners for services", *Applications and Theory of Petri Nets*, Springer, pp. 297–307, 2010.

[MAR 03] MARTENS A., "On compatibility of web services", *Petri Net Newsletters*, vol. 65, pp. 12–20, 2003.

[MAR 05] MARTENS A., "Analyzing web service based business processes", *Fundamental Approaches to Software Engineering*, Springer, pp. 19–33, 2005.

[MAS 05] MASSUTHE P., REISIG W., SCHMIDT K., "An operating guideline approach to the SOA", *AMCT*, vol. 1, no. 3, pp. 35–43, 2005.

[MAT 07] MATEESCU R., POIZAT P., SALAÜN G., "Behavioral adaptation of component compositions based on process algebra encodings", *Proceedings of the 22nd IEEE/ACM International Conference on Automated Software Engineering*, pp. 385–388, 2007.

[MAT 08] MATEESCU R., POIZAT P., SALAÜN G., "Adaptation of service protocols using process algebra and on-the-fly reduction techniques", *Proceedings of International Conference on Service-Oriented Computing (SOC '08)*, pp. 84–99, 2008.

[MED 03a] MEDJAHED B., BENATALLAH B., BOUGUETTAYA A., *et al.*, "Business-to-business interactions: issues and enabling technologies", *VLDB Journal*, vol. 12, no. 1, pp. 59–85, 2003.

[MED 03b] MEDJAHED B., REZGUI A., BOUGUETTAYA A., *et al.*, "Infrastructure for e-government web services", *IEEE Internet Computing*, vol. 7, no. 1, pp. 58–65, 2003.

[MOO 09] MOOIJ A.J., VOORHOEVE M., "Proof techniques for adapter generation", *Web Services and Formal Methods*, Springer, pp. 207–223, 2009.

[NEZ 06] NEZHAD H.R.M., BENATALLAH B., CASATI F., *et al.*, "Web services interoperability specifications", *IEEE Comput. Soc.*, vol. 39, no. 5, pp. 24–32, 2006.

[NEZ 07] NEZHAD H.R.M, BENATALLAH B., MARTENS A., *et al.*, "Semi-automated adaptation of service interactions", *Proceedings of the 16th International Conference on World Wide Web*, pp. 993–1002, 2007.

[NEZ 10] NEZHAD H.R.M., XU G.Y., BENATALLAH B., "Protocol-aware matching of web service interfaces for adapter development", *Proceedings of the 19th International Conference on World Wide Web*, pp. 731–740, 2010.

[OAN 09] OANEA O., WOLF K., "An efficient necessary condition for compatibility", in OLIVER K., LOHMANN N. (eds), *Proceedings of the 1st Central-European Workshop on Services and Their Composition,* ZEUS 2009, Stuttgart, Germany, March 2–3, CEUR Workshop Proceedings, vol. 438, pp. 81–87, March 2009.

[OUE 11] OUEDERNI M., SALAÜN G., PIMENTEL E., "Measuring the compatibility of service interaction protocols", *Proceedings of the 2011 ACM Symposium on Applied Computing*, pp. 1560–1567, 2011.

[OUY 07] OUYANG C., VERBEEK E., VAN DER AALST W.M., *et al.*, "Formal semantics and analysis of control flow in WS-BPEL", *Sci. Comput. Program.*, vol. 67, no. 2, pp. 162–198, 2007.

[PAP 03a] PAPAZOGLOU M.P., "Web services and business transactions", *World Wide Web*, vol. 6, no. 1, pp. 49–91, 2003.

[PAP 03b] PAPAZOGLOU M.P., "Service-oriented computing: concepts, characteristics and directions", *Proceedings of the 4th International Conference on Web Information Systems Engineering* (*WISE '03*), pp. 3–12, 2003.

[PEl 03] PELTZ C., "Web services orchestration and choreography", *Computer*, vol. 36, no. 10, pp. 46–52, 2003.

[QUI 07] QUINTERO R., TORRES V., PELECHANO V., "Model centric approach of web services composition", *Emerging Web Services Technology*, Springer, pp. 65–81, 2007.

[REI 07] REISIG W., BRETSCHNEIDER J., FAHLAND D., *et al.*, "Services as a paradigm of computation", *Formal Methods Hybrid Real-Time System*, Springer, pp. 521–538, 2007.

[SEG 09] SEGUEL R., ESHUIS R., GREFEN P., "Constructing minimal protocol adaptors for service composition", *Proceedings of the 4th Workshop on Emerging Web Services Technology*, pp. 29–38, 2009.

[SHA 10] SHAN Z., KUMAR A., GREFEN P., "Towards integrated service adaptation a new approach combining message and control flow adaptation", *IEEE International Conference on Web Services* (*ICWS '10*), pp. 385–392, 2010.

[SHE 02] SHENG Q.Z., BENATALLAH B., DUMAS M., *et al.*, "SELF-SERV: a platform for rapid composition of web services in a peer-to-peer environment", *Proceedings of the 28th International Conference on Very Large Data Bases*, pp. 1051–1054, 2002.

[SKO 04] SKOGSRUD H., BENATALLAH B., CASATI F., "Trust-serv: model-driven lifecycle management of trust negotiation policies for web services", *Proceedings of the 13th International Conference on World Wide Web*, pp. 53–62, 2004.

[SPA 05] SPANOUDAKIS G., ZISMAN A., KOZLENKOV A., "A service discovery framework for service centric systems", *IEEE International Conference on Services Computing*, vol. 1, pp. 251–259, 2005.

[TAH 11] TAHER Y., PARKIN M., PAPAZOGLOU M., *et al.*, "Adaptation of web service interactions using complex event processing patterns", *Service-Oriented Computing*, Springer, pp. 601–609, 2011.

[TAN 09] TAN W., FAN Y., ZHOU M.C., "A Petri net-based method for compatibility analysis and composition of web services in business process execution language", *IEEE Transactions on Automation Science and Engineering*, vol. 6, no. 1, pp. 94–106, 2009.

[THA 01] THATTE S., XLANG: Web services for business process design, Technical report, Microsoft, 2001.

[TRU 01] TRUYEN E., JØRGENSEN B.N., JOOSEN W., *et al.*, "On interaction refinement in middleware", *Proceedings of the 5th International Workshop on Component-Oriented Programming*, pp. 56–62, 2001.

[VAN 09a] VAN DER AALST W., VAN HEE K., MASSUTHE P., *et al.*, "Compositional service trees", *Appl. Theory Petri Nets*, pp. 283–302, 2009.

[VAN 09b] VAN DER AALST W.M., MOOIJ A.J., STAHL C., *et al.*, "Service interaction: patterns, formalization, and analysis", *Formal Methods for Web Services*, Springer, pp. 42–88, 2009.

[WAN 08] WANG K., DUMAS M., OUYANG C., *et al.*, "The service adaptation machine", *IEEE 6th European Conference on Web Services (ECOWS '08)*, pp. 145–154, 2008.

[WHO 06] WOHLSTADTER E., TAI S., MIKALSEN T., *et al.*, "A service-oriented middleware for runtime web services interoperability", *International Conference on Web Services (ICWS '06)*, pp. 393–400, 2006.

[WIE 97] WIEDERHOLD G., GENESERETH M., "The conceptual basis for mediation services", *IEEE Expert*, vol. 12, no. 5, pp. 38–47, 1997.

[WOL 09] WOLF K., "Does my service have partners?", *Transactions on Petri Nets and Other Models of Concurrency II*, Springer, pp. 152–171, 2009.

[WU 09b] WU Z., DENG S., LI Y., *et al.*, "Computing compatibility in dynamic service composition", *Knowledge and Information Systems*, vol. 19, no. 1, pp. 107–129, 2009.

[YEL 97] YELLIN D.M., STROM R.E., "Protocol specifications and component adaptors", *ACM Transactions on Programming Languages and Systems*, vol. 19, no. 2, pp. 292–333, 1997.

[ZHO 11] ZHOU Z., BHIRI S., ZHUGE H., *et al.*, "Assessing service protocol adaptability based on protocol reduction and graph search", *Concurrency and Computation: Practice and Experience*, vol. 23, no. 9, pp. 880–904, 2011.

List of Authors

Abdelkrim AMIRAT
University Center of Souk-Ahras
Algeria

Hugo ARBOLEDA
ICES University
Colombia

Kamel BARKAOUI
Cedric
CNAM
Paris
France

Rubby CASALLAS
University of Los Andes
Colombia

Jaime CHAVARRIAGA
University of Los Andes
Colombia

Khalil DRIRA
LAAS
University of Toulouse
France

Maryam ESLAMICHALANDAR
Cedric
CNAM
Paris
France

Anthony HOCK-KOON
Amadeus
Sopha Antipollis
France

Ahmad KHEIR
LaMA Laboratory
Lebanese University
Tripoli
Lebanon

José Carlos MALDONADO
ICMC
University of São Paulo
Brazil

Hala NAJA
LaMA Laboratory
Lebanese University
Tripoli
Lebanon

Elisa Yumi NAKAGAWA
ICMC
University of São Paulo
Brazil

Flavio OQUENDO
IRISA
Rennes
France

Mourad Chabane OUSSALAH
LINA
University of Nantes
France

Maria-Teresa SEGARRA
Télécom Bretagne
Brest
France

Jean-Claude ROYER
LINA
Ecole des Mines de Nantes
France

Mohamed ZOUARI
LAAS
University of Toulouse
France

Index

S

V, W

www.ingramcontent.com/pod-product-compliance
Lightning Source LLC
LaVergne TN
LVHW011755200926
848484LV00003B/713